GRENADA

GRENADA

Revolution and Invasion

Edited by

PATSY LEWIS

GARY WILLIAMS

PETER CLEGG

THE UNIVERSITY OF THE WEST INDIES PRESS

Jamaica • Barbados • Trinidad and Tobago

The University of the West Indies Press
7A Gibraltar Hall Road, Mona
Kingston 7, Jamaica
www.uwipress.com

© 2015 by Patsy Lewis, Gary Williams and Peter Clegg
All rights reserved. Published 2015

A catalogue record of this book is available
from the National Library of Jamaica.

ISBN: 978-976-640-555-7 (print)
978-976-640-564-9 (Kindle)
978-976-640-573-1 (ePub)

Cover illustration: Lilo Nido, detail of the mixed media Revo Installation, showing
a bootprint-trodden list of persons status unknown. This work was part of the
exhibition Grenada 1979–1983, Revolution: An Art Perspective, curated by Suelin
Low Chew Tung. Photograph by Suelin Low Chew Tung.

Cover and book design by Robert Harris

Set in Scala 10.25/15 x 27

The University of the West Indies Press has no responsibility for the persistence
or accuracy of URLs for external or third-party Internet websites referred to in this
publication and does not guarantee that any content on such websites is, or will
remain accurate or appropriate.

Printed in the United States of America

Contents

Acknowledgements

We wish to thank Carol Lawes for her careful editing of this manuscript in accordance with the style sheet of the University of the West Indies Press, and the Sir Arthur Lewis Institute for Social and Economic Studies for their financial support.

The following articles originally appeared in the journals *Social and Economic Studies* (published by the Sir Arthur Lewis Institute of Social and Economic Studies, University of the West Indies, Mona, Jamaica) and the *Round Table: The Commonwealth Journal of International Affairs* (published by Taylor and Francis, United Kingdom). We wish to thank the publishers of both journals for giving their permission to have these republished in this collection:

Merle Collins, "What Happened? Grenada: A Retrospective Journey", *Social and Economic Studies* 62, nos. 3–4 (September–December 2013): 9–13.

Nicole Phillip-Dowe, "Women in the Grenada Revolution, 1979–1983", *Social and Economic Studies* 62, nos. 3–4 (September–December 2013): 45–82.

Patsy Lewis, "A Response to Edward Seaga's *The Grenada Intervention: The Inside Story*", *Social and Economic Studies* 62, nos. 3–4 (September–December 2013): 83–111.

Jermaine O. McCalpin, "Written into Amnesia: The Truth and Reconciliation Commission of Grenada", *Social and Economic Studies* 62, nos. 3–4 (September–December 2013): 113–40.

Gary Williams, "Ferrets in the Caribbean: Britain, Grenada and the Curious Case of the Armoured Cars", *Round Table* 102, no. 2 (2013): 135–42.

Laurie Lambert, "The Revolution and Its Discontents: Grenadian Newspapers and Attempts to Shape Public Opinion during Political Transitions", *Round Table* 102, no. 2 (2013): 143–54.

John Cotman, "Coming in from the Cold: Grenada and Cuba since 1983", *Round Table* 102, no. 2 (2013): 155–66.

Wendy Grenade, "Party Politics and Governance in Grenada: An Analysis of the NNP (1984–2012)", *Round Table* 102, no. 2 (2013): 167–76.

Robert J. Beck, "The Grenada Invasion, International Law and the Scoon Invitation: A 30-Year Retrospective", *Round Table* 102, no. 3 (2013): 281–90.

Shridath Ramphal, "The US in the Caribbean: Thirty Years after American Fury", *Round Table* 103, no. 1 (2014): 41–53.

Howard Tumber, "Journalism and the Invasion of Grenada 30 Years On: A Retrospective", *Round Table* 103, no. 1 (2014): 54–64.

Abbreviations

CARICOM	Caribbean Community
CC	Central Committee
CPE	Centre for Popular Education
FCO	Foreign and Commonwealth Office
GNP	Grenada National Party
GULP	Grenada United Labour Party
JBC	Jamaica Broadcasting Corporation
NDC	National Democratic Congress
NISTEP	National In-Service Teacher Education Programme
NJM	New JEWEL [Joint Endeavor for Welfare, Education and Liberation] Movement
NNP	New National Party
NWO	National Women's Organization
OECS	Organisation of Eastern Caribbean States
PRA	People's Revolutionary Army
PRG	People's Revolutionary Government
PWA	Progressive Women's Association
RFG	Radio Free Grenada
RMC	Revolutionary Military Council
TRC	Truth and Reconciliation Commission
TRCG	Truth and Reconciliation Commission of Grenada

Introduction

Grenada

Revolution and Invasion in Perspective

PATSY LEWIS, GARY WILLIAMS, PETER CLEGG

Thirty-six years ago, on 13 March 1979, Grenada, a Caribbean micro-state measuring a mere three hundred and forty square kilometres and having a population of under one hundred thousand, the majority of whom were younger than thirty, staged a revolution of unimaginable significance, given Grenada's unimportance in international affairs. In 1979, Grenada was one of the world's newest states, having gained its independence from Britain just five years before, albeit under controversial circumstances. The months preceding independence were marked by mass demonstrations and strikes against the British granting independence to Grenada under the leadership of the repressive and eccentric Eric Matthew Gairy, who had been a domi-nant figure in Grenadian politics for nearly three decades. Five years later, Gairy was overthrown by members of the New JEWEL (Joint Endeavor for Welfare, Education and Liberation) Movement, who were part of an alliance that formed the formal opposition. Although initiated by this small group, the coup quickly garnered widespread support. However, after four hectic years of attempts, with mixed success, to put the economy on a more secure footing, to revitalize the country's political system and to more successfully engage its youthful population in voluntary community service, the revolu-tion imploded.[1] Its dramatic end, marked by a falling-out among the leader-ship of the People's Revolutionary Government (PRG) and the subsequent killings, including those of the prime minister and several members of his cabinet, the only such instance in the Commonwealth Caribbean, set the stage for a full-scale US invasion. The consequences of the invasion and of the events preceding it have been felt at the national, regional and international levels. Thirty-six years after the revolution came into being and thirty-one years after its collapse, there is an opportunity to reflect on the significance of these events internationally, regionally and nationally.

International Dimension

The Grenada Revolution cannot be viewed in isolation from two other important upheavals that occurred in close temporal proximity: the Iranian Revolution of January 1979 and the Nicaraguan Revolution of July 1979, both of which overthrew staunch American allies. Together, these three revolutions, occurring in geographical areas of significant strategic interests, dealt a strong blow to the projection of US power. The Grenadian revolution, occurring in the US "backyard", followed closely by the Sandinista seizure of power in Nicaragua, appeared to underscore the impotence of the United States in defending its spheres of influence. Unlike the Iranian Revolution, anti-dictatorial in form but guided by Shiite fundamentalists, the Grenadian and Nicaraguan revolutions adopted agendas with a "socialist orientation" and were marked by close relations with Cuba, the Soviet Union and the Eastern bloc countries. The Grenadian revolution, in particular, had wide appeal for "progressive" governments in countries of the South and more so for liberation movements throughout Africa and Latin America. It also gained support from a range of left-wing parties in Europe and especially in the United States, where the attempt of a small country in such proximity to implement an alternative political and economic agenda[2] was viewed with growing admiration. As Prime Minister Maurice Bishop declared in a speech at the City University of New York's Hunter College in June 1983, part of the appeal lay in the fact that Grenadians spoke English and were predominantly black, making the revolution's transformative agenda more accessible to African Americans. Its success was of particular importance to left-leaning movements in the Caribbean, which viewed it as an indication of what was possible. At home, the revolution unleashed the energies of the youth in the service of creating a militia for defence, of engaging with agriculture and other sectors of the economy, and of transforming communities through volunteerism. It also sought to mobilize and organize women in its support and for more direct engagement with the economy.

The revolution, located as it was in the US sphere of influence, with a government that was openly hostile, tested US hegemony. Thus, the US invasion of Grenada can be characterized as the last proxy battle of the Cold War.[3] Grenada's close relationship with Cuba, viewed by the United States as a Soviet satellite, and its broadening of diplomatic relations with the Soviet Union and the Eastern bloc countries placed it squarely within the Cold War dynamics and the battle for turf between the two superpowers. US president Ronald Reagan dramatically warned that "it isn't nutmeg that's at stake in the Caribbean and Central America; it is the United States national security".[4] When the United States invaded, the size of Cuban forces was exaggerated and the fighting presented by the media and the Reagan administration as a largely US–Cuban affair, overshadowing the resistance put up by the People's Revolutionary Army. The US victory was thus to be read as a triumph over the Soviet projection of power within the US sphere of influence, within its own backyard. The invasion of Grenada demonstrated that the United States was once again willing to use overt military force to achieve its aims, and the message was not lost on the Soviet Union or its allies in Cuba and Nicaragua. It is surely not far-fetched to say that the invasion, following what the hawks perceived as the passivity of the Carter administration, marked the flexing of US power vis-à-vis the Soviet Union, presaging and, arguably, contributing to the eventual collapse of the USSR itself.

The invasion of Grenada was the first overt use of force by the United States since the Vietnam War.[5] The Vietnam experience had left the United States wary of engaging in such operations, but Grenada, given its size and the regional political forces arrayed against it, was perceived as an opponent against whom the United States could easily win. There was a stark contrast between the complexity of the engagement in Lebanon in response to a bomb killing 241 military personnel[6] at a marine base on 23 October 1983 and the simplicity of forcefully removing the already delegitimated Grenadian military government.[7]

Grenada was also an important opportunity for the United States to test a key lesson from the Vietnam War – namely, managing the media. The media were excluded from Grenada until two days after the invasion, when they were carefully shepherded to sites "confirming" the communist threat that the island presented, such as warehouses full of weapons and other military supplies. The United States would go on to perfect this approach in later conflicts, by "embedding" the media within US forces, significantly increasing the likelihood of a sympathetic response as the media were viewing the conflict from a US vantage point, under the watchful eye and guidance of the military.

The revolution's collapse also threatened the already tenuous South/South solidarity, with countries in sub-Saharan Africa[8] and Latin America[9] expressing hostility to the Commonwealth Caribbean countries that invited, supported and, in some instances, participated in the invasion. It had the positive outcome, however, of providing the context for the international community to pay closer attention to the challenges, including those of security, faced by small states. The Commonwealth Heads of Government summit held the following November in New Delhi, which discussed the invasion at length, paved the way for the small states agenda to move centre stage with the commissioning of a study on small states, published in 1985 as *Vulnerability: Small States in the Global Society*. This was followed by a subsequent publication with the World Bank[10] and by the publication of a vulnerability index.[11] The World Bank now has a specific programme[12] dedicated to addressing the concerns of small states.[13] The small states agenda has found its way into the World Trade Organization, although with limited success to date.[14] Nevertheless, the international recognition of the special challenges of small states owes its provenance, at least in part, to the invasion of Grenada.

Regional Dimension

The revolution's collapse had a profound effect on left-wing political parties and regimes in the South and on their conviction that a third path between communism and Western capitalism was possible. This was felt most keenly in the Caribbean, where the revolution's gruesome end, followed by the US invasion, effectively destroyed the Left in the region. Its collapse led to infighting and loss of solidarity among left-wing parties, particularly between the left-of-centre parties and those considered Marxist-Leninist.[15] More importantly, it led to distrust of the Left throughout the region, resulting in the demise of some political parties and making the terrain for third parties to contest national elections more difficult.[16] Also, it served to reinforce the credibility of Westminster-style parliamentary democracy. It is now common wisdom that had the revolution not removed parliamentary elections as the route to democratic expression, the outcome might have been different.

Finally, the invasion came close to wrecking the Caribbean Community (CARICOM). The revolution had earlier tested the already strained relations within the organization, where it met with varying responses. This was mitigated by the decision of the heads of government to proceed along the lines of an acceptance of "ideological pluralism" to accommodate the revolution. The assassination of Prime Minister Maurice Bishop and others, however, revived old fears and insecurities, prompting most of the member states of the sub-regional Organization of Eastern Caribbean States, along with Barbados and Jamaica, to invite the United States to intervene. The ensuing tensions between this group and the other CARICOM countries which were against the invasion were alleviated only because of the decision to leave the Grenada events off the agenda of the Nassau summit which followed, in 1984.

National

The revolution and its demise had a profound effect on Grenada. The PRG had initially been able to neutralize much of the opposition – which, in the early days, came mostly from supporters of the ousted prime minister, Eric Gairy – by embracing them. However, in some cases where opposition persisted, the government resorted to police detention – in many instances, without trial. This served to solidify opposition, despite the revolution's continued, though diminishing, popularity. The killing of Bishop and the US invasion had the effect of cementing the existing schisms in Grenadian society and creating new ones, threatening its social fabric. Division emerged along the following lines: between those who were in favour of the revolution, seeing it as a force of good, and those who were against the revolution, convinced that it was doomed to failure; those who were pro–Maurice Bishop but were against the revolution, believing that Bishop was a good man hijacked by bad people (in other words, that he had good intentions but the revolution was essentially bad); those who were supportive of revolution and Maurice Bishop but hostile to Deputy Prime Minister Bernard Coard, who, they believed, had destroyed the revolution; and those, albeit a small minority, who reviled Maurice Bishop for betraying the revolution and paving the way for its collapse and the US invasion. In a small society with strong communal and inter-familial relations, such divisions presented serious challenges for social cohesion.

The events of the revolution, traumatic for some Grenadians, and those of 19 October 1983, when Bishop and others were killed, and of 25 October, when the US invaded, harrowing for most, have left unresolved psychological effects. The paucity of psychologists and social workers, coupled with the disuse (due to lack of custom) of the services of even those few, meant that the society received no counselling after these traumatic events, increasing the likelihood of people suffering from post-traumatic stress disorder. A truth and reconciliation commission was established in 2001 and issued its report in 2006, but it did little to reconcile the existing social schisms and to reduce the ongoing trauma from the events of October 1983.

About the Essays

Grenada: Revolution and Invasion presents a unique collection on the events that led to the dramatic demise of the Grenada Revolution, drawn from academics from the Caribbean, the United Kingdom and the United States, as well as the reflections of two significant players from this period – Richard Hart, Grenada's attorney general during the revolution, and Sir Shridath Ramphal, the Commonwealth secretary general at the time, who was instrumental in crafting a Commonwealth response that drew attention, for the first time, to the plight of small states in the postcolonial period. This book brings together in one volume varying viewpoints from the main stage of action, exploring multiple perspectives on the revolution and the invasion. These articles originally appeared in special issues of *Social and Economic Studies*, published in the Caribbean, and *Round Table: The Commonwealth Journal of International Affairs*, published in the United Kingdom. In bringing together these varied perspectives from the Caribbean, Europe and the United States, the entire volume is more than the sum of its parts, together presenting a far broader account of this still under-researched moment in history. The book is organized into sections that reflect the revolutionary period, the US invasion supported by some Caribbean forces, and reflections on the post-revolutionary period.

Part 1, Revolution, includes two chapters by Grenadians. Merle Collins's "What Happened? Grenada: A Retrospective Journey" presents a compelling account of the events that gave birth to the revolution and of the fissures that ultimately led to its fall, while Nicole Phillip-Dowe gives an account of the revolution's response to gender issues through legislation and activism, providing, at the same time, an insight into the broader challenges of transformation which the revolution faced. In "The Revolution and Its Discontents: Grenadian Newspapers and Attempts to Shape Public Opinion during Political Transition", Laurie R. Lambert presents the battles of the government-owned newspaper, the *Free West Indian*, with the voice of the opposition, the *Torchlight*, in defining the revolution, largely through the lens of the Cuban Revolution as a model. As with Phillip-Dowe's chapter, this work presents some insights into the contestation over ideas that were the battleground of the revolution. The final chapter in this section, "Ferrets in the Caribbean: Britain, Grenada and the Curious Case of the Armoured Cars" by Gary Williams, provides an important insight into the British government's treatment of the new revolution, expressed in its deliberations on whether or not to sell the revolutionary government two outdated armoured cars. It also reveals the divisions on this issue between the Foreign and Commonwealth Office and the Ministry of Defence.

Part 2, Invasion, begins with an engaging account by Richard Hart of the US invasion and of his subsequent escape from Grenada, serving as a reminder that the fall of the revolution also had significant ramifications for individuals who were part of this process. Patsy Lewis's "A Response to Edward Seaga's *The Grenada Intervention: The Inside Story*" confronts former Jamaican prime minister Edward Seaga's personal narrative of the events leading up to the invasion and of his role in it, as well as his attempt to justify the invasion. Drawing on alternative accounts, including an interview with Anthony Abrahams, a minister in Seaga's government, as well as on the reflections of the then governor general Paul Scoon from his book *Survival for Service: My Experiences as Governor General of Grenada*, she refutes Seaga's account and what she views as his attempt to rewrite history. This chapter is followed by Robert J. Beck's "The Grenada Invasion, International Law and the Scoon Invitation: A Thirty-Year Retrospective", which examines the legality of Governor General Scoon's alleged invitation to intervene, which was used by the United States and its Caribbean allies to justify the invasion. Howard Tumber's "Journalism and the Invasion of Grenada Thirty Years On: A Retrospective" examines the significance of Grenada for the US treatment of the media in situations of conflict. This section ends with Sir Shridath Ramphal's important insight into the divisions that the invasion wrought between the African Commonwealth countries and the Caribbean countries that supported the invasion, and with his account of his role in minimizing these conflicts and getting the Commonwealth to focus, instead, on the broader challenges that small states face, in the light of Grenada's experiences. This marked the beginning of the organization's delineation of the category of small states and its advocacy of their special features which require consideration from the international community.

Part 3, Grenada Redux, includes chapters that address some of the themes that persist in contemporary Grenada. These look at three aspects of the effects of the revolution and the invasion: the psychological implications for Grenadians as they attempt to address the rifts in their society; the conduct of politics in Grenada and the weaknesses inherent in Westminster democracy; and post-revolution Grenada's relations with contemporary Cuba. In "Written into Amnesia: The Truth and Reconciliation Commission of Grenada", Jermaine O. McCalpin explores the attempts of Grenada to engage with a truth and reconciliation process as a means of investigating the events that led up to the revolution, the revolution itself and its treatment of dissidence, and the events that led to its fall. He concludes that the process failed to address the need for justice of those were aggrieved, thus leaving the issue unresolved and the source of much pain. Wendy Grenade's "Party Politics and Governance in Grenada: An Analysis of the New National Party (1984–2012)" presents a picture of Westminster-style first-past-the-post democracy as it operates in post-revolutionary Grenada, by focusing on the fortunes of the New National Party, the dominant party over the mentioned period. She concludes that despite the US boast of making Grenada a model for democracy in the region, the Westminster system as it operates there allows for the trappings of formal democracy while leaving the broader issues of authoritarianism and the need for deeper democracy untouched. John Cotman's piece,

"Coming in from the Cold: Grenada and Cuba since 1983", concludes the volume by revisiting Grenada's relations with Cuba, which were re-established in the 1990s and were part of a broader re-engagement with Cuba by the Commonwealth Caribbean. In this chapter, he suggests that the impetus behind the PRG's relations with Cuba, of garnering resources to address economic and social issues, particularly of education and health, is no less real today and underscores the persistent challenges in the post-independence period that small states face in securing resources to address their development problems.

The Grenada events of 1979–1983, especially the revolution's tragic demise, brought the country to the world stage. Since then, Grenada has retreated to its place as a small state, with little significance in shaping the global political and economic landscape within which small states operate. Nevertheless, powerful resonances remain, in the island, regionally and internationally. This volume seeks both to remind us of the tumultuous past, drawing lessons for the present generation, and to begin to suggest possible political approaches for the near, if inevitably uncertain, future.

NOTES

1.   For an account of what led up to this, see Brian Meeks, "Grenada, Once Again: Re-visiting the 1983 Crisis and Collapse of the Grenada Revolution", in *Caribbean Political Activism: Essays in Honour of Richard Hart*, ed. Rupert Lewis, Caribbean Reasonings Series (Kingston: Ian Randle, 2012), 199–226.

2.   In reality, the government's economic agenda was pretty modest, proceeding along the lines of creating a mixed economy with some government ownership of estates which were put in the service of cooperatives and initiatives to encourage private sector investment, particularly in tourism. Its political agenda was more radical, as it eschewed Westminster-style democracy, which it inherited, in favour of a one-party democracy based on mass mobilization.

3.   The US covert war in Nicaragua did not end until 1989. Nevertheless, the significance of the US action in Grenada lies in the form it took, of open invasion by US troops.

4.   Ronald Reagan (US President), "Remarks on Central America and El Salvador at the Annual Meeting of the National Association of Manufacturers", 10 March

1983, *Public Papers of the Presidents of the United States, The American Presidency Project*, http://www.presidency.ucsb.edu/ws/?pid=41034 (accessed 7 July 2014). Grenada is one of the world's largest exporters of nutmeg.

5. The United States had continued to conduct covert operations in a number of countries after Vietnam – most notably, Nicaragua.

6. These included 220 marines, 18 sailors and 3 soldiers. The attack on the US marine barracks was followed by an attack on barracks of French paratroopers, killing 58. See Jim Michaels, "Recalling the Deadly 1983 Attack on the Marine Barracks", *USA Today*, 23 October 2013, www.usatoday.com/story/nation/2013/10/23/marine -beirut-lebanon-hezbollah/3171593/ (accessed 25 June 2014).

7. There is an explicit connection between the two events, as the United States diverted to Grenada warships headed for Lebanon in the wake of the attack there. This gave rise to speculation that the administration had rethought its response of retaliating to the attack, which may have embroiled the United States even further in the Lebanese civil war, in favour of an easier, more clear-cut victory in Grenada. The incident led to the United States pulling out its forces from Lebanon.

8. Ramphal's essay in this volume provides a first-hand account of the conflict that arose in the Commonwealth as a result of the Caribbean's role in the invasion.

9. The Charter of the Organization of American States was amended in 1985 to reinforce the principle of non-intervention, partly in response to the Grenada invasion. See "Organization of American States", *Dictionary of American History 2003, Encyclopedia.com*, http://www.encyclopedia.com/doc/1G2-3401803102. html (accessed 3 July 2014).

10. These included: *A Future for Small States: Overcoming Vulnerability*, Report by a Commonwealth Advisory Group (London: Commonwealth Secretariat, 1997); and Commonwealth/World Bank Joint Task Force on Small States, *Small States: Meeting Challenges in the Global Economy*, Report of the Task Force (Washington, DC: World Bank, 2000), http://www.cpahq.org/cpahq/cpadocs/meetingchal lengeinglobaleconomyl.pdf (accessed 17 January 2015).

11. Their vulnerability to climate change has overtaken the security concerns which initially triggered the focus on small states. The 1992 UN Conference on Environment and Development, which adopted Agenda 21, was followed two years later, in Barbados, by the Global Conference on the Sustainable Development of Small Island Developing States, which sought to operationalize Agenda 21 in respect of small states. Its outcome was the Barbados Programme of Action for the Sustainable Development of Small States, which set out priority areas for addressing small states' challenges. There were subsequent follow-up meetings to assess progress and to address their need for financing. See "From Barbados

to Mauritius", Intersectoral Platform on Small Island Developing States, http://portal.unesco.org/en/ev.php-URL_ID=12117&URL_DO=DO_TOPIC&URL_SECTION=201.html.

12. Activities undertaken by the World Bank in respect of small states include a Small States Forum, initiated in 2000, and held during its Annual Meeting, which brings together Finance Ministers and Central Bank governors of small states to discuss their challenges. It also provides supplementary statistics on small states.

13. The World Bank notes that over 25 per cent of its members have populations below 1.5 million (the cut-off point for considering states to be small, which was developed in association with the Commonwealth Secretariat). See "Small States Overview", World Bank, http://www.worldbank.org/en/country/smallstates/overview.

14. The Doha Ministerial Declaration 2001, paragraph 35, established a working group to investigate the trade-related challenges confronting small states' integration into the global trading system, but stopped short of identifying this group as a separate category of states. See "Doha WTO Ministerial Declaration WT/MIN(01)/DEC/1: Ministerial Declaration Adopted on 14 November 2001", World Trade Organization, 20 November 2001, http://www.wto.org/english/thewto_e/minist_e/min01_e/mindecl_e.htm.

15. For a perspective on lessons that the revolution's end held for the Caribbean Left, see Gordon K. Lewis, "The Lessons for the Caribbean Left", *Grenada: The Jewel Despoiled* (Baltimore: Johns Hopkins University Press, 1987), 161–78.

16. The Workers Party of Jamaica, which was most closely aligned with the New JEWEL Movement, the political party that was the architect of the revolution, was a major casualty, disintegrating a few years later.

Part 1.

REVOLUTION

1.

What Happened?

Grenada: A Retrospective Journey

MERLE COLLINS

ABSTRACT

The story of the revolution is as much about human emotion and simple miscommunication as it is about the greater global forces that have for centuries been exerting their superior physical and ideological powers over this tiny island of one hundred thousand people. In probing the effects of colonialism and of its inherent authoritarianism on the ideology of the Grenadian revolution and its leadership, this chapter seeks to place the men who emerged as leaders of Grenada – Eric Gairy, Maurice Bishop and Bernard Coard – in context. In attempting to untangle the deep roots of authoritarianism and the tendency to depend on a "maximum leader" in Grenada and, indeed, the Caribbean, we gain another perspective on the all-too-human dynamics of the power struggle that ended so bloodily.

Suspended in Time

To them the war was still memory, not the past, not history. When the stories pass down to the next generation, they may still be called memories because the information is passed from the mouths of the participants, but this is also the period when memories of an event become descriptions of the past, something that has little immediate relevance to the current generation.
—Nigel Hunt[1]

"When the stories pass down to the next generation . . ." – I often find myself wondering about this, where the traumatic stories of Grenada's 1983 experience are concerned. To the many traumatized by those events, it seems almost impossible that more than thirty years have passed. It seems even more incredible that many young Grenadians born in or around 1983, and those who have come after them, born fifteen years or so later, have had little extended discussion with earlier generations about the events of 1983. Parents and grandparents have often dealt with the trauma by burying it deep, saying, "That gone." They look instead to a future without much political involvement for them or, they must sometimes hope, for their children. Some parents who were involved in demonstrations as eighteen-year-olds in the 1970s would perhaps not encourage their children to do the same, fearful because of the painful lessons of their own youth.

Yet some have had such discussions, and some stories have been told, so even though the memories of war may not seem to have much relevance to the everyday lives of the current generation, the past colours everything in their world. Some young people have inherited from their parents' enthusiasm – and their pain – names like Fedon, Che, Maurice and Samora, and so they have become walking embodiments of an expressed need for revolutionary thinking, breathing memory vaults of what might have been.

Several questions present themselves: What makes us keep talking about these traumatic events, or remembering them, even when it appears we cannot discuss them sensibly? Does it make sense to remember what might have been? Can the past, traumatic and otherwise (if there is much otherwise), help map the way to the future? Is there a need for change in the social, economic and political circumstances of the people of Grenada? May any analysis of the past help to attain such change? If young people, representing the elusive future, have to be part of the envisioned change, does it not make sense for them to know and discuss details about the past?

Let me begin by reviewing details of that past, which would suggest that I answer many of the above questions in the affirmative. In 1983, Grenada (the islands Grenada, Carriacou and Petite Martinique) experienced the trauma of internal political party strife resulting in the murders of the prime minister, other ministers of government and members of the public, followed by a US invasion on October 25. For all Grenadians, but especially for the young ones born after 1983 or just before, this is one of the country's most recent open wounds, obviously there but not often discussed, still festering, just under the surface. The story that came to a bloody climax in 1983 represents a relatively recent trauma, and indeed the community would, if it could, choose to forget those days.

More recently, some Grenadians have been trying to discuss the importance of remembering. On the final, quiet afternoon of the thirty-eighth Conference of the Caribbean Studies Association, Friday, 7 June 2013, Grenadian high school students participated in a presentation aimed at recreating, memorializing and, in the process, teaching aspects of the Grenada Revolution. The presentations suggested that, for these high school students, the Grenada Revolution represented the kind of traumatic history sometimes explored in tragic plays. In fact, one student said, in a discussion after the presentation, that it was hard to believe that the things adults told them about in interviews had happened in Grenada. The student presentations were a result of the work of Grenadian theatre director Francis Urias Peters, who had been contacted by the Caribbean Studies Association. He had organized teachers to engage students in this activity. Sitting in the small audience on that final day of the conference were some who had been actual participants in or witnesses to the events of 1979–83. Their own stories, descriptions of a past they had lived, were being acted out before them. They had been actively involved in trying to change the postcolonial world they had inherited from Britain; some had talked of revolution and anti-colonialism, even anti-imperialism and Marxism-Leninism; others had simply hoped for better social and economic opportunities, for an education system not so focused on colonial ideas, for a better health system. And then everything had come crashing down.

Now, a young generation appeared to be starting the process of entering into the spirit of what happened. Imperceptibly, a door was opening to allow some much-needed future study and analysis by a younger generation. Moving and evocative, the young people's presentation suggested how lessons may be drawn from the wounds of history. One group took on the roles of major participants of the period – Eric Matthew Gairy, the prime minister who was ousted by the New JEWEL Movement (NJM) in 1979; Maurice Bishop, a member of the NJM, who later became prime minister from 1979 to 1983 and was murdered at the fort; Bernard Coard, another member of the NJM, who was Bishop's friend, became deputy prime minister and was later accused of complicity in his murder. One student played the role of a woman who had jumped from the high walls of the fort in St George's to escape the terror of bullets. Members of Urias Peters's Family Theatre, focusing on how personal relationships could reflect political conflicts, played people in the community making choices about what to believe. In a strange way, it felt like being given a particular privilege to see how the past may live in the future.

Earlier in the conference, after a lecture that had touched on the theme of trauma and narrative, I had been asked two questions, both difficult to answer briefly. In essence, the questioners, referring to the 1983 incidents, wanted to know what had happened and what may be done to ensure that events of this kind were not repeated. To consider what may be done would perhaps first require the kind of analysis that many commentaries – including this one – attempt. To the questioner at the conference who asked what happened in Grenada, I responded then, "I don't know", meaning that I thought I was not being asked to give a linear account but to attempt a philosophical interpretation of events; I meant that I knew this was a question lots of scholars have been examining, trying to find explanations at the core of the Grenada conflict of 1983, and that I did not have a quick, capsule answer. I have heard too many such unsatisfying ones. And then the questioner asked, what would you tell your children? Is that the answer you would give your children? That put the question in a very specific context. May one attempt both linear and philosophical explanations in an attempt to tell the story to the children or to the young people of a succeeding generation? These questions, coming after a presentation designed to approach answers to some of these issues, reminded me that presentations often begin in the middle of the story, with presenters assuming that the listeners share at least some of the knowledge presenters bring to the discussion, that the story is well known, that the conflict of which we speak is familiar. But this is not always the case. Indeed, at the end of many presentations about the Grenada crisis of 1983, younger people in the audience, in particular, may well ask, what really happened? Now, as I write this chapter, I think especially of young people, of those who performed on the last day of the conference and those concerned with the stories of Grenada and the rest of the Caribbean. I will attempt to explore what happened, as far as I understand it, in a way that would also help contextualize the story and explain it, particularly to young people introduced to this article. I write out of my interest in the power of narrative for examining social and economic processes. I write knowing that some would have heard or read variations of this story, that many will hear and read other variations, and that each variation approaches some aspect of a deeper truth.

First, I turn to Cathy Caruth,[2] a literary critic with an interesting analysis of trauma. In this essay, I consider only what may be useful to understand about Grenada's story, in order to avoid unwittingly wounding people further. Because even those who do not express it verbally know that the country and every individual in it, as well as many outside of it, were wounded during those dark days of 1983. What happened? I will begin with October 1983, when the events generally considered most traumatic occurred, and from there walk further back through the haunted, magical forest of history, in an effort to find some path that could have led the country to that month of trauma. In my estimation, the walking back is very important. In fact, after the first shock of 1983 had subsided, I kept thinking that I wanted to find out more about how Grenadians and other Caribbean people came to be who they are as a people. One place I wanted to visit was England, where so much of the Caribbean story rests on library shelves and in other archival spaces. How may those neglected stories, I wondered, help me understand some of the antecedents of this trauma?

On 19 October 1983, Maurice Bishop, the minister of health Norris Bain, the minister of education Jacqueline Creft, the minister of foreign affairs Unison Whiteman, trade unionists Fitzroy Bain and Vincent Noel, businessmen Evelyn Bullen and Evelyn Maitland, the production manager of the Marketing and National Importing Board Keith Hayling, member of the People's Revolutionary Army Dorset Peters, and Grenadian civilians,[3] including high schoolers and other students, were killed at Fort Rupert, situated on the hillside near the hospital in St George's, the capital. Some of these victims, including the prime minister, the ministers of government and at least one trade unionist, were, it was later admitted, lined up against the walls of the fort and executed by members of the armed forces who belonged to an opposing faction of the ruling party, the NJM. But the terrified people of Grenada were told that these individuals had died in crossfire when the fort was attacked.

After these events, a military curfew was imposed on the country, and radio announcements informed people that the government had been replaced by the Revolutionary Military Council.

The day of the murders, 19 October, is remembered as the first bloody day of these traumatic events. The second came six days later, 25 October, when troops from the United States invaded the country. They were subsequently joined by troops from the armed forces of Barbados and Jamaica[4] which played a supporting role in the months that followed. An anxious voice on the radio informed the people that a US invasion was imminent or in progress. Residents of the capital and its environs could hear military drones overhead. A strange mixture of excitement and horror pervaded the atmosphere. The Grenadian people were still reeling from the unimaginable events of 19 October and were fearful of the members of the party and the new military government, now seen as murderers. With the murders, the stage had been set for the entrance of those who, many people seemed to hope, could be new saviours.

In the days that followed, even as friends urged me to acknowledge that, given the demonstrated violence of the party and its obvious contempt for the people, there were few options and that the US invasion could not really be rejected in the circumstances, I quietly mourned the beginning of another colonial relationship. Given the political, social and economic power of the United States, given the history of British colonialism with its failure to develop Grenadian social, political and economic structures of long-term benefit to the people of Grenada and its contempt for the working people, given little demonstrated US interest (before 1983) in the social and economic advancement of Grenada, what could one expect but an unequal relationship? Would Grenada now become even more dependent and settle for a long-term relationship of subservience that could affect the sense of self of individual citizens? I asked myself these questions quietly, because the party that had promised so much and from which so much had been expected had led the country into a situation where it did not have too many choices. More Grenadians, as well as members of the invading forces, were to die during that second traumatic period in October. In my estimation, the country's self-respect was a less tangible casualty of the invasion. I could not help thinking that if there were to be a similar situation in the United States, its people were not likely, no matter what happened, to welcome a foreign power to its shores as a saviour. My friends assured me that the reality of violence from leaders reduced such concerns to the level of sentimental musings. I was not convinced, but I did not have answers. What had led to this unimaginable occurrence in Grenada?

The details of what happened on those days, and especially on 19 October, have been explored in various other accounts.[5] Each account, as different as it may be from the others, contributes immeasurably to the reconstruction of those moments and of truths about the country and the people. Again, I ask, as so many have asked and continue to ask, what happened?

To help shape a response, I go back to 1973, approximately ten years before. Grenada's premier, Eric Gairy, had by then been in leadership roles in the country for approximately twenty-two years. He had come to the fore in 1951, as a young man of twenty-nine, in a small, poor colonial state where the majority of the population depended on agriculture for its livelihood. Gairy emerged as a champion of agricultural workers, who were being exploited by the members of a planting class who, by and large, owned estates in the country. He established a union and started a political party. The union championed the workers' rights and appeared to be of more significance than the party. By the 1970s, a younger generation, some of them children and grandchildren of the workers who had supported Gairy in 1951, did not feel the same sense of allegiance to him as leader. Grenada was still a colony of Britain in 1973, but it was moving closer to independence, and there had been several constitutional changes over the years. Between 1958 and 1962, there had been an attempt at a West Indian federation, and when that collapsed, the countries of the Caribbean, beginning in 1962 with Trinidad and Tobago, and then Jamaica, acquired independence from Britain. In 1966, Guyana and Barbados joined the ranks of the independent nations, and, in 1968, the Windward and Leeward Islands, Grenada being one of the former, acquired what was called associated statehood, which meant they had control of internal affairs, while Britain kept responsibility for external affairs and defence. The leader of an associated state was called a premier. This meant that, in the 1970s, Gairy was acquiring more power as a local political leader, and the new generation of Grenadian youths, although supportive of the notion of independence, was not happy about acquiring it with Eric Gairy in office.

Through the years, Premier Gairy acquired a reputation for rigged elections, corrupt financial practices and the creation of a secret police force, which was used to brutally repress opponents. The Grenada National Party, an opposition party formed in the 1950s, was in office during the 1960s, but it never managed to capture the imagination of the agricultural workers.

Throughout the world, in the late 1960s and 1970s, young people were actively opposing governments considered repressive. I have noted elsewhere that the writer Mark Kurlansky highlights 1968 as a year in which people everywhere were showing "a profound distaste for authoritarianism in any form".[6] The Black Power movement of the 1970s also had a significant impact throughout the Caribbean, particularly in neighbouring Trinidad and Tobago and at regional campuses of the University of the West Indies. In 1968, Walter Rodney, Guyanese historian and activist working at the Mona campus of the University of the West Indies, was expelled from Jamaica. Grenadians at home and abroad were affected by this regional and international ferment. In a commentary on the works of Walter Rodney and their influence in the Caribbean, University of the West Indies professor Rupert Lewis offers the opinion that "Rodney's expulsion from Jamaica in 1968 had repercussions which spread to Trinidad, Guyana and other Caribbean territories as well as to the Caribbean populations in North America and England. It marked a new phase of regional radicalism influenced by the civil rights movement and Black Power rhetoric from the United States adapted to the Caribbean. Some of the young people influenced by this movement later on adopted Marxism."[7] Lewis names Maurice Bishop and Bernard Coard as "the most prominent examples of the transition in the English-speaking Caribbean from Black Power to Marxism". The 1970s was a radicalizing period for young Caribbean intellectuals looking for new models of social, political and economic development for their countries. Lewis's comment is important to the analysis of the events in Grenada and is worth quoting at length. He writes: "Rodney's expulsion from Jamaica gave him publicity in the Caribbean, North America, England and Africa. Bogle L'Ouverture's publication of his Jamaican lectures and speeches under the title *Groundings with My Brothers* helped to shape his political reputation as the region's premier radical-intellectual-activist. Many young Caribbean intellectuals followed in Rodney's mould in the 1970's but few were to have his intellectual depth, probity and pan-African experience."[8]

After naming some of these intellectuals, including Bishop and Coard, Lewis continues: "They had all dialogued with him but none had his experience and knowledge of the African continent and few could rival his commitment to the working people. Moreover, this commitment was linked to an overriding concern to avoid manipulation of the working people which characterized the politics of the mass parties in the Caribbean and the centralism of the left wing organizations which facilitated middle class hegemony."[9]

Let us remember this comment as we consider the story of the NJM. What I am trying to do here is to consider how the NJM's emergence during the Gairy period was facilitated by the extremes of his abuse of the system and the growing disaffection with his regime. I want also to note some of the ways in which the NJM developed, to see if there may be any clues to explain subsequent actions. The NJM was formed in 1973. It was a coming together of two organizations – the Movement for Assemblies of the People, led by Bishop, who was from the capital and had studied law in Britain, and JEWEL (Joint Endeavor for Welfare, Education and Liberation), which was led by Unison Whiteman, from rural St David's, who had studied economics at Howard University in the United States. The NJM developed rapidly, organizing young people and attracting the support of those disaffected with Gairy's leadership, and became a formidable force. In addition to Bishop and Whiteman, among those attracted to the NJM were Coard, then a lecturer in economics at the Trinidad campus of the University of the West Indies, and Kenrick Radix, an attorney who had earlier started the Movement for Assemblies of the People with Bishop. Buoyed by increasing opposition to Gairy, they and other young Grenadian intellectuals soon became focused on removing him from office.

At first, the NJM would not call itself a party. Bishop's Movement for Assemblies of the People had been a "movement" for representative "assemblies" of the people, and this movement was interested in popular democracy. These groups were all influenced by the ideas of the time. Coard has acknowledged, in an interview, that he was influenced by Black Power ideas, by Tanzania's Julius Nyerere and *Ujamaa*, by notions of African socialism. He was a student in the United States at the time and invited Stokeley Carmichael to speak at a Brandeis University summer programme during the Black Power era. He was also influenced by the example of Cuba, at first more because of Cuba's identity as a Caribbean country than because of its interest in socialism. According to Coard, he began with a broad interest in Black Power ideology, and it was the 1973–74 period in Grenada and the NJM's perception that, although it had mass support, it needed to be more organized as a party in order to remove Gairy from office that led to the party's more focused study of Marxism-Leninism and the beginning of its development as a vanguard party.[10]

Throughout the 1970s, the NJM and other groups organized opposition to Gairy's regime. In 1973, as the NJM collaborated with business groups in planning strikes to show displeasure with activities of the Gairy government, including allegations of corruption and repressive acts by the security forces, Gairy used those same security forces to counter this opposition. On 18 November 1973, six NJM members – Bishop, Hudson Austin, Simon Daniel, Kenrick Radix, Selwyn Strachan and Unison Whiteman – were beaten, arrested and charged with possession of a rifle and ammunition. The confrontation, the broad unity among the opposition forces and the arrest of the NJM members were reported in the regional press. After this confrontation, young people, particularly high school students, were at the forefront of anti-Gairy demonstrations. It is especially interesting to recall this when one notes today the way that the events of October 1983 have driven this story of student activism underground. By 1973–74, there was in the country a broad coalition of opposition to Gairy, and the NJM was a recognized leader in the struggle.

Meanwhile, the NJM was making pragmatic decisions about its participation in the electoral process. In the 1976 elections, NJM members were actually elected to office, with Bishop becoming leader of a united opposition. Other, more secret, forms of opposition to Gairy continued. As far as Grenada's response to the NJM is concerned, it is important to note that many were excited about the emergence of a group of educated young people who did not distance themselves from agricultural workers and the working class, the lawyers among them willing to take on pro bono work, and all willing to openly challenge Gairy's excesses. To a young generation wanting advancement for their country, the NJM offered hope and the promise of a more productive future. NJM members went around to secondary schools, had quiet meetings with teachers and showed an interest in the education of the youth. They supported, organized and were an important part of massive anti-Gairy demonstrations during the 1970s; one such demonstration in 1970 was organized by nurses who were agitating for better conditions at the general hospital. This was a popular cause, since conditions at the hospital were well known and much critiqued. Students were at the forefront of NJM-organized demonstrations during the period 1973–74, in the lead-up to Grenada's independence from Britain in February. The NJM appeared determined not to celebrate an independence that would give all powers, including the portfolios of external affairs and defence, to Gairy as the new prime minister.

In January 1973, in one confrontation, members of a group of thuggish young men, said to be Gairy's secret police and known as the "Mongoose Gang", jumped into the middle of an NJM-organized demonstration at the Carenage, St George's. As usual, there were many high school students and teachers. Pandemonium ensued, and terrified demonstrators tried to rush away from the areas surrounding Otway House, a union building on the Carenage. Later, it was reported that Bishop's father, Rupert, had been shot and killed while trying to shield students from the attacking Gairy forces. Another casualty of the period was the governor, Dame Hilda Bynoe, who had been appointed by Premier Gairy in 1968. Dame Hilda, the first woman and the first local to hold the post during the colonial period, was a popular but controversial figure to young people, since she had been appointed by Gairy. Offended because demonstrators had moved from shouting "Gairy must go" to add "and Bynoe, too", Dame Hilda said she would resign unless people indicated that they wanted her to stay. Incensed because the governor had even deigned to respond to the people's challenge, Gairy requested her resignation. Dame Hilda, feeling that she was not wanted by the people, had tendered her resignation via the proper channels – through the British High Commission to the Queen of England. After the fatality at Otway House and the departure of the governor, an uneasy silence settled on the land. A broad coalition continued to support anti-Gairy demonstrations, and Gairy waited for things to return to normal. Dock workers, electricity workers and all other essential-service employees remained on strike. Gairy waited. The British did nothing. On 7 February 1974, in the midst of darkness, Grenada became an independent nation in the British Commonwealth. When, in spite of the fact that the NJM had the support of the majority of people and that there were constant massive demonstrations, it was unable to unseat Gairy, the party appears to have decided to move to the organization of a vanguard that could be a tight core of leaders. As the party strove to study Marxism-Leninism and develop in vanguard mode, one major challenge was to recognize and respect that the focus of many of its supporters was opposition to the repression of the Gairy era.

On 13 March 1979, while Gairy was in New York at a meeting of the United Nations, the NJM attacked the army barracks and seized the radio station. NJM members went on radio, asking the people of the country to go to local police stations and demand that the police put up a white flag of surrender. This is an important part of the narrative of the overthrow of the Gairy regime. It shows how confident members of the NJM were of their popularity and how much support they enjoyed in the country. With the population in vocal support of their actions, and enjoying the esteem of the people because of their confident leadership of an anti-Gairy struggle, the NJM seized control of the country and, bowing to the parliamentary democratic practices inherited from the British, promised elections. It was eventually decided that elections could not be held without major disruption. Since the party had tremendous early support and this was the first change of government of its kind in the region, this may have been a mistake, but that assessment was to come much later. Perhaps it was to become more of an issue when the NJM was losing its popularity and could no longer claim legitimacy because of obvious mass support.

For four years, from 1979 to 1983, the NJM and its government, the People's Revolutionary Government (PRG), instituted many changes in Grenada. At the beginning, it was not an idle boast that the party was, in fact, focused on the people. With the support of the masses – to whom decisions were explained at meetings – the NJM/PRG challenged and tried to change aspects of the country's colonial inheritance. Party members argued that they did not have to be supportive of all of Britain's ideas and may not consider British forms of parliamentary democracy the best political option for the country; they tried to make agriculture more attractive to the population and to encourage people to eat what the country produced; they organized militias to prepare young people to defend the country against all aggressors, be they large or small; they established friendly relations with Cuba, which was regarded by the US as an enemy because of its close relationship with the Soviet Union; they set up vibrant workers', youth, women's and farmers' organizations;

they had popular public meetings to discuss the budget; they focused on what they referred to as "raising the cultural level" of the people and started an adult education programme known as the Centre for Popular Education. Since teachers needed to be trained, the National In-Service Teacher Education Programme was initiated. All of these were popular programmes, and in the early stages, they attracted many people. There was palpable excitement about the possibilities for social and economic transformation in the country.

Increasingly, as the party developed its core, the NJM rhetoric became militaristic. It developed a young, enthusiastic militia and an army, with a vocal armed-forces branch of the party. Throughout these years, the NJM was organizing as a party, studying Marxism-Leninism and working on establishing a small core group that could lead the work of the revolution. This meant that the party became very select and secretive and formed what the leadership referred to as a "Leninist vanguard"[11] group. In retrospect, and considering Rupert Lewis's comment on Rodney's insistence about not manipulating the working people, we may think about whether continuous discussion about the formation of a vanguard party in the small community opened a way for the possibility of such manipulation. Some of the young party recruits, the "most advanced elements of the working class", had had little formal education, and the party, with its programme of study, became their route to acquiring information and analytical skills. In that situation, teachers could acquire very powerful positions. In a small country of approximately one hundred thousand people, the select party group was resented for its secrecy, and the unworthy – those who were not invited to join or those who did not wish to join the party – looked askance at "the chosen".

Although the character of the party was clearly changing, people remained broadly supportive of some of the gains of the revolution – opportunities for further education, for example. In a small country that had inherited an elitist colonial education system, high school and university education were expensive and available mainly to those who had independent financial means or were able to acquire loans or scholarships. The PRG and the NJM changed this, ensuring that new secondary schools were opened and that there were more opportunities for further education. Parents, even if largely uninterested in ideology, were pleased that their children now had the opportunity to get an education. Many of the scholarships were tenable in the Soviet bloc

– Cuba, the German Democratic Republic (then East Germany), Czechoslovakia and the Soviet Union.

The United States responded to these alliances,[12] and the NJM's relationship with the public became more tense as it tried to counter such responses to its choice of political friends. While critiquing the attitude of the US government, the NJM/PRG tried to be careful to make a distinction between the government and the people, claiming that it had sympathy with the American people. Leaders reached out to the US black population. On his 1983 visit to the United States, Bishop spoke at Hunter College in New York. In his address to a packed hall, he told the audience that a "secret report to the State Department" had revealed that one reason for the US government's hostility to the Grenada Revolution was that "the people of Grenada and the leadership of Grenada speak English, and therefore can communicate directly with the people of the United States".[13] He noted that, "in some years, more American tourists come to our country than the entire population of our country"[14] and acknowledged that "if we go around and take a careful count, we may well discover that there are more Grenadians living in the United States than the whole population of Grenada".[15] This, he said, was a situation that the PRG did not want to affect negatively, although it claimed the right to manage its own affairs.

Locally and internationally, Bishop became the familiar and much-loved face of the Grenada Revolution. Locally, and especially among supporters, the Grenada political process was referred to familiarly and affectionately as "the Revo". Although, in its first two years, 1979–80, there was general excitement about the Revo, by 1981 it had lost some of its popularity. Looking back, one might say that, in the anxiety to accomplish much while simultaneously studying Marxism-Leninism and making it an important base of development for the party, the NJM members developed "battle fatigue". It was physically and mentally taxing to read, study, engage in intellectual debate and also lead the work of party and state. Perhaps without realizing the psychological toll it was taking, members of the party were themselves being traumatized. As the vanguard idea took root, a fine distinction also developed between the government and the party – the PRG and the NJM – but many operated on both fronts.

As the NJM/PRG became more overtly supportive of Cuba and the Soviet

Union, the United States became more opposed to the Bishop regime. The NJM blamed the US government for many events in Grenada. In 1981, at a rally held at Queen's Park, a bomb exploded under the stage from which leaders of the government and party were scheduled to speak, and some young people – three schoolgirls among them – were killed. Many were injured. The NJM/PRG blamed counter-revolutionaries. One night in 1981, on a stretch of road at Plains, St Patrick's, a car was ambushed and some young people shot to death. For that ambush too, the NJM blamed counter-revolutionary forces.[16] Whether or not these forces had the support of the United States, the events had the effect of contributing both to a culture of suspicion and repression within the ruling party and to a sense within the country that the NJM influence had brought to Grenada events and incidents that had not been common before.

Meanwhile, in a country the size of Grenada, it was not good for the party's public relations that it came to be regarded by the population as a type of secret society. Even as people worked in broad support of the revolution's aims to develop education and tend to the social needs of the population, they were uncomfortable with the secretive attitudes of party members and nervous about the word "communism", which became associated more and more with the party. It was not unusual to have the term – which was as little understood as was the word "capitalism" but more generally feared – applied in a disparaging manner to a political opponent. In the early 1950s, it had been used to describe Gairy.[17] Now though, the NJM's secrecy and study of Marxism-Leninism and the increasingly repressive attitudes associated with both the government and the party made the public suspicious of the NJM's ideology. The arrogant attitudes of some young leaders were not a good advertisement for either the party or its ideology. As the NJM became more suspicious about the development of counter-revolutionary activities, many people were imprisoned. Some of them, it has been suggested, may have been imprisoned with little cause. Gradually, the revolution was losing its hold on the popular imagination. It may be difficult to recall now, in the aftermath of the events of October 1983, but there was a growing sense of unease, certainly present in the country in 1982, not with one faction or the other, but with the party as a whole, its leadership of the revolution and what seemed to be the party's constant fear of "counter-revolutionary" activity. Within the Grenadian community, the designation "counter" became a quiet acknowledgement of a government and/or party assessment and an unspoken threat.

Early in 1983, Maurice Bishop spoke to the country about US opposition and planned military exercises at its military base in Vieques, Puerto Rico. There was fear about US intentions towards Grenada. Notwithstanding this, Coard today admits that the young revolutionaries could have been more dip-lomatic in their handling of relations with the United States. I would suggest that, outside opposition to and, possibly, destabilization of their revolution process notwithstanding, party members cannot be absolved of responsibil-ity for their reactions in the 1980s. Today, as people try to find ways to deal with the memory of possibility and loss, some remember, too, the attitudes and actions of members of the party. These assessments remain relevant, regardless of external interference.

Divided, the House Could Not Stand

Although the ordinary citizen did not realize it, divisions had been developing within the party. The Revo celebrated its fourth birthday on 13 March 1983. By September, a rumour had suddenly developed that Coard, a key figure within the party and generally thought to be at the helm of party work, wanted to kill Bishop. To appreciate the effect that this rumour had on the population, one has to understand the public face of the revolution during that period. Outsid-ers might critique, but as far as most Grenadians knew, the key leaders were united in their goal to build the revolution. A few short years before, they had struggled together against Gairy. The rumour now circulating suggested an impossible scenario. Even for such a scenario, it was the kind of tragic story one only read about in books. It meant that the revolutionary leadership was not as united as people had thought and that there was trouble at the core. It seemed to suggest a power struggle. Maurice Bishop was well known to the people. He was the local and international face of the revolution, a personable and charismatic young man who interacted comfortably with people at every level. When the popular imagination was stirred by the notion that someone within the government (and "government" would have been a more familiar notion than "party") was opposing Maurice (as he was popularly known), the country immediately sided with Maurice; Bernard, seen as the other powerful figure in the government (and party), became the enemy.

When the crisis came, public support for Maurice appeared to be exactly opposite to what obtained within the party. The party sympathized with Coard, and some members began to refer to Bishop as egoistic and counter-revolutionary. Coard had developed a reputation as the intellectual leader of the party. While both Bishop and Coard appeared to support the ideological perspectives of the revolution and both had moved from an attraction to Black Power ideology to the study of Marxism-Leninism, Coard, it was felt, seemed more given to analytical reading and discussion of political principles, Marxist-Leninist and otherwise, than Bishop. While both appeared generally to share the political ideas of the revolution and the leftist philosophy associated with it, Coard appeared more interested in theoretical debates, discussion and reading. Increasingly, the party appeared to be looking to Coard for intellectual leadership. Still, Bishop was the nominal leader of the party and the revolution. The party came to the conclusion that party work was not as strong as it could be, and tensions developed between Bishop and Coard. Eventually (as the public was to discover later), Coard resigned from the Central Committee of the party in September 1982. The party kept this a secret and continued as if nothing had happened. By mid-1983, it was decided (within the party) that the work of the party was not moving forward and that something had to be done. Party members decided at a meeting that the situation of stalemate could be resolved by having Bishop and Coard as joint leaders of the party. On the surface, this may have seemed a reasonable proposition, but perhaps the relations between the two groups (and their supporters) were already too tense to make joint leadership feasible.

At first, Bishop was hesitant. He then accepted the proposal, and the party appeared to be in a rejoicing mood. Bishop subsequently left for a trip abroad. When he was on his way back, party members got the news that he had changed his mind and was returning in a fighting mood. The result was that the party, which operated on what it referred to as a Leninist principle of collective agreement, felt that Maurice was betraying the principles of the party and was favouring his personal ascendancy – the ascendancy of the individual. The party later accused him of "one-manism". This, in essence, as far as the party was concerned, meant that the leader was betraying some of the basic principles of the revolution and the party that led the revolution. When Maurice returned from his trip to what was then the German Democratic Republic, the usual welcome party at the airport, headed by Coard, was noticeably absent. This clearly signalled the party's displeasure and put the two sides on a collision course. Whatever may have been Bishop's discussion outside of Grenada, and some have suggested that there was some discussion with Cuba, where Bishop made a stop on his return trip, it would have been clear to him, on his arrival, that he was out of favour with the party. He may have considered that if he was to retain his role as leader of the party and the revolution, his only option was an appeal to what had been the party's early base – the people. Bishop had apparently assessed, correctly, that he, individually, now had that base of support.

It is in this context that, shortly after his return, a rumour began circulating that Coard was planning to kill him. The party concluded, and one of Bishop's security guards later confirmed, that the rumour had been started by Bishop himself. Bishop denied it. Party members – believing indignantly that they, and not he, had made and now led the revolution and that he was undermining the principles of the party – placed him under house arrest. It was the beginning of the end – or, one may say, the signal that the end was near. The country could not comprehend that the prime minister had been, or could be, arrested. The party, with its secrecy and sense of itself as a unit, meant nothing to the people. To the public, the prime minister's arrest proved that there was some kind of scheming going on in the NJM. After this, there was a clear divide between the party and people of every walk of life.[18] Had the party remembered its own teachings about the power of the people and that its vanguard unit had information and a perception of events not shared by the people, things might have turned out differently. As wrong as party adherents may have thought the people were, they had spoken. Having been elected by popular vote on the streets and not by the ballot box, members of the NJM could not fail to realize the strength of the people's vote in this situation. But emotions appeared to intensify around notions of Leninist principles, and perhaps a disservice was done here both to Leninist principles and to the people of the country. Even though the party has been accused of succumbing to the authoritarian tendencies of Leninist thought, it may also be said that it succumbed to the authoritarian tendencies of colonial rule. It is doubtful that the NJM, as busy as its members were, had yet spent sufficient time discussing the psychology of colonialism, personality politics, the particular manifestation of this in Grenada, and the ways in which Gairy had been shaped by the autocratic example of colonial rule. The NJM had experienced Gairy's autocratic attitudes, and it is likely that party members had absorbed, more than they realized, his dismissal of the voice of the people in 1973.

On 19 October, NJM leaders and ministers of the PRG who supported Bishop walked, at the head of a mass demonstration, to the prime minister's residence, where he was under house arrest. Those guarding him appeared to abide by the revolution's ethic that the guns of the revolution would not be used against the people. They did not shoot into the crowd. People swarmed into the residence and released Bishop. The crowd left the building and surged, with Bishop, into St George's. There was some talk of Bishop addressing the crowd in the open marketplace. However, at some point, the decision appears to have been taken to go not to the market square but to the fort above the market, the headquarters of the army. Perhaps ironically, this fort, originally (and now again, post-revolution) named Fort George, had been renamed Fort Rupert to honour Bishop's father, Rupert, who had been killed during the anti-Gairy struggle. The other faction in the party, the majority group supportive of Coard, was said to be occupying a fort in Morne Jaloux, just above St George's. Symbolically, each side was now claiming a fort, and the factions seemed set for a violent confrontation. But perhaps the symbolism is clearer to us now in hindsight than it was to the participants and, one may assume, to the crowd at the time.

Accounts indicate that three armoured vehicles came from the direction of the other fort towards Fort Rupert, the one being occupied by Bishop and his supporters. This, it must be remembered, was also the headquarters of the army, and some army personnel, including members of the armed forces branch of the party, were also at that location. Some accounts indicate that there was firing from the crowd as the armoured vehicles approached and that a soldier was killed. What seems clear is that, after confrontation and various questionable actions on both sides, those sent by the Coard faction of the party to retake the fort were in the ascendancy.[19] They appear to, at first, have fired indiscriminately. People jumped off the walls of the fort to escape the bullets. A still indeterminate number of people died, while others were injured.

Grenadians remain traumatized by these events. Some accounts suggest that members of the party, too, were traumatized by the ways in which they felt moved to confront each other on that fateful day. It must be acknowledged, though, that even today many Grenadians are not sympathetic to any trauma supposedly felt by party members. Incensed by what they considered Bishop's treacherous behaviour, the party's emissaries, who claim not to have been given any direct order to do this, lined him and others, including the minister of foreign affairs Unison Whiteman, the minister of health Norris Bain (who was a minister of government but not a party member) and the minister of education Jacqueline Creft, up against a wall and summarily executed them. Several others were reported to have been killed at the fort later that day.

Grenadians locked their doors and hid in their houses, under curfew and cowed by a radio announcement that anyone disobeying the curfew would be shot on sight. A shocked silence descended over the country. Residents of St George's later said that trucks could be heard driving through the streets, away from the direction of the fort, out of St George's, in the direction of South St George. These trucks, people surmised, contained the bodies of those who had been executed. The small political party had failed to resolve its internal contradictions and had imploded. Shocked, the country mourned the loss of its leader and others who had been executed. Within a few days, news came that the United States would invade. The party belatedly attempted a rapprochement with the people, reminding the population in anxious radio broadcasts that they had trained in various militia groups to defend the country. Party members were sent out to round up members of the public to prepare for the invasion. Still traumatized, the people hid where possible, and the party was left largely alone to fight the invader. There were, however, those who were picked up and made to join the defence or those who joined, in spite of the horror, because they were also against the idea of an invasion by the United States. Although the US forces claimed to be invading to rescue students at St George's University, an American institution, the students appeared to be in no way associated with the conflict and did not appear to have been under any threat. Some Grenadians left their homes, when they could, to be on the streets showing visible, almost vengeful, support for the invasion. It was an almost gleeful betrayal of those who they felt had betrayed them by their actions. A people who had been manipulated and shown contempt no longer wanted to be described as revolutionary or to have leaders who described themselves as such. Soon, it was all over. Some Cubans who had been working on the new international airport and an indeterminate number of Grenadians were killed in the invasion. Members of the party were imprisoned and the US government established an interim government of Grenadian individuals residing in various parts of the Caribbean and further afield.

Little time has been spent acknowledging or discussing the very painful fact that Grenadians were pointing out to the American invaders not just those who they thought were involved in the executions but also those who were involved in any way with the work of the party, the government and the revolution. The whole process had been discredited. The revolution was over, and a new era of Grenadian post-revolutionary politics had begun.

It is important, too, to consider the parents of party members, who, forced to reside in a community still hostile to the role played by the party in the deaths of so many, did not have recourse to the usual community support in times of stress. Consider the parents, lovers, wives, husbands, siblings and other relatives of those who were murdered at the fort – who have never found their bodies. Consider the parents and relatives of those who went out to fight on 25 October, perhaps because they were members of the party and support-ive of party arguments, perhaps because they were co-opted, perhaps because they felt a sense of patriotism and did not want any invader on their soil, even while they condemned the murders at the fort. In other words, consider the trauma that Grenada still has not worked through. And consider the fact that this was a formerly colonized country, one where the citizens still needed to be re-educated for independence and transformation.

What preceded this situation? Where else may we find an explanation for the breakdown in communication and camaraderie? Somewhere in Grenada's history, had there developed a personality cult that made politicians of any ilk inclined to promote their ideas and personalities even when a majority of the populace seemed not inclined to support them? Why was it impossible for warring party factions to resolve their conflicts? Why, in such a small com-munity (of approximately one hundred thousand people), was it possible for young revolutionaries to execute ideological opponents who had so recently been friends? How was it possible for leaders to ignore the wishes of the majority and so to seemingly replicate the intolerant attitudes of one whom they had so recently removed from office?

Although it is possible to search even in Amerindian and early colonial history, let us go back again to 1951, to the beginning of the Gairy period. In Grenada's mid-twentieth-century colonial story, the British Colonial Office operated to maintain British systems and institutions. Exploitation of the working people by the planting classes – low wages, poor working and living conditions – created situations for the emergence of political leaders within union organizations. British authorities observed the union/party dynamic nervously because no such union/political party link existed in Britain and they could not bequeath it to the region as a British institution. Besides, union organization suggested that the working class had what they considered too much influence. As Caribbean leaders emerged in the 1950s, there were anxious discussions in the Colonial Office. Always the concern was that British models should be observed.

In Grenada in 1951, with major constitutional change allowing for universal adult suffrage,[20] there were, for the first time, no property or income qualifications for voters. All those who were over twenty-one, both women and men, were eligible to vote. Twenty-nine-year-old Eric Gairy, who had worked and been involved in worker organization in Aruba, returned to Grenada at this point, having been expelled from Aruba because of that very same involvement in worker organization. Back home, he immediately became involved in union organization and took up the cause of workers, agitating for better wages and working conditions for agricultural workers. In the first elections under universal adult suffrage in 1951, Gairy's Grenada People's Party won a majority of seats in the legislative council. Under the new constitution, in a bicameral legislature, there were eight members on the executive council, three of them being elected representatives from the legislative council. On the legislative council were fourteen members, of whom three were official (the governor, the administrator and the colonial treasurer), two nominated, one the clerk of the council, and the remaining eight elected members. Six of these were elected members of Gairy's Grenada People's Party. The scales had shifted a bit, but Grenada was still a colony of Britain.[21] As I have stated elsewhere, "With the 1951 change, elected members had little influence within the Executive body, and in the event that they succeeded in gaining support from a nominated or ex-officio member on some issue, could still be over-ruled by the Governor's power of veto."[22] The governor was the important figure. As I write this, I recall older people criticizing Gairy by saying he "think he is the Governor". In the colonial system, there was no question about where ultimate authority lay locally.

Until the 1970s, Gairy's was the main party in the legislative council. Even so, there was little real political party organization, and individual personalities continued to be the important factor. The party was really only a party in name. As the local newspaper the *West Indian* commented in 1954, "Party Politics has not yet arrived in Grenada. . . . With only one group asserting cohesion of a kind in this election and several independents opposing, talk of a party system is empty. This group, nevertheless, of itself possesses an essential party characteristic – unity – but it is difficult to determine whether the rallying point is a person or a programme."[23] Even where there was supposedly a party, the individual mattered much more than the collective.

Until independence from Britain in 1974, Gairy's Grenada People's Party, which, in the mid-1950s, was renamed first the Grenada Labour Party and then the Grenada United Labour Party,[24] was the main party in Grenada – in spite of the formation of another party, the Grenada National Party, in the 1950s. Apparent conflicts with the British elevated rather than diminished Gairy in the popular imagination. As colonial rulers, the British were watchful, aware that a personality cult was developing, as individuals emerged from union organization into leadership roles, but assessing that, in spite of their mistrust of someone like Eric Gairy, this may be the best alternative in the circumstances. Strategically, it was important to allow some individuals to emerge, in order to pre-empt more radical worker organization. Today, as we think of the contemporary Grenada story of personalities and parties, it is useful to consider the long history of the development of this tendency in Grenada and the rest of the Caribbean. Consider these comments in 1954 by K.V. Blackburne, governor of Antigua, whose opinions were valued by the Colonial Office, as correspondence from the office suggests. Participating in a discussion about whether the office should sever the union / political party link, Blackburne commented:

> Rightly or wrongly, I feel that these islands benefit more from the "boss-rule" (with certain limited controls) which they now have than from the unsettled con-

ditions which would obtain if the workers (the vast majority of the electorate) are struggling for what they think are their rights in an unorganised manner. For all of these reasons, I should prefer merely to go on preaching (as I am already doing) that political office should not go hand in hand with trade union office, and to leave it to the leaders themselves to find their own solutions.[25]

The Colonial Office, then, recognized and even facilitated the development of a cult of personality when it seemed to be in their long-term interest. They were a bit more nervous about what this portended for Grenada and Eric Gairy than they were about leaders like Bird of Antigua or Bradshaw of St Kitts. They considered requiring Gairy to give up political office if he insisted on keeping union office; however, they hesitated because they felt they could not make that requirement for Grenada and not for other Caribbean countries.[26] As we consider political processes in Grenada today and the attitudes of both the general population and the political leaders, it is useful to think about how present political attitudes have been shaped by this British colonial inheritance, not only of local politicians being watched by the Colonial Office, but of a figure like the all-powerful governor appointed by the British Colonial Office. In 1955, Governor Beetham of the Windward Islands wrote to the secretary of state for the colonies, "It could be argued that where parties do not exist on an ideological basis, the only alternative is to have parties based on personalities."[27] When we consider how colonial officials discussed issues like these, considering what to do and how much to interfere to attain what they considered best for British interests, it is amazing to think how cautious people often are today about making changes to a supposedly perfect British inheritance. Socially, economically and otherwise, Grenada and other Caribbean countries were organized with British inheritance in mind. Despite its tragic end, the NJM's anti-colonial perspectives have not, in my estimation, been discredited. There needs to be a deeper study and understanding of how colonial processes have shaped Grenada and the rest of the Caribbean, so that a response is not merely cosmetic.

Two of the many interesting aspects of the Grenada story up to 1983 are the efforts of successive generations of young people to find alternative political frames for the governing of the country, and the role of rumour in the collapse of the revolution. As demonstrated in this exploration, Grenada's political culture was historically very authoritarian, elitist and focused on the "maximum" leader. Under the colonial system, until 1951, only a small per-centage of the population was even allowed to vote. Although constitutional change came within the context of internationally connected, Caribbean-wide struggles and movements, Eric Gairy's arrival on the political scene at a key moment in the development of Grenadian politics made him seem larger than life – as the cause and effect of all the cumulative changes. Having been used to elitism in politics and the high living of political elites, the masses were not conditioned to be critical of their leader, even when he was accused of corruption. In the mid- to late 1950s and 1960s, when Gairy was increas-ingly being accused of corruption, the general attitude among the majority of his (largely agriculture-based) supporters seemed to be that others before Gairy had been corrupt and had exploited them, the people, but now it was *their* time and, since he was their representative, *his* time. Although Bishop was from St George's and of a different class background than Gairy, who was rural and closer to the agricultural classes, he was also comfortable in his interaction with the people. When the time came, he too had the kind of personality that could win him support.

As they tried to learn from the histories and experiences of left-leaning parties both within the region – Jamaica's Workers Party of Jamaica and People's National Party, Guyana's People's Progressive Party and Working People's Alliance – as well as internationally, as they tried to understand and apply principles of Marxism-Leninism (which they thought could be useful as an alternative route for the country), as they tried to consider how to use local experience in the construction of a governing ideology, Grenada's young leaders – Bishop, born in 1944, was twenty-nine when he formed the NJM with Unison Whiteman – were also grappling with the everyday problems of leadership. While the party accused Bishop of "one-manism", it would appear that the party, as a unit, opted for the authoritarian mode: they were aware that the country had views different from the party's but were unwill-ing to relax their own certainties in order to accommodate these differing viewpoints. All, it seemed, suffered the effects of the country's authoritarian political history. In effect, the NJM was a young party, new to both Left and Marxist-Leninist thinking. Members were learning as they developed. Their ambition – along with the confident and ultimately destructive arrogance of their youth – was also their downfall.

It is fascinating to consider the role of gossip in the downfall of the party and the demise of the revolution. When Bishop was returning home after his final trip, the news of what he was thinking and had decided to do reached Grenada ahead of him. Party members reacted. They themselves began to lobby those close to the party about his attitude, about his acceptance and then rejection of joint leadership and about his tendency towards "one-manism". Bishop is accused of also resorting to rumour-mongering when he realized his isolation within the party. It may thus be assumed that during the last year of NJM leadership, gossip had a role in solidifying the attitudes of the two sides towards each other. Coard had been out of the Central Committee of the party for a year without the public having any knowledge of this. This was a tremendous achievement in a community as small as Grenada. However, whether or not there was a formally organized group to support Coard – and much has been made of a core study group called Organization for Revolutionary Education and Leadership and allegedly tutored by Coard – there were friends of Coard and concerned party individuals who supposedly had discussions with him during the period of his absence from the party. It also became clear that there were similarly those who spoke to Bishop about what they considered was really going on among those who opposed him. It seems that one major tragedy here is that each side thought it was working in the interests of the country by saving it from the inadequacy and ignorance of the other. And gossip played a key role in the escalation of the tension between the two groups. If Bishop indeed started a rumour, he may have done so because he knew the power of rumour and did indeed feel himself (politically, if not personally) threatened and because the two major individuals, Coard and Bishop, did not speak directly to each other.[28] The party is left shouldering the greater blame because it showed contempt for the wishes of the people, however misguided it may have thought these wishes, and acted upon this contempt by using violence against the people and against those chosen as their representatives.

The events of 1979 to 1983 are related to all of Grenada's past stories and certainly to its continuing journey. The final day's performances at the thirty-eighth Conference of the Caribbean Studies Association suggest that the country's artists may help challenge silences imposed by the traumatic experiences of 1983.

This journey through the bewitched forest of history, with its many shadows and prickly brambles, suggests that writers today can contribute to a more complex memory of the Grenada Revolution than a Maurice/Bernard story. In Edwidge Danticat's *The Farming of Bones,* a guide who is showing tourists the ruins of Henry Christophe's Palais Sans Souci tells the group, "All monuments of this great size are built with human blood." Later, he adds, "Famous men never truly die. It is only those nameless and faceless who vanish like smoke into the early morning air."[29] Narrative is a powerful force for examining not just personalities but also complex experiences of trauma. Many people gave their lives to this initially hopeful but eventually bleak Grenadian story of revolution and trauma. The Caribbean Studies Association was wise to give the last word of the Grenada conference to tomorrow's leaders, who will continue to search for the location and nature of the wound, examining both contemporary and earlier historical events, in an effort to acquire a deeper understanding of Grenada's story.

NOTES

1. Nigel Hunt, *Memory, War and Trauma* (Cambridge: Cambridge University Press, 2010).

2. Professor of Humane Letters at Cornell University, Cathy Caruth has done interesting and informative work on trauma. Her publications include *Unclaimed Experience: Trauma, Narrative and History* (Baltimore: Johns Hopkins University Press, 1996) and *Trauma: Explorations in Memory* (Baltimore: Johns Hopkins University Press, 1995).

3. Here I have named only those who were official government personnel. Many other names have been listed on posters distributed over the years by the Maurice Bishop Patriotic Movement, and a list, with disclaimers, may also be found online at http://www.thegrenadarevolutiononline.com/page8.html (accessed 29 May 2015).

4. Trinidad and Tobago's prime minister, George Chambers, opposed the US invasion and did not join other Caribbean states and the United States in sending troops. For a recent commentary, see Rickey Singh, "Lies for Two US Invasions", *Trinidad Express,* 26 March 2013, at http://www.trinidadexpress.com/commentaries/Lies-for-two-US-invasions-200148421.html (accessed 29 May 2015).

5. See, for example, *Journal of Eastern Caribbean Studies* 35, nos. 3–4 (September

2010). This issue contains articles on the subject by Wendy Grenade, Patsy Lewis, Horace Campbell, Tennyson Joseph, David Hinds and an interview with Bernard Coard.

6. Mark Kurlansky, *The Year that Rocked the World* (New York: Random House, 2005), xvii. For a fuller discussion of the importance of the 1960s and 1970s in Grenada, the Caribbean and worldwide, see also Merle Collins, *The Governor's Story: The Authorized Biography of Dame Hilda Bynoe* (London: Peepal Tree, 2013), 9–14.

7. Rupert Lewis, *Walter Rodney's Intellectual and Political Thought* (Kingston: University of the West Indies Press, 1998), 117.

8. Ibid.

9. Ibid.

10. See Wendy Grenade, "Interview with Bernard Coard", *Journal of Eastern Caribbean Studies* 35, no. 3/4 (September 2010): 145–82.

11. See Bernard Coard's response to the question "What led to the vanguard party?", ibid., 156.

12. US/Grenada relations of the period have been discussed in several publications. See, for example, James Foran, *Taking Power: On the Origins of Third World Revolutions* (Cambridge: Cambridge University Press, 2005). Foran quotes US Admiral McKenzie as saying that Cuba, Nicaragua and Grenada "are practically one country" (187). See also Anthony Payne and Paul Sutton, eds., *Dependency Under Challenge: The Political Economy of the Commonwealth Caribbean* (Manchester: Manchester University Press, 1984), and *UFSI Reports*, issues 1–5 (Universities Field Staff International, 1983).

13. See "Maurice Bishop Speaks to US Working People", in *Maurice Bishop Speaks: The Grenada Revolution 1979–83*, ed. Bruce Marcus and Michael Taber (New York: Pathfinder, 1983), 299, 287–12.

14. Ibid., 289.

15. Ibid.

16. For comments about destabilization, see "Imperialism Is the Real Problem", *Maurice Bishop: Selected Speeches, 1979–1981* (Havana: Casa de las Americas, 1982), 189–200, and *Maurice Bishop Speaks*, 204. See also *Forward Ever! Three Years of the Grenadian Revolution: Speeches of Maurice Bishop*, intro. Jim Percy (Sydney: Pathfinder Press, 1982): 197–206.

17. See Merle Collins, "Grenada: A Political Story: 1950–1979" (PhD thesis, London School of Economics and Political Science, 1990), 81. It notes that, in 1952, the local newspaper the *West Indian* printed articles about communism. In the *West Indian*, 22 November 1950, L.C.J. Thomas, member of the Grenada legislative council, wrote, "These men are now in our midst preaching hatred and

destruction in the community on a parallel with the directives of the Kremlin . . . has Communism in its vile and ugly form invaded and gained a foothold in Grenada?"

18. For a perspective on this, see Patsy Lewis's literary interpretation of an interview, "Remembering October 19: Reconstructing Recollections of October 19, 1983", *Journal of Eastern Caribbean Studies* 35, nos. 3–4 (September 2010): 140–44.

19. Ibid.

20. For a fuller discussion of the system, see Collins, "Grenada", 54. Under the 1951 constitution, Grenada's legislative council comprised fourteen members (including the administrator as president). The administrator was the official, resident locally, who presided in the absence of the governor, whose function was to oversee the administration of all four islands of the group named the Windwards – St Lucia, St Vincent, Dominica and Grenada.

21. There were several problems with the operation of the new Constitution of 1951. For a full discussion, see Collins, "Grenada", 136–56. As stated there, the constitutional instruments were hastily assembled, and there were several operational problems. There were tensions between legislative and executive councils, with nominated and elected members struggling to assert their authority. A 1945 *Report of the West India Royal Commission* referred specifically to the "autocracy" which the Constitutions of the region involved, concluding that constitutional weaknesses might be ascribed not so much to the alleged autocracy as to the opposition engendered "between Government, on the one hand, and, on the other, those, among whom must often be counted elected members of the Legislative Council, who so vehemently and constantly criticise Government in speeches and in the Press". *West India Royal Commission Report* (London: HMSO, 1945), 57.

22. Quoted from Collins, "Grenada", 138.

23. *West Indian*, 1 May 1954, 2.

24. For earliest references to the Grenada United Labour Party, see the *West Indian*, 9 January 1955, 2.

25. K.V. Blackburne, Government House, Antigua, to Charles Jeffries, Colonial Office, 5 April 1954, CO1031/1400.

26. See Douglas Midgett, *Eastern Caribbean Elections, 1950–1982*, Development Series 13 (Iowa City: Center for Development Studies/Institute of Urban and Regional Research, University of Iowa, 1983), quoted in Collins, "Grenada", 97.

27. Beetham, Governor, Windward Islands, to Wallace, Secretary of State for the Colonies, 25 July 1955, CO1031/1407.

28. See Coard's comments about this in the interview with Wendy Grenade mentioned in note 5.

29. Edwidge Danticat, *The Farming of Bones* (New York: Soho Press, 1988), 280.

2.

Women in the Grenada Revolution, 1979–1983

NICOLE PHILLIP-DOWE

ABSTRACT

This chapter is an exposition of the lives, feelings, expressions and views of the Grenadian women who took part in the revolution, ranging from those who were in the highest echelon of the People's Revolutionary Government to the rank and file. It provides an analysis of the National Women's Organization and the programmes of the People's Revolutionary Government that affected women, of how they sought to address the needs of Grenadian women at the time and of whether the socialist revolution really empowered the women of this small Caribbean nation.

Labour Riots Set the Stage for Revolution

In Grenada, the year 1951 is synonymous with *strike, riot* and *revolution*. The strike action of February of that year led to the widespread burning of estates. The radicalism that had swept through the rest of the Caribbean in the 1930s had finally and belatedly exploded at home and was presided over by Eric Matthew Gairy. This period saw an increase in wages and an improvement in working conditions for agricultural workers, most of whom were women. It also saw the establishment of a number of women's groups, including the Young Women's Christian Association, Soroptimists, Lioness Club, Home Industries Association, Home Makers Association and the Grenada Women's

League. These groups were mainly charitable organizations that catered to the needs of poor women, especially those in rural areas. For example, the YWCA and the Home Makers Association provided advice on domestic science and home management. With the exception of the Grenada Women's League, these groups had no political affiliation. The Grenada Women's League was the women's arm of Gairy's Grenada United Labour Party (GULP). However, like the other women's groups, its vision was limited to charitable work.

The Gairy regime encouraged the movement of women into positions of power by appointing Dame Hilda Bynoe as the first female governor of Grenada and, incidentally, the first in the British Commonwealth. Gairy also appointed two female ambassadors. Three women won their parliamentary positions on a GULP ticket. One became a minister, and the others parliamentary secretaries. The Gairy government also encouraged the establishment of a commission on the status of women, and Grenada hosted the regional seminar on women in 1970.

There were, however, those who were not happy with the Gairy regime. Some women joined and took an active role in the opposition parties, the Grenada National Party and the New JEWEL Movement (NJM). These women felt that, despite Gairy's projection of the image of promoting and encouraging women, many of their demands were not being met. For example, few day-care centres had been built; scholarships for women were not available; equal work for equal pay was not implemented; and women in positions of power within the Gairy regime (indeed, like the men) were not expected to oppose the decisions of his government. The women's groups in existence at the time had raised these issues, but they were not addressed satisfactorily.

On 13 March 1979, the NJM staged a military coup that marked the beginning of a new political epoch for Grenada and for the entire English-speaking Caribbean. At this point, women who had supported the Gairy regime either continued to do so or supported the new People's Revolutionary Government (PRG) (or else, they remained indifferent). A second group of women, who had opposed the Gairy regime, did not follow the socialist line. A third group felt that the way forward was through the establishment of a women's organization guided by Marxist ideology. It is this third group that I have focused my attention on.

The St George's Progressive Women's Association (PWA) embodied the ideals of the second group. It opposed the Gairy regime but did not view changes along socialist lines. Formed in early 1977, its aims and objectives included demands for better wages, improved working conditions for women, employment opportunities, proper housing, medical facilities and sanitation, as well as the extension of civil and other democratic rights.[1] Membership was open to any woman residing in Grenada who accepted the goals of the organization. Membership fees were fifty EC cents a month, while unemployed women were given free membership. According to Dessima Williams,[2] Grenada's representative to the Organization of American States, 1979–1983, the PWA served as a small but effective urban forum for politicizing and organizing middle-class women – housewives, teachers, professionals, students – and a core of the urban working class. Its unique advantage was that, although it opposed the Gairy regime, it was allowed to operate without molestation. There is no evidence of the PWA being victimized by the Gairy regime. This was due in part to the prestige of the PWA's leadership, which was made up of upper-class and upper-middle-class women.

Between 15 and 17 June 1979, the PWA held a national conference for women. At the conference, supported by the newly formed PRG, Prime Minister Maurice Bishop called for women to join men in solving their own problems and that of the society as a whole. He noted:

> The woman cannot do it by herself; the man cannot do it himself. It is by the combination of men and women together attempting to build a new process; to build a new society, to build a new civilization, attempting to produce more; attempting to find the new value systems, to identify ideas and new ways of pushing our country forward. It is only if we achieve this unity of the man and the woman that we would be able to move forward.[3]

Phyllis Coard, member of the Central Committee of the ruling NJM and president of the National Women's Organization (NWO), called on women "to remember that it's only our struggle that is going to win our revolution. We, the women, can bring women's rights and total liberation and justice for all our peoples".[4] The conference drew up a number of resolutions to define further action: it recognized the deplorable state of the health service, the importance of political education for national development, and the existence of discrimination against women in education, employment and the law. It set down the following resolutions:

- A steering committee made up of representatives from every parish and women's organization should be formed to find solutions to the above problems and women should take the lead in working towards changing the unjust societal conditions that they face.
- Women should take an active part in carrying forward and consolidating the revolution.
- More centres were needed for pre- and post-natal care, immunization and parental training for mothers.
- More educational and training opportunities were needed to meet the particular needs of the society, especially those of girls and women.
- There should be equal economic opportunity for women in all areas of the workforce, particularly in the development of agricultural production, such as agro-industries.
- A programme for political education for nationals and particularly for women should be adopted through the use of mass media.
- Antiquated and unfair laws, especially those pertaining to women, should be revised and there ought to be a just legal code for the entire society.[5]

The PWA dissolved soon after the conference, one of the reasons cited for its demise being that an autonomous organization had no place within a one-party socialist state. Since members of the NJM participated in the organization and made decisions based on party discipline and solidarity, it was impossible for the PWA to operate autonomously. It was perhaps predictable that independent and articulate members would sooner or later be in a confrontational situation with NJM members. Indeed, directly following the conference, an emotional confrontation occurred between Phyllis Coard and Alice McIntyre, the chairperson of the conference, concerning the former's failure to check with the committee before inviting some of the speakers. Prior to this, there were differing views on the PWA's plans to establish a women's reading centre at Marryshow House, the University of the West Indies Centre in Grenada. Allegedly, Coard saw this as a threat to the revolution. In May 1979, to counter the PWA proposal, she suggested that the NJM Political Bureau should immediately plan to start a bookshop for progressive books in order "to avoid opportunists and CIA elements bringing in revision-ist Maoist and Trotskyite literature".[6]

The PRG was of the view that none of the women's groups in Grenada had, up to that time, effectively challenged the status quo, and therefore they could not hope to bring about any meaningful change in the lives and sta-tus of women in the wider society. They believed that the only way women could effect transformation was through the state apparatus facilitating such changes. Only a broad-based, well-organized "revolutionary" women's orga-nization capable of mobilizing women – politicizing and unifying them into a powerful revolutionary force – could achieve this. The NJM's NWO took up this challenge, operating from within the ruling party.

Early in 1979, several women's groups supporting the revolution were formed. Claudette Pitt, an executive member of the NWO, claimed: "Women called in to say we want to form groups. They called and asked us to come and speak to them. We were bombarded by this."[7] According to Phyllis Coard, this was where Cuba played a role. Isabel Jamoron, representative of Cuba's Fed-eración de Mujeres, noted, on a visit to Grenada in May 1981, that what was done in Cuba "was the establishment of a mass organization". She observed that the Cuban communist party was small, plus there were problems of sectarianism. She further noted that this was "why Fidel Castro placed so much emphasis on building the mass organizations plus building the party".[8]

The issue was discussed at the NJM's Central Committee, and it was decided that the NWO should become a national group. In the words of Phyl-lis Coard, "It was a good idea for Grenada. We were building a government that was broad based and we needed a broad-based women's group. It was a struggle at first to persuade NJM women to have Gairyite women join. There was such hostility previously between the two groups."[9] In December 1980, the first general meeting took place, and a decision was reached to drop the "New JEWEL Movement" from the group's name and call it simply the National Women's Organization. Phyllis Coard was elected president and Rita Joseph vice president. The executive included Claudette Pitt and Tessa Stroude. By that time (late 1980), the NWO comprised fifteen hundred members operating in 47 groups in all the parishes except Carriacou. By November 1982, membership stood at sixty-five hundred women organized in 170 groups, with 11 groups in Carriacou and 1 in Petit Martinique.[10]

The NWO followed a structure that resembled a hierarchy:

Congress
National Executive and National Secretariat
National Council of Delegates
Parish coordinating teams
NWO groups

At the congress, which was held every six years, the work of the organization during the previous six years was thoroughly assessed; aims, objectives and overall direction of work in the coming six years were decided; an in-depth programme of work for the first two years was discussed and adopted; and a national executive body was elected.[11] Each NWO group elected two delegates to serve on the national council of delegates and represent their group at the congress. The national executive was the highest body of the organization when the congress was not in session. The national executive comprised the president, vice president, and five other elected members – three delegates from St Andrew and St George, and two each from the other parishes. The national executive appointed the national secretariat, which included the president, vice president, a financial secretary and public relations officer, and a secretary. It ensured that decisions of the national executive were carried out and oversaw the day-to-day running of the organization. The national council of delegates consisted of two delegates elected from each NWO group. The parish coordinating teams comprised the parish delegates to the national council of delegates and other members of each group within the parish. Each team was responsible for supervising and guiding the work of the NWO groups in its parish and ensuring that the current NWO programme was carried out. It also submitted monthly reports to the national executive outlining the work of all the NWO groups within the parish. It elected a chairperson, a secretary, and various committees on organization, education, finance, publicity and employment.

Theoretically, the structure of the NWO was linked to the PRG's adoption of grass-roots democracy (as an alternative to the Westminster model) to allow ordinary Grenadians to have a say in the development of their community. Tessa Stroude, a member of the NWO national executive, gave a detailed description of how this process actually worked. She noted:

> The [NWO] groups would identify what they wanted to do in their community. For the groups to function by themselves we [the National Executive] had a system of training . . . we could not ensure that the groups functioned properly because the women were not exposed. For example, they were not sure what was the role of a chairman or a secretary or treasurer. So we did a lot of training with the leaders of the groups to ensure that they functioned. We developed a work plan at a congress meeting. We could not have all the members there but say for example there are twelve groups in St. Patrick, each group would nominate four or three women and they would come with their ideas and we looked now at what could be the emphasis for the year.[12]

The main aim was to have programmes to cover the needs of women of all types – NJM, Gairyite, Grenada National Party, old, young, and of all classes.[13]

The Women's Desk was established in June 1979 and acted as an intermediary between the government and the NWO. Tessa Stroude and Rita Joseph were full-time workers at the Desk. Stroude explained how the Desk worked in collaboration with the NWO:

> Although the Women's Desk was responsible on the government level, the NWO had workers in the field. They were the ones to identify people of need. . . . We tried not to make it partisan, so it wouldn't really be people that belonged to us, NJM supporters, that would get the benefits but the people who really needed it. It was said that we [NJM supporters] did all the work but Gairy people getting all the benefits, but Gairy people were the poor people and they were the ones that needed it.[14]

The NWO, working alongside the Women's Desk, set its work plans for 1981. These were to do the following:

- Ensure efficient and fair distribution of free milk, and the effective operation of the house-repair programme.
- Ensure that health centres were repaired and epidemics were prevented through constant clean-ups of the communities.
- Ask the Ministry of Health to organize mass health and first-aid education.
- Discuss with the Ministry of Communications and Works the areas that were most in need of water.
- Maintain an active interest in bringing electricity to rural areas.
- Ensure equal education for girls, to educate women on their legal rights.

- Organize the full participation of all women in the Community School Day Programme.
- Mobilize women to step up their work in the CPE (Centre for Popular Education) programme.
- Encourage NWO members to play an active part on farmers' boards and trade unions.[15]

Despite the efforts of the NWO to expand the organization into a mass movement, it can be reasonably argued that it remained a tool of the PRG. Every government agency or party arm, whether socialist or capitalist, tends to propagate the views of the regime in power. Though the NWO remained to a large extent an arm of the PRG, it fulfilled its function as part of the ruling party. This reality does not diminish the accomplishments of the NWO, as discussed later on. In fact, the NWO sought to address for the current government one of the criticisms aimed at the Gairy regime – its lack of accountability to the people. The PRG sought to rectify this by holding monthly or bi-monthly public meetings and explaining the programmes of the revolution to the people. The NWO groups met once a week and discussed matters relevant to their individual communities. Once a month or once every two months, a member of the NWO executive attended these groups and explained the programmes of the revolution.

An examination of the activities of the NWO, the Women's Desk and the policies of the PRG as a whole give some insight into the successes and failings of these work plans. The NWO was able to distribute approximately four thousand kilogrammes of free powder milk every month as well as cooking oil to the needy.[16] Through its efforts, various cooperatives were established, which provided employment to both women and men. For example, Patsy Romain, an executive member of the NWO, remarked on the establishment of the Byelands Bakery Cooperative: "The government had a campaign going around to grow more food. It was the idle-lands-for-idle-hands program to help ease unemployment. When we looked around Byelands there were no idle lands. . . . Then the suggestion came for a bakery. The National Cooperative Development Agency did a feasibility study. The bakery has helped to employ ten sisters from NWO in Byelands and four men."[17] At Requin in St David, an agricultural cooperative was established, which employed three women, one of whom, a foundation member, became its president. According to her, the cooperative planned to grow pumpkin in four and a half acres, and tomatoes, carrots and cabbages in smaller plots.[18] A dried-fruit project was also established in Mount Rose.

The NWO, along with the Women's Desk, took an active role in voluntary projects like road repair, building of community centres, community clean-ups and island-wide beautification programmes, painting bridges and walls, clearing drains and overgrown shrubbery, and house rebuilding. By December 1982, one in every nine families had received house-repair materials. These families would have been selected by field officers of the NWO from among the poorest families on the island.[19] With financial aid from the Women's Desk, a schoolbooks-and-uniforms programme got underway. Stroude explained the difficulty in implementing the programme since there was a majority of very poor families and most people were part-time wage earners. This presented a problem in identifying those who were most needy. In spite of this hurdle, it was one of the main social welfare programmes of the NWO. By 1981, the NWO was also responsible for the creation of six new preschools and a day nursery. Two of the former were in the island's largest parish, St Andrew, in the villages of Byelands and Conference.[20] The government provided training and salaries for the women who ran these schools.

The NWO sought to provide political education for women so that they could be aware of the problems that the country faced. Dessima Williams aptly explained this concept:

> We spent time explaining the structure of the world economy to rural women so that when they produce bananas, carry them on their heads for long distances, sell them to the National Marketing Board and are paid the small prices that they are, they do not think the government is keeping back some of the money and paying them meagre wages. We teach them that we, as one small country, do not control the price for bananas internationally.[21]

In addition, the PRG took measures to ensure that female students had the opportunity to be educated to the same standard as male ones. These measures included:

- A mass literacy campaign – for example, the CPE, which began functioning in September 1980. A high proportion of students were women.
- First, the reduction of school fees from EC$37 to EC$12.50 per student, and then, free secondary education.

- The adoption of a policy of teaching technical subjects – for example, agricultural science, carpentry and metalwork – to both girls and boys.
- A greatly increased number of scholarships to universities and further education at institutions abroad (108 scholarships in 1979 as compared to 3 in 1978), 22 per cent of which went to women.[22]

The CPE conducted a preliminary census in April 1980 that revealed an 8–10 per cent illiteracy rate. In November 1980, the CPE registered 2,738 illiterates, 58 per cent of whom were women.[23] However, more women than men volunteered to be teachers in the programme.

The national coordinator of the literacy programme was twenty-four-year-old Valerie Gordon (later Cornwall). A teacher by profession, she grasped the opportunity to serve her nation in its literacy drive. Her duties included coordinating the work of the CPE in all the parishes, fundraising for the National Technical Commission, planning programme design, developing methodology and pedagogy, and co-authoring the CPE books. She felt that the programme was very successful in teaching reading and writing, in organization building in the community and in bridging the intergenerational gap within communities.[24] It also served as a good learning experience for the nation. Grenadians learned about their communities and their culture and wrote their own textbooks, which was a major achievement in terms of the quality of the books. Minister of education Jacqueline Creft declared that the "new education" was geared to educating "all people, not just a few, with the self-knowledge and self-confidence which would motivate them to make important decisions about and participate fully in their country's development".[25]

In an attempt to further enhance education, the PRG implemented the National In-Service Teacher Education Programme (NISTEP) and the Community School Day Programme. The programmes complemented each other. NISTEP ensured that a number of female and male teachers would attain their teacher's certificate while they remained in the service. The teachers were to attend the NISTEP courses one day a week during the school year and five days per week for several weeks during the vacation. On the day that the teacher attended the NISTEP courses a volunteer teacher from the community taught the students. The students were taught a wide range of practical subjects like handicraft, agriculture, sewing, fishing, the island's cultural heritage and its oral history. Most of the teachers of this Community School Day Programme were women. While they were not highly paid, it offered a source of income and a sense of meaningful participation.[26]

The NWO also encouraged women to take up the challenge of doing non-traditional jobs. According to Phyllis Coard, the NWO's ideological stance embraced the dictum that "women were equal to men. They were equal in society". She noted that women were registered for carpentry, welding and woodwork courses at the Technical and Vocational Institute. A project in motor mechanics for women was established at Queen's Park in St George's. Women also registered at the True Blue Fisheries School in St George's. When the National Transport Service buses came on stream in 1980, it was decided at the parish council level that all the conductors should be female.[27]

Women also gave their assistance in the development of the youth through work in the National Youth Organization and the Pioneers. Both groups aimed at organizing the nation's youth and beginning the process of instilling in them the necessary qualities of discipline, self-confidence, creativity, commitment, leadership and patriotism. Pioneer activities included talent searches, quizzes, drama exercises and debates. All these activities came to a head at the Pioneer camp in 1981. Lorianne Felix, executive member of the National Youth Organization responsible for the Pioneers, noted that the children were "encouraged to grow and be the new people and the new society, to study, work and play hard".[28]

One of the NWO's most difficult tasks, according to Peggy Nesfield, a member of the St George's NWO, was the attempt to break through the patriarchal and macho attitude embedded in the fabric of Grenadian society. Within approximately four to five months of taking office, the PRG launched two significant initiatives for women, maternity leave (which was written into law in October 1980) and equal work for equal pay. The Maternity Leave Law entitled women who had worked for more than eighteen months for the same employer to three months of maternity leave, with full pay for two months. It also guaranteed women the right to re-employment with the same employer after those three months. Women had to work for at least 40 per cent of the work week or fortnight to qualify for the three-month maternity leave. The worker would have to notify her employer at least three weeks before she chose to take her leave and also have to mention that she intended to come back to work after the leave. Daily paid workers were entitled to one-fifth of their annual pay, about two-and-a-half months' pay.[29] Before these initiatives were drawn up, the maternity leave proposal was sent to different organizations, including other women's groups like Lionesses, Soroptimists, the Presbyterian Women's Guild and the Women's League. The organizations gave their suggestions in areas that they thought should be amended.

Prime Minister Maurice Bishop used threatening language to warn employers of the consequences they would face if they discriminated against women or demanded sexual favours in exchange for employment. Yet there were those, both female and male, who were against this form of empowerment for women. Some older teachers and nurses scoffed at the idea of maternity leave. Their view was that, since they had not been given the privilege, it should not be extended to the younger generation. In May 1981, one female employer was fined five hundred EC dollars for failing to comply with the Maternity Leave Law. Restaurant-owner Evelyn Thompson fired her twenty-five-year-old waitress Jessica Williams because she was pregnant. Williams had been employed since May 1979 and worked from seven a.m. to five p.m. for six days a week for a salary of one hundred dollars. Thompson admitted that she had dismissed Williams due to her pregnancy and gave this response to Judge Lyle St Paul. She stated, "I never got maternity leave in the days when I had my children."[30] Peggy Nesfield noted that this attitude extended into the personal and intimate lives of women. NWO activists, she observed, had a hard task educating women about the role that men should play in their homes. She noted that women complained of men shirking their responsibilities as fathers. Many single mothers felt frustrated as they sought to keep their jobs and manage their homes. The NWO and Women's Desk had to also deal with the problem of incest and offered sex education for women.[31] But these attitudes were difficult to change and remained a thorn in the side of the NWO throughout the revolutionary period. In fact, male chauvinism in relation to women's work in the home reared its head at the highest level of power in the PRG, namely the Central Committee, as will be discussed later in this chapter.

The PRG passed the School Children's Immunization Law (or People's Law No. 41 of 1980). Under this law, twelve thousand six hundred children were immunized against five infectious diseases.[32] A new maternity unit was constructed in 1981–82. The X-ray unit and laboratory facilities at the St George's General Hospital were refurbished. There was a reduction in the doctor-to-patient population ratio from 1:4,864 in 1977 to 1:2,816 in 1982. There was also a reduction in the dentist-to-patient population ratio from 1:53,706 in 1977 to 1:21,400 in 1982.[33] In 1981, Dr Annette Alexis became the first Grenadian female ophthalmologist to practise in Grenada.

In May 1979, the PRG passed the Trade Union Recognition Law (People's Law No. 9 of 1979). It made the recognition of trade unions compulsory for employers. The result was that the percentage of unionized workers jumped from 30 to 80 per cent between May 1979 and May 1980.

Women dominated three of the largest trade unions at the membership level. Prior to the passage of the law, trade unions were male-dominated. The Grenada Manual and Mental Workers Union, which spearheaded radical changes for workers, did have a number of female organizers at the village level. However, there were no women on any of the union executives until the mid-1970s. By 1975, there were women representing categories of workers in trade unions. For example, the Grenada Civil Service Association (now Public Workers Union) had women representing nurses and clerical workers. According to the records, J. Japal represented the nurses in 1975.[34] Jeanette Dubois headed the Grenada Union of Teachers, one of the largest unions, from 1981 to 1983. More than 60 per cent of its members were women. Dubois's leadership role in the trade union movement began in the late 1970s, when she held the post first of secretary, then of vice president, of the St John's branch. As president of the union, she chaired executive meetings and represented the union at regional and international conferences and meetings, collective bargaining sessions and dispute settlements. During her period in office, the health plan and the credit union were started. The union fully supported the PRG's on-the-job training programme. Dubois's contribution to the union included the revival of branches in rural areas – for example, St Andrew, St Patrick and St David. By 1983, she was president of the Trade Union Council.[35]

In the areas of decision- and policymaking, women were given more power. Between 1979 and 1982, Jacqueline Creft was minister of education, youth and social affairs, while Phyllis Coard was deputy minister of women's affairs, president of the NWO and a member of the Central Committee. Claudette Pitt was deputy minister for community development, and Dessima Williams was Grenada's representative to the Organization of American States. Marcella David was cabinet secretary, Dorcas Braveboy was permanent secretary in the Ministry of Health, while Lew Bourne was her counterpart in the Ministry of Housing, Gloria Payne-Banfield in the Ministry of Planning and Florence Rapier in the Ministry of Legal Affairs. In programme-planning, women held key roles in education, telecommunications, health and agriculture. Valerie Gordon was national coordinator for the CPE; Sharon Fletcher headed the Community School and Day Programme; Candia Alleyne led the Food and Nutrition Council; Yvonne James was health planner in the Ministry of Health; Jane Belfon was director of tourism, and Pamela Buxo secretary for tourism; Joan Ross was programme director for Television Free Grenada; Regina Taylor was general secretary of the Agency for Rural Transformation; Angela Cape was deputy manager of the National Marketing Importing Board; and Bridget Horsford was manager of the agro-industries plant. Monica Joseph became Grenada's first female judge in 1982. She acted as a diplomat, negotiating with James Mitchell's administration in St Vincent on the issue of escaped prisoners.[36]

The PRG and the NWO also encouraged women to join the militia and the army. And they did, with some learning to fight, while others joined as cooks, first-aid attendants and news-runners (who carried information in times of crises from one part of the island to the other without being caught). Albertina Alexander (seventy-three at the time she was interviewed) beamed with pride when she remembered her stint in the militia. She recalled, "There were three of us in the kitchen [army camp Fort Frederick]. We cooked three separate set of food. We checked the men and the plates. The men use to say, 'Ah want mammy Tina food.' When it was ready, one of us would call out 'Come an' get it' and you would see them running coming down."[37]

By 1981, women constituted 35 per cent of the militia corps.[38] The majority of casualties of the 19 June 1980 bomb blast, which was probably intended to eliminate the leadership of the PRG, were women.[39] Far from intimidating women, the bomb blast catapulted them into a new consciousness and a new militancy. Slightly over 50 per cent of all new militia volunteers after the tragedy were women. Of the ninety recruits in the Grand Roy militia, thirty-four were women. Prior to the bomb blast in June 1980, there were only five women among the twenty-seven members.[40] An eighteen-year-old recovering from injuries after the blast epitomized the defiance of women in the face of threats on their lives: "That still can't stop me from going to rallies. For as long as I have strength, I going."[41]

Women avidly expressed their support for the militia and the revolution, in poetry, songs and interviews in the local newspapers. The revolution saw a burst of cultural expression from the Grenadian people, and women were by no means excluded. Merle Collins and Christine David (poet/writer) made their mark on the world stage during this era. For the first time in Grenada's history, a woman, Lady Cinty, won the National Calypso Monarch title in 1983. An example of this creative explosion is the poem of Helena Joseph, a young teacher from the parish of St David. She made her poem famous by frequent public readings around the nation. She wrote:

> I Militia
> I conscious militia
> You Mr Exploiter . . .
> You spread propaganda
> About Grenada
> Through the media
>
> I Militia say
> I conscious Militia say
> You can't leave us to suffer
> Is the heavy roller for you Mr Exploiter
> Ah pick up me AK oppressor
> To fight you counter
> To free the worker
> To build Grenada
> I Militia will never surrender.[42]

In the face of regional and international pressure spearheaded by the United States, Grenadian women pledged their support and willingness to defend their revolution.[43] Susan Lake[44] of St George's noted: "We must always be on the alert. We must defend our revolution, the free milk, free health care, free education, the road projects, and so on."[45]Aletta May of the Prime Minister's Ministry called on the people to "[s]tand firm. We should encourage other comrades to be alert and be vigilant. Comrades should be prepared to defend the revolution, to look out for all counter-revolutionaries and be on our guard. I am prepared to defend the revolution."[46]

Claire Steeples gave testimony about being in the People's Revolutionary Army. She said she had not been discriminated against because of her gender: "[The commanders] put [her and her sister] in front during training sessions, to do as much as the guys did."[47] She noticed that a number of soldiers had entered the army with literacy problems and decided to become involved in remedial education within the army. Courses were offered for those doing the School Leaving Certificate and O-level exams. Even though she taught and worked in the armed forces, her own education was not neglected. She proudly stated that she received the first scholarship of the revolution. The army funded her A-level education at the Institute for Further Education. She was responsible for counter-intelligence in the army: she gathered information on what was happening in the country and possible threats against the revolution. Her daily routine was to "change from school to army uniform, teaching, sentry duties and [participating in military] training as well".[48]

As a women's group, the NWO was always questioned on its stance on feminism. The organization took the orthodox Marxist line and stated that "the NWO is not a feminist organization. We have taken the egalitarian approach. Women make up at least 50 per cent of our people; they therefore make up half of Grenada's potential for development."[49] They saw men as partners in the struggle, working side by side to overcome the forces that kept their society oppressed – poverty, illiteracy, dependency, underdevelopment and neo-colonialism. They sought to show that advancement could be attained through women's active participation and leadership in the revolution as a whole.

Women derived substantial benefits from the work of the NWO, the Women's Desk and the PRG. Phyllis Coard gave a detailed account of what she saw as the most important benefits of the revolution to Grenadian women:

> I would like to emphasize that the main benefit which the revolution in general and the NWO brought to women was a psychological one. It was the giving to women of respect from their society which led to a tremendous rise in self-

respect among women. . . . The leaders of the revolution, especially Comrade Bishop, spoke frequently of values, about the respect to be accorded to women, then they backed it up with actions – the Maternity Leave law, the CPE, the primary health care, the distribution of free milk and the insistence by Comrade Austin that members of the People's Revolutionary Army support their children. In how many Caribbean countries would you find hundreds of women with no more than primary education confidently leading group meetings, as well as organizing cultural activities, fundraising, field trips and many other activities? . . . This is why I said that the tremendous rise in self-respect, self-confidence and leadership skills were the main success of the NWO; though of course they were equally the successes of the revolution itself with regard to women.[50]

Rita Joseph, Claudette Pitt, Tessa Stroude and other women of the NWO executive shared Phyllis Coard's view. But what was the view of the ordinary women? How did they feel about the NWO and the work of revolution as it affected them? A seventy-two-year-old great-grandmother of Birchgrove had this to say: "I am with the revolution and the government one thousand and nine per cent. After the revolution we formed our women's group here in Birchgrove. Progress gave me new energy. I wanted to fight on for my grandchildren because I saw in it some future. Woman is real, real out now – we feeling more confident. We heart open now."[51]

Twenty-two-year-old Catherine Mapp of L'Esterre village in Carriacou reported: "Above almost everything, the revolution has been a revolution for women. Women definitely see it as a change in their direction, something which they could benefit from directly. Free secondary education, free milk distribution, electricity at last in our village and the maternity leave law. These are the things which affect their daily life and make a real difference to them."[52] Anti-PRG views were not recorded in Grenada during the period of the revolution.

The NWO could boast of a number of achievements during the period 1979–83. However, for most groups formed as an arm of a political party, the collapse of the party usually leads to that of the group as well. The NWO was no exception and, as such, failed to continue after 1983. The group had its shortcomings, and the PRG was hardly above criticism in its relations with women. There were Grenadian women who vehemently opposed the revolution, and others opposed aspects of the process. The NWO revealed its recognition of its own inadequacies in its work plan for 1983–89, which included political education, organizational and leadership training, community news boards and the NWO newsletter. It noted that there were few members at the executive level able to effectively deal with political education and leadership training. Sufficient supervision at the national level was lacking, as was transport to take women to meetings, especially on the west coast, St Patrick and St Mark.[53] The organization also faced the problem of women not attending meetings since they had no one to take care of their children. There were programmes to develop day-care facilities. However, childcare was not provided during meetings, and women were expected to come to meetings without their children. While the NWO was involved in vital work, it did not address other important areas like sports, legal reform and research into women's problems.

The NWO has been criticized for encouraging women to enter the field of male-dominated jobs yet failing to re-evaluate the female-dominated fields. The NWO, it has been argued, should have given similar encouragement to boys and men to enter these fields – for example, home economics, early childhood education and secretarial studies. The organization has also been criticized for not measuring up to its claim to be a mass organization. It has been pointed out that it did not involve middle-class women's groups. It made no attempt to ally with the existing women's groups or encourage their participation, whether or not they had been supportive of the revolution. The older organizations went dormant during the PRG, losing their younger members and their craft and nutrition teachers to the NWO. The only exception was the Airport Development Committee, which was organized and led by women.[54] In answer to this criticism, Phyllis Coard noted:

> I am not certain whether a women's organization could have been built including all classes of women, without the upper-middle-class women dominating the groups, simply because of their higher educational level and much greater self-confidence. Given that the revolution was a revolution of and for the working people, the NWO had to be an organization in which the majority – working-class, peasant and lower-middle-class women – led and benefitted the most. However, I think the failure was not even to be aware that this would be a problem, and would cause serious hurt feelings and a sense of being excluded among the upper-middle-class women who were, after all, part of the society

too. Had I been aware of the problem at more than a superficial level, I would then have taken some form of action to reach out to them. As it was, I let my total preoccupation with building an organization that could develop working-class women blind me to the fact that another section of women of the upper middle class largely felt marginalized. As president of the NWO from 1979 to 1983 I have to take responsibility for that.[55]

The NWO has been charged with being too aggressive in its rhetoric and proposing radical ideas such as marriage being outdated. Furthermore, certain crucial laws affecting women were not dealt with. For example, the sentence for rape remained at a maximum of three years, and restrictive laws against illegitimate children remained unchanged up to 1983.[56] The organization was further criticized for not confronting the issue of violence and abuse of power within the revolution. While the NWO gave support to the involvement of women and youth in the armed forces,[57] the revolution as a whole has been criticized by women both inside and outside Grenada for the resulting extension of violence in the society, the breaking up of families and the reduction of regular churchgoing during the period. Mary Jane noted that the community clean-up was held on Sundays, but some of the older folks preferred to go to church, and they were "reported" by their own children. Older persons, who did not understand the revolutionary process or were opposed to it, were seen as being subversive.

Mary Jane complained of children being made to handle guns such as AK-47s from an early age. She recalled seeing blindfolded boys between eight and ten years old putting guns together in the Grenville car park in St Andrew.[58] Mary Jane also claimed that, prior to the revolution, pregnancy outside of marriage was seen as shameful. During the revolution, young women were encouraged to have children, especially those who joined the militia and army. They were reportedly told they would produce the flowers of the revolution.[59] Mary Jane had risked imprisonment in the mid-1970s to sell the *New Jewel* newspaper, yet, by 1983, she had reservations about the revolution. She noted: "I was turned off when, on the first anniversary of the revolution, Daniel Ortega gave Maurice Bishop a gun from the freedom-loving people of Nicaragua to the freedom-loving people of Grenada. Guns meant death and destruction. I just stopped."[60]

Lucy Lace complained of a lack of freedom of speech: "You could not say anything with a semblance of disagreement. You had to be careful what you said."[61] One woman noted that she did not get involved in the revolution because "[i]t was a coup and it was not as popular as they tried to make it".[62]

Another claimed that "a Russian" viewed the St George's harbour from her home. She claimed that the plan was for "the Russians to take over the area overlooking the harbour". She believed that the proposed international airport was really "a jumping-off point for the Russians to take over South America".[63] This fell in line with the theory floated by some writers that Grenada was to be used by the Soviet Union as a launching pad for a move into South America.

The NISTEP and corresponding Community School Day Programme faced problems, including not attracting enough volunteers willing to take over classes when the teachers went off to their training. Often, at the Methodist school in St Andrew, only three teachers were left to handle the children.[64]

While the PRG did take the placement of women in areas of decision-making further than the previous regime, it has still been criticized for not taking the process far enough. For example, there were no female majors, lieutenants or colonels in the army. Bernard Coard (deputy prime minister of the PRG and a member of the Central Committee) gives an explanation as to why this was the case. He noted that the under-representation of women in positions of power in the military was a global issue, since the army has "always been conceived of traditionally as a male preserve".[65] However, in relation to Grenada, he recalled that there was one woman in the armed wing of the NJM, the National Liberation Army, which had been in existence since 1973. He said: "She received exactly the same military training as the men. She was on par with them militarily, in terms of skill and training. However, when the revolution came, she branched out into other areas of work, non-military areas of work. Had she stayed in the military, she would have been one of the top commanders."[66] He further noted that the men who filled the positions of commanders in the People's Revolutionary Army were members of the National Liberation Army. They had proved themselves through the years and attained senior positions in the army. He was of the opinion that, over time, some women would have risen to the top, but, by 1983, none of them had.

The women who did hold decision-making posts in the PRG had the serious problem of balancing their work with their home life. In May 1982, Phyllis Coard, as chair of the Women's Committee of the NJM, noted the complaints of her colleagues and wrote a letter to the Political Bureau. The main problems identified were as follows:

> The special problems of women with children are rarely if ever considered when fixing hours of study classes and committee or PCB [Parish Coordinating Bodies] meetings. When some women members raised the problems of having no one to leave their babies with at 5.00 a.m. or no one to get the children break-fast or ready for school, the attitude of many heads of the PCBs, committees and study groups has frequently been that "you just have to solve that problem". As a result, some women members have been deemed "indisciplined" for missing meetings, others have taken serious risks with their children like leaving babies in the care of young children of ten or twelve years. Some have faced criticisms from the masses for "neglecting" their children.
>
> The maternity leave law must be respected by the party. The experience over the past two years shows us that even some senior party comrades expect that women members will continue political work almost until she gives birth and will take on work again shortly afterwards. Furthermore, women with babies or young children should always be consulted before being directed to go abroad for the party, to ensure that arrangements can be made to look after their children.
>
> The party should seek actively to change the attitude of party men to the questions of babysitting, child care, housework and should ensure that all fathers support their children equally, both financially and psychologically. The party should make male party members understand that it is their duty to spend equal time looking after their children, whether or not they live in the same house as the mother. Party men are *pressing* sisters to have babies for them. Yet, afterwards, they take little or no responsibility for them. All party men and women must share housework and baby care equally in order that both should have an equal opportunity to develop as party cadres. Otherwise, women party cadres will always be held back in their development . . . relative to what they are capable of.[67]

At a meeting on 22 September 1982, the Political Bureau answered these complaints. It concluded that there was a lack of day-care centres and pre-primary schools, that men had shown a lack of concern and support for these women, and that the women had developed an attitude of laziness and ill-discipline.[68] By July 1983, the matter reached the Central Committee, yet little was done to assist the women, and the chauvinistic attitude of the men remained unchallenged and unchanged. According to the Central Committee, the work of the women's committee was weak, due to "deep petty bourgeoisie trends" in some of the members. However, concrete attempts were being made to solve the problems faced by women, through the provision of day-care centres, kindergartens, pre-primary facilities and skills training. The committee further noted, following standard Marxist rhetoric, that it "would not encourage weakness, or breed cynicism or put the party in the position of a privileged clique or encourage disunity between men and women in the party's rank and file".[69]

It has been alleged that one of the flaws of the revolution was that men within the PRG and NJM used their positions of power to elicit sexual favours from women. Byron Campbell, chairman of the National Transport Service, claimed that some women were penalized for not acquiescing. He presented evidence of at least one such woman, who was accepted to study in Bulgaria but was denied access to the scholarship because she refused the sexual advances of a member of the PRG. He admitted: "We accuse the Gairy regime, but we have to be honest with ourselves. This happened to some extent during the revolution. It may not have been widespread, but there were incidences of it happening."[70]

In general, Marxist ideology does not deal with gender relations. Sheila Rowbotham noted that: "Marx's thought could be applied by women to reveal and illuminate aspects of their oppression, but in his work, women's relations to men and women's capacity to shape society and culture are extrinsic. Although Marx was formally committed to the legal emancipation of women and to their right to work, his intellectual passion was not directed towards the relations between men and women, but towards class."[71]

Frederick Engels, in his seminal Marxist work *The Origins of the Family, Private Property and the State*, did not shed much light on the issue either. While he saw women's subordination as being linked to certain social processes, along with biological differences, he did not address relations between men and women. He stated that women's emancipation could only take place when their participation in social production would increase and domestic work claim only an insignificant amount of their time. He did not say whether they could obtain this with the support of men. Within the Grenadian context, the Central Committee followed orthodox Marxist doctrine, which did not provide them with a blueprint for more equitable gender relations. In spite of the attempts of the Political Bureau and the Central Committee to sweep the problem under the carpet, it was a very real one and remained a thorn in the side of the regime until its collapse. Two of the women in positions of power explained how they coped. Tessa Stroude noted:

> Every day of the week there was something to do (NWO meeting, militia, selling of party papers, community work and party meetings). You hardly had enough time to yourself. We were doing it because we were committed to a cause and we were doing what was best for a cause and we were doing what was best for the country. You found ways and means to continue family life but it was difficult.[72]

She recalled taking the children with her to do party work:

> I used to take the children with me. As NWO organizer I used to do spot checks. I would go up to the country and I took the children in the back of the car with me. . . . As party members [she and her husband, Lieutenant Chris Stroude] had to sell the party paper on Saturdays. We would make it a family thing. We would sell the paper together and take the children with us for the walk. On Sunday morning, also compulsory for us was to go to a community and do community work. We took the children. The children enjoyed it. They had fun, they could play and it was good for them too, to understand the concept of community. In the evening [on Sunday] we took the children to the beach.[73]

Another such couple, the Pitts, called in babysitters: "They did the work of mother and father for us."[74] Claudette Pitt recalled that there were "serious debates" in the party on the issue and that the men approached it "chauvinistically".

The End of the Revolution

The remainder of this chapter will examine the role of women in the collapse of the revolution. Some of the women within the PRG and NJM agreed to the proposal for joint leadership which led to the demise of the revolution. These discussions were held in mid-September 1983. The proposal for joint leadership was the culmination of a year's worth of discussions on methods to enhance the "application of a Leninist standard of discipline, consistency, and seriousness" within the party and the government. The members of the Central Committee who proposed joint leadership were of the opinion that little or nothing had been done towards the "consolidation of a Leninist vanguard". Joint leadership was an attempt to combine Bishop's and Coard's strengths. Bishop would attend to working among the masses, with a focus on propaganda, production and the organs of democracy, to militia mobilization and to regional and international affairs; while Coard would concentrate on party organizational development, strategy and tactics.[75]

The Central Committee was divided on the issue; while the majority agreed, George Louison, Unison Whiteman and Fitzroy Bain disagreed. Bishop felt the proposal for joint leadership was a vote of no confidence against him. Phyllis Coard, as the only female on the Central Committee, agreed with the idea "not only for a short term, but on the long term basis". In retrospect, she says:

> I had mixed feelings. On one hand it was necessary with the amount of work the revolution had undertaken. Maurice became exhausted; he had too much on his plate. It was done based on their strengths. Bernard was not on the Central Committee at the time. It was embarrassing for me. I did not wish to be seen as pushing my husband. It was a difficult situation for me. I represented the women in the party. I had to take the position of what the other women would have wanted, not a personal position. They wanted joint leadership. They were totally frustrated. Women spoke of resigning from the party. Therefore I voted for joint leadership on the 16th September.[76]

While the Central Committee had agreed to joint leadership, the issue was taken before the General Meeting of the NJM on 25 September 1983 for a final decision. Here, some party women voiced their opinions. It can be seen from their responses that the failure to resolve their problems was intricately tied to what was viewed as the weakness of the party as a whole. It was disappointing to them that, by 25 September 1983, Bishop was still hesitant in implementing joint leadership, the sole strategy, in their view, to deal with the problems of the party and to push the revolution forward. Edlyn Lambert expressed her shock and disappointment at Bishop's attitude to the decisions of the Central Committee and to "democratic centralism and free, frank and honest criticism". She reminded Bishop that in May 1983 he had called on every party member to walk the extra mile. She then asked, "How can we walk the extra mile if you don't set the pace for us?" She asked him to think of the many lives that would be lost if the party did not come out of the crisis so the revolution would move forward.[77]

Claudette Pitt reminded Bishop that, in a weekend party seminar, he had said that democratic centralism was a norm of party life. She expressed her shock at hearing his current position and his unwillingness in practice to accept the committee's decision on joint leadership, and reminded him that, in the years before the revolution, he had always singled out Coard for praise for his hard work, energy and foresight. Loraine Lewis noted that the NJM's main weakness was its members' failure to be firm. Faye Thompson noted that Bishop's behaviour was unexpected and rude. Maureen St Bernard noted that Bishop's problem was that he did not mingle with the rank and file of the party and that was why he could not understand the changes that were taking place within it. Murie Francois called on Bishop to accept the criticism.[78]

Bishop agreed to joint leadership after this meeting on 25 September 1983. On his return from a trip to Eastern Europe, however, he reconsidered. He allegedly spread a rumour that Phyllis and Bernard Coard were trying to kill him, and he was placed under house arrest. There is a continuing argument about whether or not Bishop actually spread the rumour. It has been argued that he did it to discredit the Coards in the eyes of the Grenadian public. By doing so, he would neutralize the effectiveness of any perceived threat from Coard to his leadership. It has also been argued that the Coards used the rumour as a pretext to have Bishop arrested and make it easier for them to seize leadership of the government. While negotiations were still being held between Bishop and the Central Committee, the Grenadian public took matters into their own hands and staged demonstrations in St George's and Grenville. They had got wind of the conflict brewing in the government. They had heard disjointed bits of information about the proposed joint leadership, the alleged threats to kill Bishop and his house arrest. The demonstrators demanded that the government give a statement on the precise nature of the disagreement. Members of the public eventually stormed Bishop's house (Mount Wheldale) and took him to Fort Rupert, where he and a number of colleagues were killed. One woman from the St Andrew parish described her involvement in the demonstrations. She said she made placards in the back of her shop. On 18 October 1983, the demonstrators blocked the runway of Pearls Airport "with barrels and stones". As early as two o'clock on the Wednesday morning (19 October), people left Grenville and commandeered every vehicle they could find to take them to St George's to free their "Comrade Leader" (Bishop).[79]

Phyllis Coard was convinced that Bishop had spread the rumour, and it made her realize how strongly opposed he was to joint leadership. She said she and her husband felt threatened on 19 October. On freeing Bishop from his house, which was in close proximity to the Coards', the angry crowd had threatened: "We coming back for you all." She sent her children to Mount Moritz, and she and Bernard went to Fort Frederick. She said that they felt the best thing to do was to leave the island until everything had simmered down.[80]

Claudette Pitt mused, in retrospect, that perhaps joint leadership had been the wrong approach to solving the issues in the party. However, she claimed that those who instilled the fear in Maurice Bishop of losing power were the ones responsible for his death. She argued:

> Maurice did not have the qualities to be leader. Decisions had to be made and you could not please everybody. Maurice tried to do that. Bernard was the party organizer. Most of the projects of the revolution were created and started by him. . . . Any problem anyone had, you went to Bernard. If you went to Maurice, he would say, Go to Bernard. Dynamism and charisma are not the only qualities for leadership. This goes back to cultism. There were some who created confusion in his [Maurice's] mind. I blame those who did so for his death.[81]

While she was vehemently opposed to the killing of Bishop, Claudette Pitt tried to analyse why it happened and the possible thoughts in the minds of his killers. She explained: "They were so mad, disappointed and confused. They had no life. Their whole life was dedicated to the revolution. They felt totally disappointed by October 19. Maurice had betrayed them."[82]

Faye Thompson further described the mood of some party members on hearing of Bishop's failure to comply with joint leadership. She noted: "That was the utmost betrayal as a party member. That was what incensed people. . . . Coming out of the September 25 meeting, everyone that was present was on such a high, because you thought that you had thrashed it out. People had spoken frankly . . . and now for the first time we are on the same wavelength, we are on the same page, reading the same book and we could move forward."[83] Thompson felt that Fort Rupert, as a military installation, should not have been overrun by civilians. Yet, she noted, there was absolutely no justification for the killings. She did give an idea of the mood in the fort on that fateful day, and, from her recollections, it seemed as though the battle lines had been drawn. She recalled:

> It was after the release of Maurice we took the decision to put the guns in the tunnel (safe spot on Fort Rupert). We spent most of the morning doing that, up until the point when the masses arrived. That was when the soldiers in charge of the fort were arrested and cached. It shows you, then, that the party lines were drawn. As party members, there were nineteen of us. We were told: "Wait there and we will deal with you." From there [the room into which they were ordered], we saw people moving with guns that had been retrieved from the tunnel. Vincent Noel was down on the bottom landing saying, "All those with militia training, come forward and arm yourself because we have some hooligans to deal with on Fort Frederick" [where Coard, Austin and other members of the PRG had congregated].[84]

Nancy Lou was with Maurice Bishop and Jacqueline Creft in their last hour and witnessed the carnage at Fort Rupert. She recalled:

> I was making cups of coffee. I gave the first to Maurice but he said, "Give it to St Paul." Matron Grant, Senator, Norris Bain's wife, Marcelle Belmar's mother, Merle Hodge, Chris Stroude, Porgie Cherubim, Avis and Jackie were in the room. Jackie said, "I don't like this. I am scared. I know these guys go do something stupid." Avis said, "I never see so much people in one place." Then there was a loud explosion. Something pushed me against a wall, physically lifted me. When I looked, Avis was totally dismantled. There were fatty tissues floating in blood and body fluid. Where I was, heavy gunfire was hitting the wall. If I got up to run I would get hit. I decided to stay right there. Matron Grant was praying, "Stop the hands of the slaughterers, Jesus." Maurice said, "See where the firing is coming from." I lost it. I said to myself, If I have to die, let me die with no pain. I was about to stand up; Senator threw himself at me and locked my neck. Porgie said, "I will try to see if there is anything I could do." He called out, "Langaigne, hold your fire, there are many injured people in here." We heard the reply: "Drop your f*****g guns and come out with your hands in the air." Porgie said: "There

is no one with guns in here." The threat was repeated. Maurice said, "Let the women and children go." I was covered in blood. I could not lift my right hand; a bullet had hit me. I felt like sticks were poking me in my side. Jackie Creft held on to my pants, what was left of my jeans. Gemma Belmar was still breathing even though there was a bullet straight through her head. Vincent Noel was lying in the veranda. He said, "Help me, help me." I proceeded to go down the steps. Jackie held on to my sleeve. Someone said, "Look at Jackie Creft. Don't let the motherf****r get away." I got to the hospital gate.[85]

Maurice Bishop, Jacqueline Creft, Unison Whiteman and five others (trade union leaders and supporters of the revolution) were marched to the parade square at the upper level of the fort and executed. Within a week, on 25 October 1983, US and Caribbean forces invaded Grenada to try to restore order and return the island to a democratic system of government.

The testimonies of three women shed some light on what happened in the aftermath of the killings. Lady Esmai Scoon, wife of the governor general Paul Scoon, recounted her night of horror at Government House:

> They [the People's Revolutionary Army (PRA)] were shooting at the building [Government House]. It was coming from Richmond Hill. We were lying on the dining room floor. There were US soldiers on the compound of Government House. PRA armoured cars were coming through the gate from St Paul's side during the night about 8.00 p.m. A helicopter flew over and blew it up. That was frightening. I wept bitterly. At eight the next morning sixty marines walked with us to Queen's Park. We passed the back way, Mt. Royal to River Road, down the steps. There were shots coming from down the steps. I felt I would get one of the bullets. When we got to River Road, the people said, "Sir Paul, we behind you. God bless you."[86]

Mary Louise, a former NWO executive member, recalled her experience after 25 October 1983:

> I had lost everything. All I had was the clothes on my back. . . . At Point Salines we used the bathroom at night. It was open and you had to climb up to it. To bathe, a pipe ran overhead with a hose. Four of us had to bathe together, the soldier said, "Wet" and he opened the water, then he closed it and said, "Soap", then "Rinse". . . . In prison, Lana McPhail's parents found out where we were and sent us three panties and a toothbrush. We shared the panties and this one toothbrush. . . . Phyllis and the men were kept in small box-like cells and every

morning at about 4 a.m. the soldiers would beat the cells with pieces of wood and iron.[87]

Claire Steeples, the third informant, recalled her experience in the military, defending her country in the wake of the foreign invasion: "At home, I dressed in my uniform and took my gold chain and my school ring, the only two pieces of jewellery I had, and gave them to my mother and said if anything happens to me, take care of my boys and give each of them these. [She has twin boys.] When I remember this, I get very emotional because I was willing my children to my parents."[88] She recalled the disappointment she and her fellow soldiers had felt that Cuba had not come to the rescue. She said:

> Being in St. George's cemetery, according to military training, our formation was poor and disorganized. We could easily get killed. I was lying on a Syrian grave and I felt a oneness with that grave. On the Park Bridge there was absolutely no cover. We saw F16s and we thought that they were MIGs. We were disappointed. We expected help from Cuba. We would fight for some time and they would come and assist us. The other female soldiers were freaking out and crying and when I looked around after a while, I was the only female – the rest had gone home.[89]

She recalled the brutishness of military training and the effect it had on the psyche: "As a soldier, one learned who the enemy is and they become not a person who has ideas and thoughts and could reason, but a mere ant that could be crushed. During the invasion, I wanted so much to kill a Yankee soldier, to slit his throat and feel the knife cutting into his flesh. It is amazing what war can do to you."[90] She was interrogated by US soldiers and then set free.

In the aftermath of the US invasion, eighteen people, including Phyllis Coard, were accused of the murder of Maurice Bishop, his cabinet ministers and others. A trial later ensued, in which, among others, seven female witnesses, including the wife of Norris Bain and the mother of the late Gemma Belmar, gave evidence about when they last saw their loved ones. Anne Bain recalled: "Norris was flat on the floor in front of me. I was clutching his belt and praying. . . . As we were leaving, I looked back and saw Norris for the last time. He was in a line of people coming from the room with their hands up."[91] Sylvia Belmar, mother of Gemma, recalled going from the fort to the hospital, where her daughter had been taken by schoolmates. There she saw Gemma bleeding from a wound to her head and her school uniform and sneakers soaked in blood.[92]

Seventeen of the accused were convicted, including Phyllis Coard, and were sentenced to be hanged. In 1992, a mercy committee met to decide on their fate, and they were granted life imprisonment. Between 1992 and 2009, they filed several motions with the High Court, the Court of Appeal and the Privy Council. In 2001, Phyllis Coard was released for medical reasons. All the other detainees were released between June 2007 and September 2009.

How did the women whose husbands were in jail cope in the immediate post-revolution era? Tessa Stroude, wife of Lieutenant Chris Stroude, noted: "I think what helped us wives is that we stuck together through everything. We used to go out together. We used to organize surprise birthday parties for each other. We were always together discussing each other's problems."[93] As far as keeping her family together was concerned, she continued: "Chris, as father, was always in contact with his children. He wrote them every month. He was the one that explained puberty to them. I didn't have to do those things. I do not make any decisions about the children without consulting him."[94]

Valerie Gordon, who would later become the wife of Major Leon Cornwall, said that that time was extremely difficult. She had been married less than five years, and her former husband was "violently extracted without notice". She had to support her husband and two children, aged just three and one, financially and emotionally. She said what kept her going was "a deep faith in God, and the sisterhood" helped her to make it through.[95]

Most Grenadians have been close-mouthed about the events surrounding 19–25 October 1983. These women have chosen to let their voices be heard. It is a significant breakthrough in the prolonged silence.

The majority of women in the higher echelons of power in the PRG were in favour of joint leadership as a means of solving the problems of the government, as were their male counterparts. These women would have viewed Maurice Bishop's failure to adhere to this policy as a betrayal of the wishes of the Central Committee and the membership of the party. Despite this betrayal, they would not have been in favour of his assassination and that of other colleagues.

The events of October 19 would have plunged Grenada into a malaise of fear, uncertainty and scepticism. Yet, some women chose to defend their country against invasion by a super power – the United States. They held the belief that Grenada's situation, as grim as it was, could have been settled internally, and there was no need for the intervention of an external power that was profoundly anti-revolutionary.

Empowerment during the Revolution

Were Grenadian women "empowered" in the period 1979–83? Did the revolutionary process transform their lives? Under the Eric Gairy regime, some women were placed in positions of power within the government. The PRG took the process further. However, how much further the process was taken may be questioned.

Grenada was on par with Barbados in this period, in terms of the number of women in the highest echelon of power. There were four women in Grenada's senate between 1976 and 1981. Three women served in the Barbados House of Assembly between 1976 and 1983. There were two female Grenadian ministers between 1976 and 1981.[96] However, Dominica and Montserrat fell behind. Between 1979 and 1983, there were two women in the highest echelon of power in Dominica – the prime minister and a minister of government. Between 1979 and 1983, Montserrat had one female minister of government.[97] With regard to the number of permanent secretaries in government ministries, Grenada ranked among the best in the region. Yet, it can be argued that, in spite of its socialist revolution, the positions of power held by women in Grenada were of the "kitchen cabinet" type. Grenadian women were allowed to head ministries like education and women's affairs. So while the revolution may have increased the number of women in positions of power, the type of portfolios they held remained unchanged. The woman as minister was limited to her traditional role as social worker and teacher.

Although the PRG passed legislation mandating equal pay for equal work, evidence from estates such as Douglaston and Westerhall showed that, up to 1983, men were still paid more than women. The PRG issued the Maternity Leave Law in 1980. Oral evidence has established that rank-and-file Grenadian women benefited. However, Phyllis Coard noted that women in the party were expected to work immediately after delivering their babies. When confronted with the contradictions, the Central Committee took a doctrinaire stance that did not deal with the issue at hand.

The shortcomings of the policies of the PRG and the work of the NWO and the Women's Desk beg the question whether Marxist ideology in its strictest sense, superimposed onto a Grenadian context, had worked. Could Marxist ideas of a classless society work in Grenada or any Caribbean territory with its inherent chauvinist and macho influences? Marxist ideology did not advocate the equality of women as a priority. If Grenadian women had demanded it, would it have been given to them in this relatively short period (1979 to 1983)? Grenadian women would have had to experience a revolution within a revolution to address their needs.

The argument rages on as to whether or not socialism, rather than capitalism, was instrumental in enhancing the conditions of women, generally. According to Sheila Rowbotham:

> Marx was primarily concerned with the social consequences of class antagonism, not conflict between men and women. By the time he wrote *Capital* he concentrated on exploitation and alienation of the worker who sells his or her capacity to labor to the owner of capital, who gives only part back in the form of wages. Though this covers the situation of the working-class woman as a wage earner, it does not explore the position of women working in the family, the sexual relations between men and women, our relationships to our bodies. In *Capital* Marx takes for granted the necessity of women's labor in maintaining and reproducing wage earners, but he does not examine this in any detail or discuss its implications for women's consciousness.[98]

The failure of Marxism to deal with this issue manifested itself, in the Grenadian context, in strained relations between men and women in the PRG and the NJM. The problems included the responsibility for childcare and household chores devolving largely on women when both sexes had to attend meetings or functions. Also, women within the party were not expected to take maternity leave. The concern of the revolutionary leadership to end women's confinement to traditional roles too often seemed limited to making their labour available to the regime. Women became as free as men to work outside the home, while men remained free from work within it.[99]

The revolution of 1979 attained victories for women in the areas of education, health, housing and representation in government. Yet, there were shortcomings, such as limited equal work for equal pay, problems of implementation of maternity leave for NJM members, and the absence of women in positions of power in the army. It would be fair to say that the transformation was not complete.

NOTES

1.   Constitution of the St George's Progressive Women's Association, 1977, Public Library, St George's, Grenada.
2.   Dessima Williams, "Grenadian Women under the New JEWEL Movement", *TransAfrica Forum* 4, no. 3 (1987): 55.
3.   Maurice Bishop, "Women Step Forward", in *Maurice Bishop Speaks: The Grenada Revolution 1979–1983*, ed. Michael Taber and Bruce Marcus (New York: Pathfinder, 1983), 37.
4.   Williams, "Grenadian Women", 56.
5.   Rosemary Porter, "Women and the State: Women's Movements in Grenada and Their Role in the Grenada Revolution 1979–1983" (PhD diss., Temple University, 1986), 333.
6.   Phyllis Coard, memo to NJM Board, 1979, Public Library, St George's, Grenada.
7.   Claudette Pitt (executive member of the NWO), interview by the author, Bathway, 27 February 1999.
8.   Phyllis Coard's notes in Isabel Jamaron's report on the NWO, May 1981, Public Library, St George's, Grenada.
9.   Phyllis Coard (president of the NWO), interview by the author, 16 February 1999.
10.   NWO, "The Part the NWO Must Play in the Development of Women in Grenada from 1983 to 1989", 1983, Public Library, St George's, Grenada, 5.
11.   Ibid., 6.
12.   Tessa Stroude (executive member of the NWO and Women's Desk), interview by the author, 2 February 1999.
13.   Coard, interview.
14.   Stroude, interview.
15.   National Women's Organization, Draft Resolution on the Work Programme of the National Women's Organization for 1981, Public Library, St George's, Grenada, 1981a, 1–2.

16. National Women's Organization, pamphlet published in November 1981, Public Library, St George's, Grenada, 1981b.

17. Miranda Davis, *Third World Second Sex: Women's Struggles and National Liberation* (London: Zed Books, 1983), 158.

18. "Requin Co-op Gets Off the Ground", *Free West Indian*, 6 December 1980, 2.

19. NWO, "The Part the NWO Must Play", 6.

20. "Preprimary Schools Open in St. Andrew", *Free West Indian*, 6 June 1981, 10; and "Successful Year of NWO", *Free West Indian*, 21 November 1981, 5.

21. Dessima Williams, ed., "Women Must Define Their Priorities: Grenada 1979–1983", in *Women in the Rebel Tradition: The English-Speaking Caribbean* (New York: Women's International Resource Exchange, 1987), 24.

22. Rita Joseph, "The Significance of the Grenada Revolution to Women in Grenada", *Bulletin of Eastern Caribbean Affairs* 7, no. 1 (1981): 17.

23. Report by the national coordinator of the Centre for Popular Education, *Free West Indian*, 28 February 1981, 8.

24. Valerie Gordon Cornwall (former coordinator for the Centre for Popular Education), interview by the author, 24 February 1999.

25. Jacqueline Creft, "The Building of Mass Education in Free Grenada", in *Grenada Is Not Alone: Speeches by the PRG at First International Conference in Solidarity with Grenada* (St George's: Fedon, 1982), 52.

26. "CSDP Looks Forward to a Brighter Year", *Free West Indian*, 25 July 1980, 7.

27. Coard, interview; "Fisherwomen Join True Blue School", *Free West Indian*, 31 January 1981, 6.

28. "50 Pioneers at First Camp", *Free West Indian*, 25 April 1981, 8.

29. *Free West Indian*, 11 October 1980, 1.

30. "Boss Fined for Firing Pregnant Worker", *Free West Indian*, 2 May 1981, 3.

31. Peggy Nesfield (employee of the Ministry of Education and Foreign Affairs from 1979 to 1983), interview by the author, 5 February 1999.

32. Michael Aberdeen, *Grenada under the PRG* (Port of Spain: People's Popular Movement, 1983), 61.

33. Ibid.

34. Madonna Harford (former president of the Grenada Union of Teachers), interview by the author, 31 October 2006.

35. Jeanette Dubois (former president of the Grenada Union of Teachers), interview by the author, 31 October 2006.

36. Monica Joseph, interview by the author, 17 March 1999. See also Ecumenical Program for Interamerican Communication and Action (EPICA) Task Force, *Grenada: The Peaceful Revolution* (Washington, DC: EPICA Task Force, 1982), 99.

37. Albertina Alexander (domestic worker from the village of Morne Jaloux, St George's), interview by the author, 9 February 1999.

38. *Free West Indian*, 26 July 1981, 10.

39. A bomb was set off at Queen's Park at a rally on 19 June 1980. It was probably intended to wipe out the leadership of the PRG. Instead, three women died – Bernadette Bailey, Laurice Humprey and Laureen Phillip.

40. Collen Lewis, "Interview with Phyllis Coard: Women's Growing Role in Revolutionary Grenada", *Intercontinental Press/Inprecor* 18 (1980): 1,193.

41. Merle Hodge, "Leading Role in Production and Defense: Women in the Grenadian Revolution", *Intercontinental Press/Inprecor* 18 (1980): 943.

42. Chris Searle, *Grenada: The Struggle against Destabilisation* (London: Writers and Readers Publishing Cooperative, 1983), 109–10.

43. US president Ronald Reagan had repeatedly commented that the new Grenada airport was being used as a military base.

44. The names used in this account are pseudonyms.

45. "We Stand Ready to Defend Our Revolution", *New Jewel*, 27 March 1983, 5.

46. Ibid.

47. Claire Steeples (pseudonym), interview by the author, St George's, Grenada, 10 February 1999.

48. Ibid.

49. Rita Joseph, interview by the author, 9 February 1999.

50. Coard, interview.

51. Merle Hodge and Chris Searle, "Is Freedom We Making", in *The New Democracy in Grenada* (St George's: Government Information Services, 1981), 48–49.

52. Searle, *Grenada*, 108.

53. NWO, "Part the NWO Must Play", 8–9.

54. Porter, "Women and the State", 349.

55. Coard, interview.

56. Beverley Steele (former resident tutor of the University of the West Indies Centre, Grenada), interview by the author, 19 February 1999.

57. Peggy Antrobus, "Lessons from the Grenada Revolution: Zoning in on Peace", *CARICOM Perspective* 22 (November–December 1983): 10.

58. Mary Jane (pseudonym), interview by the author, 22 February 1999.

59. Ibid.

60. Ibid.

61. Lucy Lace (pseudonym), interview by the author, 24 February 1999.

62. Mary Theresa (pseudonym), interview by the author, 9 March 1999.

63. Mary Annie (pseudonym), interview by the author, 26 March 1999.

64. Jane (pseudonym), interview.

65. Bernard Coard, interview by the author, 17 August 2000.

66. Ibid.

67. Chairperson, Women's Committee, NJM, "Problems Affecting Women Party Members", letter to the Political Bureau, NJM, 11 May 1982, Document 79, 1, *Grenada Documents: An Overview and Selection* (Washington, DC: United States Department of State and Department of Defense, September 1984).

68. Minutes of Public Bureau Meeting, 22 September 1982, Document 81-2, *Grenada Documents*.

69. Central Committee Report on First Plenary Session, 13–19 July 1983, Document 110, 18, *Grenada Documents*.

70. Byron Campbell (National Transport Service chairman, 1979–83), interview by the author, 30 June 2000.

71. Sheila Rowbotham, *Women in Movement: Feminism and Social Action* (London: Routledge, 1992), 141.

72. Stroude, interview.

73. Ibid.

74. Pitt, interview.

75. Extraordinary Meeting of Central Committee of the NJM, 14–16 September 1983, Document 112, 2121, *Grenada Documents*.

76. Phyllis Coard, interview.

77. Extraordinary General Meeting of the Full Members of NJM, Sunday, 25 September 1983, Document 113, 37, *Grenada Documents*.

78. Ibid.

79. Jane (pseudonym), interview.

80. Phyllis Coard, interview.

81. Pitt, interview.

82. Ibid.

83. Faye Thompson, interview by the author, 24 August 2000.

84. Ibid.

85. Nancy Lou (pseudonym), interview by the author, 12 March 1999.

86. Lady Esmai Scoon, interview by the author, 17 March 1999.

87. Mary Louise (pseudonym), interview by the author, 9 February 1999.

88. Steeples (pseudonym), interview.

89. Ibid.

90. Ibid.

91. "Maurice Bishop Murder Trial", *Grenada Newsletter*, 17 May 1986, 2.

92. Ibid.

93. Stroude, interview.

94. Ibid.

95. Valerie Gordon Cornwall, interview.

96. See Kenneth O'Brien and Neville Duncan, *Women and Politics in Barbados 1948–1981* (Cave Hill, Barbados: Institute of Social and Economic Research, 1983), 50–52.

97. See Lennox Honeychurch, *The Dominica Story: A History of the Island* (Roseau: Dominica Institute, 1984), 275–76; and Verene Shepherd, ed., *Women in Caribbean History: The British Colonized Territories* (Kingston: Ian Randle, 1999), 183–84.

98. Sheila Rowbotham, *Hidden from History: Rediscovering Women in History from the 17th Century to the Present* (New York: Vintage, 1974), xxiv.

99. Catherine MacKinnon, "Feminism, Marxism, Method, and the State: An Agenda for Theory", *Signs* 7 (1982): 523.

3.

The Revolution and Its Discontents

*Grenadian Newspapers and Attempts to Shape
Public Opinion during Political Transition*

LAURIE R. LAMBERT

ABSTRACT

*What role did the newspaper play in attempting to influence public opin-
ion in the early stages of the Grenada Revolution and what are the terms
in which printed discourses on the revolution were conceptualized? The
Grenada Revolution was a discursive political process where branding and
narration were necessary elements in securing the revolution's authority
and legitimacy. This chapter argues that Cuba functioned as a metonym
through which the revolution was translated in Grenadian periodicals.
Even before the coup of 13 March 1979, Grenadian media represented the
New JEWEL Movement – the revolutionary party – as Cuban-inspired
and socialist. In order to examine how socialism in general, and the
socialist character of the People's Revolutionary Government in particular, was narrated, a comparison is staged between two newspapers – the
government-run* Free West Indian *and the privately owned the* Torchlight. *Competing discourses on Cuban communism are analysed for the
ways in which they stood in for the Grenadian people's hopes, aspirations
and anxieties in the midst of radical political change. Issues including
race, gender equality, property ownership, freedom of religious practice
and freedom of travel are examined in relation to capitalism and socialism and to the People's Revolutionary Government's efforts to maintain
narrative authority of the revolution.*

Introduction

In the late 1970s, Grenada served as an important venue for the fusion of Black Power politics with Marxism-Leninism. By this time, it was clear that the project of independence, which, in the anglophone Caribbean, began with Jamaica in 1962, had failed to excise colonial-style oppression from the region. For the generation witnessing the promise and subsequent disappointment of independence, Marxism became a viable alternative to free-market capitalism. In the midst of the Cold War, many Caribbean people, not just those sparking protests across university campuses in Jamaica and Trinidad, perceived socialism as a solution to the economic stagnancy that defined the region's nascent postcolonial history. It is from this context that Cuba emerged as both model and cautionary tale in Grenadian politics.

In a newspaper editorial entitled "Who the Cap Fit" from the 28 January 1979 issue of the *West Indian*, the editor accused the New JEWEL Movement (NJM) of "playing at revolutionaries and imitating personalities like Che Guevara with the same blind idolatry as a beatnik would a Beatle".[1] At the time, the *West Indian* was a biweekly newspaper controlled by Eric Gairy's government in Grenada, and the NJM was the leftist rival party, led by the young lawyer Maurice Bishop. The editorial continues with a critique of the Cuban Revolution as a failed political process. It marks the Cuban government as morally bankrupt because of human rights violations and its refusal to recognize any political party besides the Communist Party of Cuba. On the NJM's apparent desire to emulate what Castro had achieved in Cuba, the editor had this to say: "The only consolations are that the voting public [of Grenada] will have had a glimmer of the 'human rights' and 'democratic solutions' the neo-Cuban revolutionaries have in store for us."[2] Even before the NJM seized power, its political opponents used the NJM's relationship to Cuba to create a menacing public image for the party. With an election on the horizon, the pro-Gairy editorial sent a clear message to its Grenadian readers: If you think you would rather have the NJM in power, look at what is going on in Cuba and think again. Already, the existence of the NJM as the centre of the political alliance serving as the official opposition suggested the confluence of Black Power and Caribbean socialism. It was important for Gairy, therefore, to employ red-scare tactics, popularized in the West, in order to represent the NJM as dangerous, firebrand radicals.

In this chapter, I examine newspaper coverage on Cuba and Grenada-Cuba relations in the *Free West Indian*, which was government-run, and the *Torchlight*, which was privately owned by Grenada Publishers Limited. The *Torchlight*'s managing director and chief shareholder was Grenadian businessman D.M.B. Cromwell, a former director of Grenada's Inland Revenue office, with close ties to Grenada's business sector. The *Trinidad Express* was another major shareholder, with 25 per cent interest in the *Torchlight*.[3] Given Cromwell's background, the *Torchlight* was generally seen as representing the interests of the Grenadian bourgeoisie. One finds very different narratives of Cuba emerging out of the Grenadian press when these two periodicals are read alongside each other, as would have been done by the reading public in Grenada during the revolution. These narratives served to forecast for Grenadians what the revolution might have in store for them. From the revolution's beginnings in March 1979, the coverage on Cuba in the *Free West Indian* was uniformly positive. By contrast, in the *Torchlight*, we find shifting perspectives on Cuba. Early articles reported rumours that Cuba had provided military support for the NJM's coup. The *Torchlight* dismissed these rumours, however, and initially supported the notion that the People's Revolutionary Government (PRG) would help Grenadians build a more just society.[4] But as the revolution progressed, the tone of the *Torchlight* changed. The newspaper began to critique the government's anti-imperialist rhetoric and its refusal to hold elections – both of which were interpreted by the *Torchlight* as signs of Cuba's undue ideological influence on Grenadian politics.

Both newspapers used representations of Cuba in their attempts to influence public opinion on local matters. This chapter examines how the revolution was as much about narration and branding as it was about ideology and political practice. Cuba, I argue, served as a metonym through which Grenada was translated, at a time when it seemed too challenging, and perhaps too frightening, to confront the radical change the revolution had announced.

Testimonio: I Lived in Cuba

After Cuban leader Fidel Castro pledged significant support for Grenada, the PRG used the *Free West Indian* to narrate Cuba in favourable terms.[5] Cuba was an ideal ally for the PRG because of its Marxist-Leninist orientation and also because it was the most successful model of socialism in the Caribbean. The paper promoted Grenada-Cuba cultural exchange initiatives where Grenadians could visit Cuba for short periods to gain exposure to various aspects of Cuban life.[6] It painted the relationship between the two nations as a positive example of the fraternal unity required to ensure the successful establishment of sovereign Caribbean nations on a global stage. In an interview entitled "I Lived in Cuba: A Grenadian Talks of His Experiences in Our Sister Island", published on 2 June 1979 in the *Free West Indian*, Aaron "Cubano" Young, a Grenadian who had lived in Cuba for decades, offers an idyllic narrative of revolutionary Cuba.[7] The interview is modelled on the *testimonio*, a literary genre made popular in Latin American writing. Literary critic Joanna R. Bartow describes *testimonio* as a first-person narrative of a "real individual or group of individuals, commonly referred to as informants, witnesses, testimonial subjects, speakers, or narrators".[8] This narrative typically reflects a collective experience that had not previously been expressed. It can be written by the speaker or related to a third-party mediator such as a journalist. Bartow emphasizes the centrality of *testimonio* to the Cuban and Mexican revolutions, theorizing how "[t]he political power and subversive potential of ceding published space to the 'authentic' voices of marginalized groups served to begin breaking down limits on concepts of authorship".[9]

Young's interview serves just this purpose by providing Grenadian readers with a first-hand account of the Cuban Revolution. It reflects strategies of the Left for combating red-scare tactics; and it not only promotes Young as the proletariat author, but also gives a sense of the importance of public opinion in Grenada. The PRG was using the *testimonio* to convince the Grenadian public of the viability of its vision. Young explains that he lived in Cuba between 1921 and 1969, under the governments of Gerardo Machado, Fulgencio Batista and Fidel Castro. The governments of Machado and Batista were corrupt and oppressive. Women and the poor were continually exploited, and wealthy Americans and elite Cubans owned and controlled the island's resources. The revolution led by Castro was supported by poor Cubans, Young recalls, and Young's two sons fought on the side of the revolutionaries. According to Young, the 1959 revolution transformed Cuba in the best possible ways. He explains: "After the Revolution everything changed. All the corruption that was practiced was finished with. The rich people no more could exploit us. All the big business that made huge profits and sent it to the US were taken over by the people, who worked it for Cubans' benefit."[10] Young's picture of Cuba is one of an egalitarian society where US imperialism and class exploitation are eradicated. It is also one in which Grenadians participated in the Cuban Revolution in solidarity with Cubans: the rich people no more could exploit *us*, he says. Young's identification with Cubans stresses an inter-Caribbean solidarity. The interview communicates a "them versus us" dichotomy that identifies "rich Cubans and foreigners", mainly Americans, as the chief exploiters of the working poor, while representing an active alliance between the Grenadian and the Cuban workers. Grenadians' reactions to Young's testimony must have been mixed. On the one hand, the Cuban government could offer services such as education and healthcare to its citizens, while Grenadians had to pay steep prices for these same services. On the other hand, Grenadians found Castro's twenty years as leader unsettling. At least Gairy's control over Grenadian politics had been suspended for a time by Herbert Blaize.

Covering an array of topics, Young responded to the reporter's questions about education, employment, infrastructure, housing, rations and freedom of religious practice in Cuba. All his accounts of Cuba were positive. On the question of religious freedom, Young said that he was a practising Roman Catholic and felt confident that Catholics held "the same rights" as everyone else in Cuba. Young's narrative does not stage a direct critique of capitalism, but rather takes the approach of praising communism through the description of life in Cuba as simultaneously idyllic and productive. The interview addresses some of the different images of Cuba that were circulating in Grenada in 1979 as the Grenada Revolution began. The Gairy government (and American media) had already primed the public to associate Cuba with censorship, oppression, militarism and infringement of individual rights and freedoms. As a result, the PRG's close ties with Cuba raised questions about these issues "spreading" to Grenada.

It did not make much difference that some of these problems were already prevalent in Grenada under Gairy's tenure. Prior to the Grenadian revolution, the anglophone Caribbean had not experienced a coup. The post-independence political culture of the region dictated that national elections were the only legitimate method for changes of government, even though, in Grenada, they had produced little change. Grenadians, therefore, were not sure what to expect from the PRG, and, given that other forms of media – specifically, radio and television – were controlled by the government, the newspaper was an ideal venue wherein Grenadians could read and debate diverse views on their circumstances. Putting the Young *testimonio* in conversation with the earlier *West Indian* reports of the NJM as pseudo-guerrillas, a more complex picture of Cuba begins to emerge. Young's account of Cuba reads as an attempt to insert a Grenadian eyewitness account into the discourse on the Cuban Revolution. The rhetoric shifts to include revolutionary heroism embodied by the people, as opposed to focusing solely on representations of figures such as Castro. Young, as a supposed representative of the common man, moves beyond images of guerrilla warfare to offer an account of revolution as part of the everyday lives of regular people in Cuba, including Grenadians. The subtext was that the Grenada Revolution was for "everyday" people as well.

Cuba, *Otra Vez*[11]

The following week, another article appeared in the *Free West Indian* with the same photo of Young, this time with a report that the previous article on him had met with enthusiasm and curiosity from readers and that Grenadians were eager for more information about Cuba. As proof of this enthusiasm, the article reprinted a letter from a reader who had several questions about Cuban society. The reader, B. Edwards, wanted to know about topics including freedom of international travel for Cuban citizens and the status of black Cubans. He wrote, "Nobody is telling us about what Cuba is really like, so Mr Editor I am asking you please to give us more information", implying that, prior to the Young interview, proper media coverage on Cuba was lacking.[12] To answer these questions, the reporter interviewed Julian Rizo, Cuban chargé d'affaires to Grenada. While the interview with Young maintained some semblance of veracity by emphasizing the element of testimony and the quotidian experience of the masses, the interview with Rizo reads as a thinly veiled attempt to whitewash Cuba for the Grenadian public. Rizo's responses are not untrue; however, they do at times elide the complex structures through which communism was developed in Cuba, via the revolution. Based on his responses, it is clear that Rizo and the PRG were committed to crafting a portrait of Cuba that would make the Grenadian public more comfortable with the idea of Cuba serving as both an example for and ally of the Grenada Revolution.

With regard to travel, Edwards asked why "we do not see Cubans visiting Trinidad, Grenada, and so on as tourists, apart from Government officials". In response, Rizo claimed that there was no legal restriction on Cubans travelling but that the US embargo had severely limited Cuban access to "hard currency", making it extremely difficult for the Cuban government to grant their citizens the funds required to travel internationally. As a result of this, he said, it is much easier for Cubans to travel to other socialist countries with which Cuba shares trade relationships. An answer closer to the truth would have explained that the extensive process of application for an exit visa placed severe restrictions on travel for the average Cuban citizen and that freedom to travel was not a legal right for Cubans.[13]

On the topic of race, Edwards wanted to know the size of the black Cuban population and their status in Cuba. On this much-debated topic, Rizo demurred: "The Cuban government does not keep statistics which include people's skin colour, and besides we are very much a mixture of races, so it is hard to be absolutely accurate. But between 30–40% of Cubans (roughly) are non-white."[14] He cited Juan Almeida, "the third in government (after Fidel and Raul Castro)", as a black Cuban with significant political power, but added the caveat that "persons in Cuba do not hold positions because of skin colour, but because they are the most qualified and the most hardworking".[15] Edwards' question suggests a Grenadian identification with other revolutionary populations not only within a Caribbean context but also within the African diaspora. It also suggests that there were reservations about the status of black people in Cuba, and that these reservations extended to a deeper concern about what position the Cuban government might take towards Grenada's own population, of whom more than 95 per cent were of African descent. If Cuba's government did not treat its own blacks with respect, then what sort of interest could they have in helping Grenada? Rizo cited racism as the chief motivating factor behind the political and economic oppression of black Cubans in pre-revolutionary Cuba. He maintained, however, that the revolution had placed black and white Cubans on a level playing field.[16] On this point, his response paints a more realistic picture of the Cuban Revolution during that period as, in the early decades of the revolution, the Communist Party of Cuba worked aggressively to achieve racial equality, at least in economic terms.

These two articles serve as an example of the public relations work the PRG pursued to set the stage for their growing entanglement with Cuba as the Grenadian revolution evolved. Several newspaper issues included positive coverage on the 1979 Caribbean Festival of Arts (Carifesta) hosted in Cuba[17] and on the Cuban dance troupes touring Grenada and Carriacou.[18] The government used the *Free West Indian* as a platform for the explication of its political agenda. Its representations of Cuba were designed not only to convince Grenadians that Cuba was an ally to Grenada, but also to illustrate what a revolutionary future might look like for Grenadians under the PRG. The *testimonio* from Young offers a representation of everyday life in Cuba where a premium is placed on the use of revolution to establish genuine freedom in terms of racial, social and economic equality. The Rizo interview elucidates how this view of everyday life in Cuba is actually part of the Communist Party of Cuba's mandate for the island. Together, the two pieces work to show how cooperation between the government and the masses produces harmony in Cuban society and to suggest how the process might be duplicated in Grenada.

A Tale of Two Communisms

Weeks later, the *Torchlight* published a serial piece on Cuba spanning seven issues. The series, entitled "Inside Cuba Today", was excerpted from a book of the same title by American photojournalist Fred Ward.[19] Its appearance in the *Torchlight* was accompanied by the subtitle "A Compelling Account of Life under Communism in the Caribbean". Each of the instalments attempts to comment on key aspects of Cuban life. The series offers Grenadians a Western, liberal impression of Cuba that, while sympathetic to the Cuban people, maintains the belief that communism is doomed to failure because of the strictures it places on individual freedoms and liberties. It is a view that endorses free-market capitalism as the only viable option for nations in the twentieth century. The Cuban people are not depicted as communism's participants, but rather as its survivors subject to Castro's dictatorship.

The first instalment begins, "Work is a fundamental obligation of the people for themselves and the state under the system that Fidel Castro and his supporters have instituted."[20] Ward writes that the Cuban government views work according to the communist directive "[f]rom each according to his ability, to each according to his needs". This practice is failing in Cuba, he argues, because working people are more interested in monetary incentives as opposed to the moral incentives communism supposedly champions. Ward's analysis of the Cuban situation points to a number of downsides to communism, including limited access to consumer goods due to the system of rationing whereby each household is entitled to a fixed number of items. As Ward sees it, part of the problem in Cuba is one of memory: "Cubans do not live in a vacuum without memory. Older people remember the capitalist days and what was available. Anyone can observe the streets recalling that once they were filled with autos and now there are few. Cubans are all exposed to outside publications, radio, and foreign visitors, all revealing conditions in the international marketplace."[21] The international marketplace is represented as the modern present, while communism is faulted with forcing Cuba into a pre-modern existence. Ward describes a nostalgic link between capitalism and a period of availability. Capitalism is naturalized; therefore, it is an integral part of the good old days. The *Torchlight* editors seemed to have anticipated a similar identification on the part of Grenadian readers – one where communism would feel utterly unfamiliar and capitalism would be sufficiently internalized to seem the only "right" way of doing things. Grenadians still had access to the pleasures of capitalism, but it was not clear how and when the PRG would change things. Much of Ward's series stresses the limitations of the rationing system and how Cubans lack things that Americans take for granted, such as toilet paper, processed foods and household appliances. He writes about the function of the black market, where Cubans can access the various products and brands that are not made available to them by their government, and details the small concessions the government has made in response to problems arising from communism. These concessions include "legalizing private enterprise in limited sectors".[22] Underscoring Ward's analysis is the idea that all Cuba's problems would be solvable with the reintroduction of capitalism.

On the question of travel, Ward states plainly, "working-age Cubans are prohibited from leaving the country, while retirees sometimes receive permission to join their families abroad".[23] His view stands in stark contrast to the one offered by Rizo a month earlier in the *Free West Indian*. Instead of conceding that there exists a channel for applying for exit visas and that it is possible, though extremely difficult, for Cubans to travel, Ward simply states that travel is prohibited. He emphasizes the communist-capitalist dichotomy and implies that nations have only these two choices when deciding how to shape their economies. As they read this column, Grenadians must have wondered how to define their own context, where their government was espousing socialist rhetoric while the economy continued to function within a capitalist framework. By reprinting parts of this series, the *Torchlight* was providing a counterpoint to the *Free West Indian*'s account of Cuba and offering Grenadians reasons to be sceptical of the PRG's goals.

With regards to religion, Ward's observations again run contrary to those of Aaron Young's.[24] Ward cites the government takeover of schools from the auspices of the Catholic Church as an example of the Communist Party of Cuba's encroachment on religious freedom: "The Government claims to guarantee freedom of religion, as it did in the recently ratified constitution. However, these guarantees are somewhat specious."[25] Active participation in religion can actually function as a form of resistance, Ward observes. One of his "informants", poet Roberto Fernandez Retamar, explained it as such: "Religious beliefs are an honorable way of saying you are against socialism. You can say, 'I want to defend Christianity, the belief of my parents.'"[26] The Cuban government, however, was known to jail or otherwise sideline individuals who were deemed religious dissidents.[27] The idea of the suppression of Christianity would have given many Grenadian readers pause for thought. Christian roots were deep throughout the nation, with a large majority of Grenadians identifying as practising Christians.

Ward also finds the communist approach in Cuba to gender equality problematic. He tells readers that gender equality was "formalized by the government" in Cuba and that this has led scores of women out of the home and into schools and the workplace, including professions formerly dominated by men. In his evaluation, the Political Bureau and Central Committee of the Communist Party of Cuba were the only two highly visible places where women remained under-represented.[28] This was a remarkable development, given the feminist struggles taking place across the globe at the time; still, Ward finds a way to read this in a negative light. He views increased access to education as problematic because women's professional advancement and the movement towards gender equality that education has afforded them have disrupted the traditional gender roles within the "Latin culture" of Cuba. In Ward's text, one exemplary of mainstream American press on Cuba, communism is seen as masculinist because it allegedly accommodates the figure of the dictator as state father and provides state actors with unusual powers to reshape the workforce and gender relations. The relationship between the state (the government) and the nation (the people) is represented as unnaturally patriarchal. Communism, therefore, creates a deviant masculinity that leads to the active undermining of normative, "macho" Latin masculinity. In short, the communist drive towards gender equality has placed macho Cuban masculinity under threat. Citing the Family Code that required Cuban men to share the responsibilities of housework with their spouses, Ward concludes, "Obviously domestic tranquillity has been jolted."[29]

Ward's critique of communism paints a picture of a political system at odds with traditional, Western family values that centre on the nuclear family governed via patriarchal authority. Communism is represented as an all-encompassing system that allows the government to disrupt the private lives of citizens. The PRG introduced early initiatives to promote women's rights, including legislation on equal pay, maternity leave and affordable childcare, and Ward's critique of the disruptive shift in gender roles reads as a warning to the Grenadian family about the changes socialism could pose.

The Cold War in Caribbean Context

The underlying premise of the *Torchlight* series is that the primary social, cultural and political context for Cuba is the Cold War and the American-Cuban conflict. Beyond his gesture towards "Latin" gender roles, Ward ignores the possibility of a distinctly Caribbean context for Cuba's communism – one that accounts for social, cultural and political practices that are tied to, and yet different from, those of the United States. This oversight reflects Ward's expected readership and his subject position as an American, but also a more general assumption of a totalizing US hegemony in the region. Cuba is removed from its context as one of the largest nations in the Caribbean and instead cast as antagonist to the United States. In the Grenadian context, however, Caribbean regional dynamics would have been more urgent, with reports in both the *Torchlight* and the *Free West Indian* of Cuban, Jamaican, Guyanese and Trinidadian resources (including human resources and capital) having an impact on their revolution. American political hegemony was a given in most of the anglophone Caribbean at the time of the Grenada Revolution, especially with the failure of democratic socialism in Jamaica.

When the PRG came to power, new possibilities began to surface for Grenadians. By reprinting parts of the Ward series on Cuba, the *Torchlight* was asking Grenadians to consider whether socialism was truly an alternative to what they had experienced under Gairy. Suddenly, Cuba served as a metonym for the ideological crossroads at which Grenadians found themselves. If public opinion on Cuba could serve as an unofficial referendum on the direction Grenadians wanted for their own nation, then the editors of both the *Free West Indian* and the *Torchlight* seized on representations of Cuba in order to make their cases for and against radical political change in Grenada. This question of what, precisely, constituted "radical change" came to revolve around discourses on state power and what, traditionally, had constituted mechanisms for political change on the island and, more generally, in the anglophone Caribbean. Communism required that the state interact more intimately with its citizens. The *Torchlight* coverage on Cuba feeds on the idea that Grenadians would not be comfortable ceding so much control to the government, while coverage in the *Free West Indian* stresses mass participation as the foundation of good governance.

The *Torchlight*'s reporting irritated the PRG and, although the paper never had a circulation of more than a few thousand, it became the target of government censorship because it challenged the government's narrative authority. The PRG's inability to tolerate the dissenting opinions expressed in the *Torchlight* was more an expression of the government's need for total control of the narrative of the revolution than a case of ideological inflexibility. Coverage of the revolution in the *Torchlight* was sceptical about the benefits for Grenada in becoming embroiled in the Cold War. It did not seem worth taking on the juggernaut of the US government. What the *Torchlight* overlooked, and what the PRG understood most clearly, was that Grenada, as with the rest of the Caribbean, could not help but be involved. Geography and history had resulted in the United States perceiving the Caribbean as their backyard and of vital importance to national security. The Soviet Union's close relationship with Cuba and involvement in Central America during the 1980s made the region a hot spot in the Cold War.

As the revolution progressed, the *Torchlight* editors and writers continued to skirt the line when it came to making claims about the PRG. Most of the circulated discourse continued to involve Cuba, communist ideology and Bishop's increasingly frosty rhetoric towards the United States. As one writer put it, "Why did Bishop have to go and drink bush for Castro's fever?"[30] The *Torchlight*'s insistence that there was something foreign and therefore threatening about the PRG's pro-Cuba/anti-United States rhetoric revealed a deep anxiety in Grenada about the meaning and purpose of the revolution. A key question remained: Was socialism even possible for such a tiny nation that was indelibly linked to its neighbours both large and small?

Conclusion

The final issue of the *Torchlight* was published on 10 October 1979. The headline "Rastas to Protest" covered the front page with an illustration of three dreadlocked men and an accompanying article detailing the dissatisfaction of a segment of Grenadian Rastafarians with the PRG. The *Torchlight* had aligned itself with the unlikeliest of bedfellows. The Rastas had been supporters of the NJM and the overthrow of Gairy; they were expecting changes but found that, with the PRG in power, they were experiencing the same disdain that they were subject to under the Gairy government. It seemed that capitalism and socialism had at least one thing in common in Grenada: neither mixed well with the cultural resistance of Rastafari. Rastafarian leaders stated their solidarity with the paper: "The 12 Tribes of Israel congratulate *Torchlight* for its brave stand in this time . . . if the PRG close down the *Torchlight*, [it] is the same Gairyism they [are] dealing with."[31] The article reported that Rastafarians would stage a protest to demand, among other things, greater political representation. One of their spokesmen is quoted as saying, "we are not supporters of Cuba and Russia, we see [these countries] as enemies of the Rasta since they do not acknowledge Rastafarian doctrine". Again, Cuba was singled out as a source of contention between Grenadians and their government. This article was the final straw in the government's conflict with the newspaper.

On 13 October 1979, the PRG ordered the *Torchlight* to be closed until further notice. The closing of the paper was front-page news in the *Free West Indian*, which reported that the ban on the *Torchlight* was only temporary and the PRG expected that the paper would be up and running again soon.[32] The article also mentioned that, the day before the paper was closed, "Rastafarian members of the People's Revolutionary Army" formed their own protest against the *Torchlight*, with placards reading "Rasta Don't Work for No CIA", "Rasta Stand Firm with PRG" and "Rasta Say Down with Torchlight, Up with People's Revolution". A few weeks after the newspaper was closed, Prime Minister Bishop delivered a speech accusing the *Torchlight* of inciting violence by printing lies about the PRG's treatment of Grenadian Rastafarians.[33] He cited the newspaper's ownership by Cromwell and the *Trinidad Express* as proof of its imperialist interests and claimed that the newspaper was purposefully ignoring the voices of the Grenadian masses in an effort to destabilize the revolution. Despite the PRG's statements about working with the *Torchlight* editors, the newspaper was never published again.

The circulation of debates on Cuba in Grenadian newspapers demonstrated that, during the Grenada Revolution, the struggle for hearts and minds was forged as forcefully with the pen as with any other weapon. The PRG needed an airtight script for the revolution because their rise to power brought a cadre of internationalists to Grenada from the Caribbean, the United States, the United Kingdom and Canada. The claiming of Grenada as a revolutionary space created the opportunity for the consolidation of a transnational network of Caribbean nationalists, Black Power activists and socialists in a last-ditch effort to make the struggles of the late 1960s and 1970s pay off. By 1979, there was too much at stake for the revolution to fail; but the majority of the PRG were young people in their thirties, and some in leadership positions throughout the army, police force and other government-run services were still in their twenties. The combination of transnational pressure to "get it right" with the collective inexperience of the national leaders created a recipe for conflict. The strain of being pro-socialist while in the geopolitical sphere that the US government considered its own "backyard" was particularly stressful, especially once the White House, the Central Intelligence Agency and the Department of Defense decided Grenada was a threat. At the end of the day, Cuba was more than a metonym for Grenada. It was a barometer by which forces for and against the Grenada Revolution measured the potential for success or failure. Control over the narrative of the revolution made the newspaper an integral part of the apparatus of government and state sovereignty as well as an equally important tool for political dissent.

NOTES

1. "Who the Cap Fit", editorial, *West Indian*, 28 January 1979, 65(7), 4.
2. Ibid.
3. K. Gordon, *Getting It Write: Winning Caribbean Press Freedom* (Kingston: Ian Randle, 1999), 80.
4. Editorial, *Torchlight*, 18 March 1979, 22, no. 19: 4.
5. The PRG renamed the *West Indian* the *Free West Indian*, to emphasize the impact of the revolution on the newspaper.
6. Advertisement, "Grenada and Cuba Friendship Society", *Free West Indian*, 9 June 1979, 2; and advertisement, "Visit Cuba for Carifesta", 9 June 1979, 9.
7. "I Lived in Cuba", *Free West Indian*, 2 June 1979, 3.
8. J.R. Bartow, *Subject to Change: The Lessons of Latin American Women's* Testimonio *for Truth, Fiction, and Theory* (Chapel Hill: University of North Carolina Press, 2005), 12.
9. Ibid., 13.
10. "I Lived in Cuba", 3.
11. *Otra vez* is Spanish for "again".
12. "The Truth about Cuba", *Free West Indian*, 9 June 1979, 6.
13. S. Farber, *Cuba since the Revolution of 1959: A Critical Assessment* (Chicago: Haymarket, 2011), 44.
14. "Truth about Cuba", 6.
15. Ibid.
16. Ibid.
17. "Grenada to Participate in Carifesta", *Free West Indian*, 11 April 1979, 4.
18. "Valentino, Daida Visit Carriacou", *Free West Indian*, 9 June 1979, 9.
19. The entire piece was published earlier as a book – F. Ward, *Inside Cuba Today* (New York: Crown, 1978).

20. F. Ward, "Inside Cuba Today", *Torchlight* 22, no. 50 (8–29 July 1979): 6.

21. Ibid.

22. Ibid.

23. Ward, "Inside Cuba Today", *Torchlight* 22, no. 53: 8.

24. Although there is an eight-year time lag between their observations (Young left Cuba in 1969, and Ward visited Cuba in 1977), I would argue that the comparison is still effective because Rizo's account of Cuba is from 1979 and serves to supplement Young's *testimonio*.

25. Ward, "Inside Cuba Today", *Torchlight* 22, no. 54: 9.

26. Ibid.

27. Farber, *Cuba Since the Revolution*, 21.

28. Ward, "Inside Cuba Today", *Torchlight* 22, no. 54: 8.

29. Ibid.

30. G. Smythe, "Diplomatic Finesse", *Torchlight* 22, no. 68 (12 September 1979): 7. Drinking bush tea for someone else's fever is a colloquial saying in Grenada. Literally it means that you are drinking bush medicine (herbs) for a sickness that is someone else's. More accurately, it suggests that one may be seeking a solution to a problem that may not be attentive enough to one's specific contexts.

31. "Rastas to Protest", *Torchlight* 22, no. 76 (10 October 1979): 1.

32. "*Torchlight* Closed. Bishop Is Home. Plotters Jailed. Detainees Released", *Free West Indian*, 20 October 1979, 1.

33. A. Wilder, "Free Press and the Role of the Media (10–12 November 1979)", Bishop speech excerpt, "The Grenada Revolution", http://www.thegrenadarevolution online.com/bishtorchlightretro.html (accessed 31 October 2012).

4.

Ferrets in the Caribbean

*Britain, Grenada and the Curious Case
of the Armoured Cars*

GARY WILLIAMS

ABSTRACT

*When the Marxist-Leninist New JEWEL Movement seized power in
Grenada in March 1979, they set about securing and defending their
"revolution" against the threat of a counter-coup organized by the deposed
prime minister Eric Gairy. Military aid was quick to arrive from expected
allies, namely Cuba and Guyana. Grenadian prime minister Maurice
Bishop also requested arms from Britain and the United States. The
People's Revolutionary Government's ties to Cuba and evasiveness over
election plans ruled out the United States providing any support. Britain
remained more open-minded about the PRG's intentions. Using recently
declassified British government documents, this chapter will examine
London's deliberations over supplying armoured cars to Grenada. It
argues that the Foreign and Commonwealth Office focused on the bigger
picture of steering the PRG away from Cuba at the cost of considering
how the sale of the armoured cars to the PRG would appear to a wider
audience and that the PRG's increasingly authoritarian behaviour ultimately vetoed the sale.*

When the Marxist-Leninist New JEWEL Movement (NJM) overthrew the
government of Eric Gairy in Grenada on 13 March 1979, it was understand-

ably concerned about the threat of a Gairy counter-coup. Gairy had been in New York when the coup happened; he requested military assistance from the United Kingdom and the United States but was turned down by both. This was as far as his efforts to regain power went, and he remained in exile in the United States until 1984. Gaining diplomatic recognition from some neighbouring countries (Barbados, Trinidad and Tobago, and Guyana) and larger powers (the United States, Canada and the United Kingdom) gave the new People's Revolutionary Government (PRG) some sense of legitimacy and security. Nonetheless, the spectre of a Gairy counter-attack preoccupied the PRG leadership. Hence, within two weeks of the coup, Prime Minister Maurice Bishop had established the People's Revolutionary Army (PRA), invested with the same powers of search and arrest as the police, and a militia to defend the revolution. At a press conference on 6 April 1979, Bishop claimed that he had received reports of Gairy recruiting mercenaries; in the days that followed, he made official requests to Britain, the United States, Venezuela and Cuba for arms. The swift arrival of secret military assistance from Guyana and Cuba prior to these official requests has been well documented.[1] Drawing on recently declassified UK government documents, this chapter will examine Britain's response to the request for arms and, in particular, the deliberations that occurred over whether to supply armoured cars to the new government.

Requesting Arms

Bishop's official request for arms to British and American diplomats in Grenada on 7 April 1979 did not include any particular details, although, when pushed by US officials later, he asked for several hundred automatic and semi-automatic machine guns plus ammunition. The rapid decline of US–Grenada relations in the weeks after the coup, due largely to the PRG's evasiveness about elections and its growing links with Cuba, ruled out the United States providing arms. Washington soon restricted its relations to normal diplomatic contacts only, while providing military support to Grenada's Eastern Caribbean neighbours to address a perceived vacuum of security and promote stability. Britain had so far pursued a more relaxed "keep a line open" approach to the PRG and also supported US efforts to improve regional security and stability by providing police training and equipment to Grenada's neighbours.

British diplomatic representation in the Caribbean was limited to the larger islands, and so Grenada was covered by the Trinidad mission. The British high commissioner there, Harry Stanley, was in Barbados when the request for arms was received and took the opportunity to consult his American and Canadian counterparts. Although the diplomats considered that the PRG sincerely feared a Gairy comeback, they believed that the arms requests were possibly "designed to provoke early negative or foot-dragging responses from [the] West which he [Bishop] could use to justify [the] appeal to Cuba, whose intervention was already arranged".[2] In London, the Foreign and Commonwealth Office (FCO) echoed this line of thought, but the feeling was that "we do not wish to force Bishop into the arms of Cuba if that is not his real intention. Furthermore, if we promptly respond to Bishop's request, this would remove his excuse for resorting to extraordinary measures and delaying the holding of free and fair elections."[3] London agreed with the suggestion of the UK high commissioner in Barbados Stanley Arthur that a visit by a security expert was the best way of "keeping Bishop in play" by gaining time and diverting the PRG from plans for new equipment in favour of practical issues such as organization and training.[4] The FCO's overseas police advisor Michael Macoun, accompanied by Brigadier J.W. Gray from the Ministry of Defence's Directorate of Military Assistance, visited Grenada on 19 April. The terms of reference for the visit reveal that Macoun and Gray's remit extended beyond providing an assessment of, and advice on, the PRG's security requirements. They were told by FCO officials to "tread very carefully" and seek to persuade Bishop that there was no need to solicit advice and assistance from beyond Grenada's traditional circle of friends,[5] although, with Cuban and Guyanese arms already on site, the aim was also to establish how dependent the PRG was on Cuba and Guyana.

Bishop responded positively to the offer of police training, but did not require it immediately, as some reorganization and consolidation of the existing force would be necessary first – under Gairy, there had been a progressive decline in professionalism and morale and an absence of training. Bishop declined the offer of military training, revealing that other "friendly" Caribbean Community (CARICOM) countries had met Grenada's needs, but did welcome the offer of a Ministry of Defence full consultancy on the future role, strength, deployment and training of a small defence force, in the near future. He also asked for some general military equipment to raise the PRA's morale and identified as urgent the need for a multipurpose marine and air patrol capability. Brigadier Gray quizzed Bishop on the Gairy counter-coup threat, asking him about the likely strength of mercenary forces, how they would reach Grenada, how they would be recruited, armed and trained without attracting attention, and so on. Gray concluded that Bishop "had no answers to any of these questions, he could not quantify the threat and it is clear that no objective analysis has been made. There is probably no hard intelligence to show that such a threat exists at all – other than in Bishop's mind."[6] Macoun and Gray reported back that the discussions with Bishop had been "cordial and frank", although the complete lack of reference to the Cubans gave the talks "an air of unreality".[7] No senior military or police personnel had been made available, so it was difficult to establish how dependent Grenada's forces were on Cuba and Guyana. It was clear from Bishop's response to the offer of training and the lack of a request for arms that Cuba and Guyana had made substantial inroads already in these areas. Nonetheless, Macoun recommended that the United Kingdom should offer some equipment as a sign of goodwill, follow up on the consultancy in a couple of months and offer to survey the out-of-order marine craft.[8] Peter Gay, Second Secretary at the British High Commission in Trinidad, was instructed to present Bishop with a list of available equipment to see whether he was genuinely interested, although the FCO was "not yet entirely convinced that it would necessarily be in our best interests to be open-handed, especially with military equipment, at this stage".[9] High Commissioner Arthur's reaction certainly supported this viewpoint. He cabled London on 8 May, arguing that refloating Grenada's marine craft would be seen in the region as increasing Grenada's military capability at a time when the other Eastern Caribbean islands had little defence capability and when St Vincent and the Grenadines, Dominica, and Antigua and Barbuda all had craft in a similar state of disrepair. As for providing military equipment, Arthur was emphatic: "such a gesture would simply not be understood in the rest of the Eastern Caribbean. Any aid we offer to Grenada should be strictly outside the military field at the present time."[10]

Ferrets to Grenada

In June, a British plant-hire firm, Canham and Rodwell, applied for clearance to sell two second-hand armoured cars with mounted machine guns to Grenada.[11] The FCO's Mexico and Caribbean Department was wary: "this could reflect badly on us if we are supplying heavy goods at this time".[12] High commissioners Stanley and Arthur were asked for their opinions. As before, Arthur doubted that the Eastern Caribbean would approve of the sale, more because the armoured cars could be used for domestic suppression than due to any threat they posed to regional stability. By contrast, Stanley felt that Trinidad would be reassured if Britain were to provide arms, as they would not allow anything excessive and there was a clear advantage in not having the PRG look exclusively to Cuba.[13] The FCO attached more weight to Stanley's assessment as Grenada was part of his bailiwick and his view coincided with theirs. The FCO deputy permanent undersecretary Anthony Parsons noted that the case for selling the cars was "finely balanced, but I do not think that we should embargo arms supplies to Grenada so long as the situation there is not in our judgment irreversible. To do so at this stage would be likely to hasten this process."[14]

At this point, events in Grenada gave the FCO cause for concern. In July, two public meetings organized by the opposition Grenada National Party, the first since the coup, were quickly disrupted by pro-PRG hecklers and eventually cancelled. The media fared no better: the independent *Torchlight* had welcomed Gairy's removal and been generally supportive of the PRG but became the target of repeated criticism in public and threats of criminal libel actions by the PRG in private, for publishing supposedly destabilizing stories. Citing the publication of "extremely serious, dangerous and totally false allegations", the PRG shut the paper down in October.[15] Grenadians who had been willing to give the PRG a chance were beginning to feel deceived; there was no sign of elections or a restoration of the constitution and no decrease in the number of people being detained without charge. Added to this were the growing links with Cuba, which was arming and training the PRA and sending groups of technical and medical experts to the island. On 9 July, a formal agreement between the two countries had been signed, covering technical and economic aid. At the Sixth Summit of the Non-Aligned

Movement in Havana in September, Bishop gave a clear indication of where Grenada was heading when he said that Cuba "is now the best example in the world of what a small country under socialism can achieve. That is what socialism is all about."[16]

Reconsidering the Licences

When the UK Department of Trade and Industry's Export Licences Board informed the Ministry of Defence and the FCO that the order for the armoured cars had been amended slightly and resubmitted in September, the ministry approved the sale within a week. At the FCO, the head of the Mexico and Caribbean Department, Alan Payne, suggested that it would be worth canvassing the views of the high commissioners in Trinidad and Barbados again, as the situation in Grenada had changed. His superior, Assistant Undersecretary Richard Stratton, did not agree, feeling that the reasons Parsons had given in his July decision still held, although he accepted that consulting the high commissioners would do no harm. High Commissioner Stanley had been in favour of approving the licences in June, but his response in October was more cautious: "If it were decided that we should make a comprehensive attempt to win over the PRG, including floating the possibility of further aid, I would grant the licences: if not, not."[17]

A discussion paper by Payne, dated 15 October, recommended that the sale should go ahead. The case in favour of proceeding was that: it had already been agreed; the United Kingdom could retain some influence with the PRG rather than alienating it further; the PRA was well armed by Cuba, and the Ferrets would make little difference; if the United Kingdom did not provide them, then Cuba would; the equipment was already outdated; the United Kingdom did not have any policy inhibiting the sale of arms to Grenada's neighbours; and the supplier would be upset. The case against the sale was that it could be interpreted as an act of overt support for a government that had seized power by force and suspended the constitution, was supported by Cuba and had demonstrated repressive tendencies, and that the arms requested bore little relevance to external threats but could be used for internal repression.[18] The case in favour was hardly compelling but reflected the FCO's belief that the PRG could be steered away from Cuba and back towards the West. However, when the recommendation was placed before FCO minister Nicholas Ridley, he decided that the deal would not go ahead. As well as placing most weight on the views of high commissioners Stanley and Arthur, Ridley was firmly of the opinion that elections in Grenada would have to precede any sort of aid. Bishop first got wind of the decision via a meeting with Peter Gay on 9 November. Gay had been authorized to say that the licences were unlikely to be granted. Bishop apparently took the news calmly and said Grenada would obtain the cars from elsewhere.[19]

"Britain Bans Arms Sales to Grenada"

When the Ministry of Defence was informed that the FCO had decided not to support the sale, only finding out FCO's reasoning in a cable circulated to missions in Bridgetown, Washington and Havana, Roger Harding from the ministry's Defence Sales fired off a "more in sorrow than in anger" memo to Payne stating his "surprise and disappointment" at the decision, which he felt was at odds with Permanent Undersecretary of State Sir Michael Palliser's letter to ambassadors asking them to support defence arms sales. Harding dismissed the FCO's concerns, saying that it was "going a bit far to claim that the sale of two second-hand Ferrets to Grenada represented a spread of arms".[20] What was really irritating the Ministry of Defence was the feeling that they had not been consulted by the FCO and were then handed what seemed like a fait accompli. Payne was "astonished" by Harding's memo and drafted a lengthy reply defending the FCO's decision and stating that the ministry had been informed but, clearly, the message had not reached Defence Sales. Payne explained that the public line, a desire to avoid the spread of weapons in the Caribbean, would not reflect the real concerns about supplying arms to a clearly authoritarian regime that had reneged on its promise to hold elections; obviously, in this situation, the political implications far outweighed any commercial ones. With a hint of condescension, he explained that a "necessary part of FCO policy [is] to differentiate between those who understand and support what it is we are trying to do in the region and therefore deserve what backing we can give them, and those whose policies and attitudes both domestic and foreign are directed towards objectives clearly hostile to our own".[21]

Before the official refusal to deny the licences was signed off on, on 12 December, the story broke in the press. The Grenadian high commissioner to the United Kingdom, Fennis Augustine, had contacted David Jessop, editor of the London-based monthly *Caribbean Insight*. A front-page article entitled "Britain Bans Arms Sales to Grenada" was published in the December edition; ironically, it appeared alongside a piece reporting Cuba's recently announced substantial assistance for the PRG's new airport project. The FCO had expected the Ferret decision to attract attention but was irked by Jessop's "unhelpful" piece and the suggestion that the decision was political and part of a wider attempt to isolate the PRG and encourage early elections, that it was "without precedent" and would possibly be subject to parliamentary discussion.[22] As mentioned above, Bishop's initial reaction to the FCO's decision was calm, but now a public reaction was called for. In a radio broadcast, he defiantly stated that Grenada would not accept any aid with strings attached and that the decision not to provide the armoured cars was "childish and foolish", as it was obvious that Grenada could obtain them elsewhere.[23]

Conclusion

Grenada's militarization was initially prompted by the seemingly genuine concern of a Gairy counter-coup, although Bishop understood well that a revolution needs a bogeyman, and, by early May 1979, he was accusing the US Central Intelligence Agency of having a three-point "pyramid plan" to destabilize Grenada.[24] The PRG's aim to secure and defend the revolution, as well as its desire to establish close relations with Cuba, meant that access to relatively large quantities of military aid was straightforward. The United Kingdom's willingness to provide police training and equipment revolved around two factors. First, the FCO had always seen a strong police force as the most important precondition for security in the region. Second, and most significantly, the FCO saw the police as a potential counterweight to the PRA and also to the growing Cuban influence on the PRA. However, the PRG sidelined the police force as the army quickly took over responsibility for law and order and possession of the police barracks, transport, arms and the radio communications network.[25]

The initial decision to support the sale of two armoured cars was finely balanced. The FCO consulted high commissioners Stanley and Arthur in Trinidad and Barbados respectively; Stanley was supportive and Arthur strongly opposed. Essentially, the decision rested on the FCO's continuing belief that there was still all to play for in Grenada and that it was possible to influence Bishop to steer the PRG towards a more moderate path and away from Cuba. Additionally, the sale of the Ferrets was an opportunity to confirm the United Kingdom as an alternative source of supply to the Cubans and to establish a link with the PRA, getting an idea of its strength in the process. In June 1979, this seemed a realistic, if perhaps optimistic, path to pursue.

After June, the PRG had increasingly revealed its authoritarian colours, most notably with the closure of the independent *Torchlight* newspaper and a string of political arrests, which gave more significance to the possible usage of the armoured cars. The slight amendment to the order in September led the FCO to reconsider the sale. The Export Licence Board had approved a licence and the Ministry of Defence supported the sale. Senior FCO officials recommended that the sale proceed, against the advice of High Commissioners Arthur and Stanley (with the latter too now questioning its appropriateness). It hit the buffers only when it reached the level of FCO minister Nicholas Ridley, his response reflecting his own beliefs about the juxtaposition of aid and politics. Apart from being left out of the loop, the ministry acknowledged that the situation had changed since the June approval but felt that the FCO's official line, that London did not want to see a spread of arms in the region, was unconvincing – two outdated armoured cars would be a drop in the ocean next to Cuban military supplies. Successive British governments had emphasized the importance of increasing Britain's share in the arms trade, and the lower end of the market, such as the Ferrets, was proving particularly lucrative. As far as the Ministry of Defence was concerned, the refusal to sell to Grenada, followed in quick succession by a similar refusal to supply Guyana with six unarmed Saracen patrol cars, would undermine "our credibility as a reliable arms supplier in a traditional UK market".[26]

There is no record of whether the United States was informed of the intention to sell the armoured cars. At a tripartite meeting of the United Kingdom, the United States and Canada about Grenada and the Caribbean in May 1979, FCO officials had said they would not sell the PRG any arms. At a similar meeting in October, there was the briefest of mentions that a sales licence would not be issued. High Commissioner Arthur was surely correct that Grenada's neighbours would have taken a dim view of Britain supplying arms. The smaller Eastern Caribbean states had condemned the coup and refused to recognize Grenada, fearing that the PRG posed a threat to the security of the region. Barbadian prime minister Tom Adams had expressed his concern about the purpose of Macoun's trip, let alone the prospect of selling armoured cars.

The FCO got itself into a tangle over the Ferrets, prioritizing the bigger picture of steering the PRG away from Cuba, at the cost of giving adequate weight to how the sale of armoured cars would appear. Payne's memo to Harding in the Ministry of Defence explaining why the sale had been denied was a dramatic about-face, the FCO having recommended the sale only weeks before: "the sale would have constituted an unmistakeable gesture of support for a government which not only we, but the more moderate and respected voices in the Caribbean find thoroughly distasteful".[27] Ultimately, the delay and refusal of a licence gave Bishop an excellent opportunity to publicly criticize UK policy and justify his turn to Cuba for military assistance. London was left in the awkward position of explaining, somewhat unconvincingly, that the decision did not reflect deterioration in relations but was driven by a desire to avoid the unnecessary spread of weapons in the Caribbean.[28] The Ferrets decision marked the point at which the FCO concluded that a proactive strategy to move the PRG away from Cuba and towards constitutional rule would not work; the PRG's actions that summer had made its authoritarian tendencies and ideological allegiances clear. London subsequently confined its policy to watching and reporting, as was reflected in the decision to establish a permanent diplomatic presence on Grenada in January 1980.

NOTES

1.   US Department of State and Department of Defense, *Grenada: A Preliminary Report* (Washington, DC: Department of State and Department of Defense, 1983), 18–30; G. Williams, *US–Grenada Relations: Revolution and Intervention in the Backyard* (New York: Palgrave Macmillan, 2007), 39–40.

2.   S. Arthur to British High Commission, Port of Spain, "Port of Spain Telegram

No. 61: Grenada: Requests for Arms", 091850Z, 9 April 1979, Bridgetown 17, FCO 99/363, the UK National Archives (hereafter TNA). This cable was written by High Commissioner Stanley.

3. J. Shakespeare to R. Stratton, "Request for Arms from New Regime in Grenada", n.d., FCO 99/361, TNA.

4. Arthur to Port of Spain, "Telegram No. 61", TNA.

5. "Terms of Reference for the Visit of the Police/Military Advisory Team to Grenada", n.d., FCO 99/363, TNA.

6. J.M. Gray, "Report on DDMAO's Discussion with the Prime Minister of Grenada and Some General Impressions on Defence Matters", 23 April 1979, FCO 99/363, TNA.

7. R. Kealy to FCO, "For Shakespeare M and CD from Gay", 202115Z, 20 April 1979, Port of Spain 70, FCO 99/363, TNA.

8. M. Macoun to J. Shakespeare, FCO, "Grenada: Police/Military Mission – 18–20 April 1979: Appendix A", FCO 99/363, TNA.

9. R. Chase to P. Gay, "Follow Up to the Police/Military Mission to Grenada", 1 May 1979, FCO 99/363, TNA. Gay gave the equipment list to Bishop on 3 May. Bishop subsequently requested six Land Rovers and one hundred camp beds. R. Kealy to FCO, "Military Equipment for Grenada", 181835Z, 18 May 1979, Port of Spain 85, FCO 99/363, TNA. The total cost was £18,450. K. Savell to P. Gay, "Half Ton Cargo Landrovers [sic] for Grenada", 11 September 1979, FCO 99/363, TNA.

10. S. Arthur to FCO, "Grenada: Brooke Marine Craft", 081300Z, 8 May 1979, Bridgetown 146, FCO 99/ 363, TNA.

11. The order was for one Saladin and one Ferret, subsequently changed to two Ferrets, worth about £6,000. Both models were produced from the 1950s to the early 1970s.

12. J. Shakespeare to R. Stratton, "Arms for Grenada", 25 June 1979, FCO 99/363, TNA.

13. H. Stanley to FCO, "Your Tel Number 57: Grenada: Military Equipment", Port of Spain 114, 28 June 1979, FCO 99/363, TNA.

14. A. Parsons to N. Ridley, untitled confidential memorandum, 13 July 1979, FCO 99/363, TNA.

15. A. Wilder, "The *Torchlight* and the NJM/PRG", *The Grenada Revolution Online*, http://www.thegrenadarevolutiononline.com/torchlight.html (accessed 25 October 2012).

16. M. Bishop, "Imperialism Is Not Invincible", in *Maurice Bishop Speaks: The Grenadian Revolution and Its Overthrow 1979–83*, ed. B. Marcus and M. Taber (London: Pathfinder, 1983), 55.

17. H. Stanley to FCO, "Your Tel No. 97: Supply of Military Equipment to Grenada", 122035Z, 12 October 1979, Port of Spain 206, FCO 99/363, TNA.
18. A. Payne to R. Harding, "Arms for Grenada", 15 October 1979, FCO 99/363, TNA.
19. H. Stanley to FCO, "Grenada: Military and Police Equipment", 131815Z, 13 November 1979, Port of Spain 239, FCO 99/363, TNA.
20. Harding to Payne, "Grenada", 23 November 1979, FCO 99/363, TNA.
21. Payne to Harding, "Sale of Arms to Grenada and Guyana", n.d., FCO 99/363, TNA.
22. D. Jessop, "Britain Bans Arms Sales to Grenada", *Caribbean Insight* (Caribbean Council for Europe), 12 December 1979, 1.
23. R. Kealy to R. Chase, "Ferrets for Grenada", 6 December 1979, FCO 99/363, TNA.
24. L. Rossin, *United States–Grenada Relations since the Coup: A Background Paper* (Barbados: US Embassy, 1982), 29.
25. Minutes, "Anglo/US/Canadian Talks on the Caribbean on 18/19 October Agenda Item (II)B Measures to Bolster Local Security Forces Points to Make", n.d., FCO 7/3557, TNA.
26. A. Payne to R. Stratton, "Arms Sales to Guyana and Grenada", 17 December 1979, FCO 99/363, TNA.
27. Payne to Harding, "Sale of Arms".
28. A. Payne to M. Perceval and K. O'Neil, memorandum, 15 November 1979, FCO 99/363, TNA. The United Kingdom was providing arms to Barbados at the time.

Part 2.

INVASION

5.

The "Grenada Diaries"

RICHARD HART

Friday, 14 October 1983

Kenrick Radix [minister for legal affairs, People's Revolutionary Government (PRG)] visited my office and told me there has been a "coup" and that "Maurice [Bishop] is under house arrest". My first reaction was one of incredulity, and I wondered whether Kenrick was unwell, but he seemed calm enough. He claimed "Bernard [Coard – PRG's deputy prime minister] and the young Turks" had seized power.

At 10:00 p.m., I drove to Maurice's residence as arranged but was told by the outer sentry I could not see the comrade. I then went up to the Cuban embassy, where I saw Julian Rizo, the ambassador. He had returned with Maurice on the plane from Havana on Sunday and told me that he had been completely taken by surprise and he was sure Maurice had also, "otherwise he would have taken steps to prevent it". There are rumours thick and fast about what has happened to Maurice.

Tuesday, 18 October

Everything is still very calm in Grenada. It appears that the Central Committee here had informed the Cuban party of its suspicion that they were interfering in Grenadian affairs by encouraging Maurice, and Fidel Castro has very angrily denied this. The Central Committee has withdrawn the suggestion.

Wednesday, 19 October

There have been important developments today. This morning, the market square was full of people, and there was a demonstration by schoolchildren in uniform who had come in from the country. The slogans shouted were pro-Maurice and anti-Coard. Then, a crowd marched up to the prime minister's residence, in which the children played a prominent part. The sentries seemed to have done no more than fire into the air, and the crowd forced entry and freed Maurice, who then travelled to Fort Rupert.

According to Shahiba Strong [PRG's chief of protocol], who had been at Fort Rupert before coming to our flat, some ministers were with Bishop, and several supporters came out with guns. While Shahiba was there in an upstairs room, with a crowd milling about in the grounds, soldiers appeared in armoured vehicles and there was some shooting. The building in which Maurice and others were located was surrounded. The crowd then scattered, and one woman was badly wounded.

Tonight, at about 10:00 to 10:30 p.m., there was a communiqué from General Hudson Austin [head of the Revolutionary Military Council (RMC)[1]], in which he spoke of the crowd led by Unison Whiteman [PRG's minister of foreign affairs] which went to the prime minister's residence this morning. He said the sentries had been ordered not to shoot at the people, and realizing this, they broke in and brought Maurice out. He then led them to Fort Rupert, the military HQ, where also the soldiers had orders not to fire on them. They entered the barracks, disarmed the soldiers and handed out arms to members of the crowd. A communication from the armed forces command was answered by a statement by Bishop that there would be no compromise and that the leaders of the New JEWEL Movement (NJM) and the army would be arrested and shot. The army then sent a detachment to recover possession of Fort Rupert, which was fired upon and two soldiers were killed and one wounded. The soldiers then returned fire, and in the recapturing of the Fort, Bishop, Whiteman, Norris Bain [minister of health and housing], Jacquie Creft [Bishop's former partner and ex-minister], Fitzroy Bain [trade unionist and NJM Central Committee member] and [three] others were killed. A curfew has been imposed from 9:00 p.m. tonight for three-and-a-half days, and no one is to leave their homes during that period, except essential workers who will be given special passes and transport. Anyone disobeying the curfew will be shot on sight.

In another announcement on RFG [Radio Free Grenada] tonight, the formation of the Revolutionary Military Council to govern Grenada until the situation returns to normal was announced.

Thursday, 20 October

Andrew [Richard's son] phoned from London at about 3:00 a.m., and I brought him up to date on developments here. He asked how our future plans will be affected. It is too early to say, but it seems to me I should continue to do my job.

Friday, 21 October

The curfew was lifted today from 10:00 a.m. to 2:00 p.m. to enable people to go out and buy food for the weekend.

Saturday, 22 October

There is a serious Reuters story that [a] US task force is heading for Grenada to protect the lives of the US University students.

Sunday, 23 October

This afternoon, after about 4:00 p.m., there was an announcement that at the Caribbean Community (CARICOM) meeting this morning a decision was taken by the Organisation of Eastern Caribbean States (OECS) with the support of Jamaica and Barbados to invade Grenada, with the aid of US forces. The Revolutionary Military Council expects the invasion tonight. We asked a friend to phone Andrew and ask him to call us, but, in case he did not get through, to give him certain information concerning our assets, which I dictated to her.

Monday, 24 October

Happily, the night has passed without the planned invasion materializing. Everything seems normal here this morning. Shops and offices are open and, at the St George's University Medical School, classes have resumed.

Tuesday, 25 October

The US attack on Grenada started at 5:40 a.m. Radio Free Grenada announced the news and kept up a series of stirring patriotic calls to resistance for hours. It appears one US helicopter was shot down over the sea. RFG went off the air finally at 7:45 a.m., and somebody phoned to tell us that they had instructions to destroy the transmitter and abandon the station.

I saw one plane fly over in the early morning. Later, there was a whole flock of helicopters that came over the town on the other side of the Carenage [inner harbour], and there was a lot of firing. In the afternoon, one helicopter was shot down in the same area and crashed on the Tanteen playing fields. We saw it go down and heard the explosion, followed by the sound of exploding ammunition and black smoke. We heard a lot of shelling by heavy guns and, later, some bombing by jet planes but could not make out what they were bombing.

There have been several bombing flights by jet bombers that passed over the house and dipped down and rose again, dropping their bombs or firing missiles as they crossed the hills opposite. They seemed to keep well to the left of Fort Frederick – possibly that is where the anti-aircraft fire is coming from, though we do not see any smoke from the guns. The bombers scored a direct hit on one of the institutions about three hundred yards or more to the left of the fort, possibly the Mentally Handicapped Persons Hospital. If that is what was hit, the patients and staff must certainly be dead [eighteen people were killed].

Wednesday, 26 October

The whole of the town was brightly illuminated at about 1:00 a.m. by flares which were suspended in the air and drifted very slowly downwards. We did not know whether this was some sort of US reconnaissance or part of the PRA's [People's Revolutionary Army] defence against night-flying aircraft.

This afternoon, there is still the sound of gunfire, which seems to be coming from the direction of Tempe or the hills beyond, and there is a lot of smoke from there. The water is off. Today, we have seen many people coming along Simmons Street and going down the steps by our house, loaded with new suitcases, radios and other goods, obviously looted from shops on the Market Square side of town. Somebody even looted our garbage!

The pounding of heavy guns is still going on, though we cannot see where the firing is coming from or what it is directed at, but it is really heavy. We can also hear jet planes but cannot see them.

Thursday, 27 October

Just after 6:00 a.m., small groups of heavily armed US soldiers were moving along the Carenage on foot. They were moving cautiously in single file, about fifteen yards apart on either side of the road. It does not appear that there is any sniper fire, and this is their first entry into the town, or at least the part of the town we can see. I think things would have been very different if the people had not been stunned and divided by the death of Maurice. There would have been thousands more, determined to resist.

At about 9:45 a.m., two jet planes passed over the Tempe area, going north. Barbados Radio says that Fort Frederick has fallen just before midday. We can see that the flags on Fort Frederick are down. Also, there are now a number of US soldiers walking along the Carenage on either side of the road, and an army vehicle is moving slowly along the road with them, so it looks as if the invasion force is now in control of St George's. Also, with the aid of binoculars, I can now see what appears to be some US soldiers looking out from Fort Frederick.

There was a tremendous sound of an explosion that shook the house. A bomb or a shell must have landed in the town, though I cannot see any smoke on this side of the town. The pounding of big guns or bombs has lasted for over half an hour, and it is now 4:42 p.m. There was a lull in the firing, and then, at about 6:00 p.m., it started again and got quite heavy, and there was the sound of jet aircraft again. Another explosion shook the house at about 6:30 p.m., and the firing got much heavier and there are more aircraft.

Friday, 28 October

At just before 7:30 a.m., we could hear the firing of heavy guns starting again, and aircraft are again flying overhead. This morning, the Food Fair supermarket, which backs on to Scott Street just below us, was looted. We could see people coming up the steps from Scott Street beside our house, carrying bags of flour and so on, and baskets of loot.

At 11:15 a.m., an armed US launch came into the Carenage and chugged slowly around the harbour. At 4:00 p.m. this afternoon, we are still hearing the sound of bombardment or bombing in the distance.

Saturday, 29 October

At 7:00 a.m., there is again the sound of heavy bombardment. The PRA is not such a pushover as the Americans had expected. It is really quite magnificent that, despite the overwhelming odds, they are still holding out. The occupation forces do not appear to be doing any policing functions, at least not on this side of the town, or, I suspect, on the other side either, or in the suburbs such as Belmont. Looting is continuing with impunity – all this within a quarter of a mile of the large US military encampment at Queen's Park.

At about 3:40 p.m., a military party came to the flat. The officer who spoke to me said he was a Jamaican with the "multi-national force"; he asked whether Shahiba Strong was living here and said that they wanted her to go with them to the prime minister's home to answer some questions. The officer said that he would bring her back safely. At about 4:35 p.m., they brought Shahiba back, and she told us she had been informed that she could leave Grenada immediately, so she packed quickly and left to be put on a plane to Barbados, according to the officer.

As the officer left with her bags, Shahiba stopped at the door and said to me that she had been spoken to by Lieutenant Colonel Ken Barnes [head of the combined Caribbean Security Forces], who had told her that they were trying to get me out too. Now, that does not sound too likely, and he may have told her this just to make sure that she would remain calm, and we do not know whether there is anything in it at all, but, of course, we [Richard and wife Avis] will have a holdall and suitcases packed and ready, just in case an opportunity to leave does come up.

About an hour later, we got a phone call from Shahiba. She was calling from Queen's Park, where she was waiting for a helicopter to take her to Point Salines, and she said she had learned that they were also taking out British citizens and had asked whether there was room for two more and had been told that this would be okay if they came right away. We grabbed a few more things, and I put a few important business files into the suitcase, put on a suit and grabbed my briefcase, and off we went to Queen's Park. On the way, we passed the shell of the burned-out Central Police Station.

Queen's Park was swarming with American soldiers. Shahiba met us and we had our suitcases cursorily checked (presumably for arms and explosives) by a US officer. He suggested I keep my briefcase. It was then I realized that the last thing I had done was to put the book I was reading into the briefcase and that it was the book by Fidel Castro that had been presented to me by the Cuban delegation to the Conference of the American Association of Jesuits – the book prepared for the Non-Aligned conference in India! The officer who had checked our baggage had taken no interest in books and papers, but, presumably somewhere higher up the line, we would encounter an officer who would take an interest in such matters. I therefore thought that I should seek an opportunity to get rid of the book at Queen's Park before we boarded the helicopter.

At about 7:00 p.m., we were taken out in front of the stands to await the helicopter, together with our luggage. There were about twelve of us who were supposed to go, but after they had loaded the luggage, including our holdall and suitcases, they said they could take only four people. So away they went with our luggage. They said the helicopter would return for the rest of us in half an hour, but it did not return, and at about 10:30 p.m., we were finally told we could not go until tomorrow. We were eventually put in a room under the stairs and given some chairs and blankets. I slept in the chair for part of the time and on the floor for part of the time. We were each given a plastic package with rations – tasteless but at least capable of assuaging hunger.

Sunday, 30 October

This morning, there was a lot of movement of armoured vehicles, and a lot of Jamaican soldiers came into the pavilion and took up positions on the playing field. I kept out of sight. The reason for all this was that Edward Seaga [prime minister of Jamaica] was coming in by helicopter from Point Salines for a meeting with [Prime Minister] Tom Adams of Barbados and the governor general [Paul Scoon]. When Seaga had arrived, he and his escort eventually departed. But we were still waiting for a helicopter to take us to Point Salines. We got rid of Fidel's book behind crates of empty bottles on a shelf under what must have been a bar.

At about midday, we were finally put on a helicopter for the flight to Point Salines. It was very sad to see Queen's Park, the scene of so many rallies of the PRG, swarming with American soldiers and very sad to see it disappearing behind us as the helicopter moved over the shore line. I was sitting next to Shahiba and could see her tears and my own eyes were quite moist. It was even more distressing to arrive at Point Salines and see the place swarming with US military vehicles and aircraft and arrogantly confident US soldiers. One had the feeling that their presence was desecrating this airport, which the Cubans had done so much to create for revolutionary Grenada. We were put to wait just in front of the unfinished terminal buildings, and this too was a most distressing experience.

The representative of the British high commissioner of Barbados was at Point Salines, and he promised to telephone Andrew and tell him we were okay, but there was no sign of John Kelly, his representative in Grenada. Kelly had promised to inform me if any arrangements were being made to evacuate British citizens, but he did not do so, and, but for Shahiba's quick thinking, we would not have known that this escape route was possible. But our chances of getting out seemed to depend on whether the Americans, who were running the show (there was not a Grenadian anywhere in charge of anything), realized what my position in Grenada was. Two Barbadian immigration officials had been flown into Point Salines to process people being flown to Barbados, because, as the British representative told me, there were some people the Barbadian government did not want in Barbados. When I heard that, I wondered whether I had any chance of getting in, but they processed our passports without any trouble. However, no one would admit to any knowledge of the luggage that had been taken away from us yesterday evening.

After an interminable delay, a Hercules cargo plane went off with some of the people waiting to go. However, we did not get on this flight. Avis and I had been told to wait for the next flight, but the Americans were steadily tightening up on departures, and another stage was added to the departure routine, in the form of a US intelligence officer who checked the departure list and selected for questioning people who aroused his suspicions or curiosity. Assisting him was Thomas Langton, a detainee who was serving a sentence for escaping from custody. He pointed out Margaret Regisford [an NJM activist] as a "communist", but did not have any idea who I was as he was detained before I came to Grenada and had not gone into court during his case. Nevertheless, I was selected for questioning, presumably because my passport showed me to be a solicitor.

I was asked what I was doing in Grenada, to which I replied that I was a legal consultant recruited in England. I was asked whether I had worked for any other government and told him I had worked for British local government for seventeen years. I was asked what countries I had visited and was able to omit Cuba because my Cuban visa had not been stamped in my passport. But the thing that had really aroused his suspicions was that my passport was a new one, and he wanted to know why I had got a new passport. I had the expired passport on me, and he scrutinized all the visas and eventually must have come to the conclusion that I was a harmless career lawyer because he passed us through. But Margaret Regisford, who was relatively "small fry", was not allowed to go on the flight. This officer had asked to see my luggage, and, in a strange way, the fact that it had been stolen or lost worked in my favour. Had he opened the suitcase, he would have seen a file containing my instrument of appointment of attorney general and would then certainly have put me in the detention centre.

The Hercules cargo plane had seats on either side of the body of the plane – plain but not uncomfortable for a short journey. The sight that met us on arrival at the Barbados airport was incredible. Hundreds of warplanes of the US air force, or so it seemed – a never-ending row of helicopters and helicopter gunships and planes after planes. It was a really incredible sight. What an incredible illustration of the extent to which Tom Adams has put Barbados at the disposal of the US government.

When we landed, we were taken into the old airport terminal building, which the Americans had taken over. While we were there, we were standing next to two Barbadian immigration officers, and an American was instructing them on how to question us to find out what we were doing in Grenada and get as much information about us as possible, saying "we have to keep tabs on these people" or something like that. But when he had left, the immigration officers simply asked whether we had been processed by Barbadian immigration officers in Grenada before leaving, and when we said yes, they said OK and asked nothing more. We were able to walk right out of the building, where we were collected and taken to a friend's house. Everyone was very emotional.

NOTE

1.   The RMC was a virtual entity that never met. Austin was the figurehead and had no aspirations to be its permanent leader. Rather, Coard had control behind the scenes. However, he was not a member of the RMC and kept a low profile, knowing that the Grenadian people would not accept his leadership.

6.

A Response to Edward Seaga's *The Grenada Intervention: The Inside Story*

PATSY LEWIS

ABSTRACT

In 2009, former Jamaican prime minister Edward Seaga published a short monograph entitled The Grenada Intervention: The Inside Story, *in which he sought to justify his decision to intervene in Grenada in October 1983. Seaga, in his position as prime minister, played a pivotal role in convincing the United States government to intervene militarily in Grenada, following the arrest, then execution of the Grenadian prime minister, Maurice Bishop. In the wake of the invasion, Jamaica provided contingents from the Jamaica Defence Force, which acted as support troops. Seaga's short account seeks to explain his role in the intervention. This chapter critiques Seaga's account of the sequence of events that led to the US invasion and his role. It draws on alternative accounts by Grenada's governor general at the time, Sir Paul Scoon, whose purported "invitation" was one of the bases on which attempts to justify the invasion under international law hinged. It also draws on an interview with Jamaica's minister of tourism and information at the time, Anthony Abrahams. Finally, it presents an analysis of the case for intervention on the basis of the invitation from the Organisation of Eastern Caribbean States, under international law.*

Background

In the early morning of Tuesday, 25 October 1983, troops from the United States of America invaded Grenada. They were later supported by contingents of soldiers from the Jamaica Defence Force, the Barbadian Defence Force and police officers from countries in the Organisation of Eastern Caribbean States (OECS), who provided mainly police functions in the months that followed.[1] The invasion followed the October 19 killing of Prime Minister Maurice Bishop and some members of his cabinet, among others, following a split in the ruling New JEWEL Movement (NJM), the party behind the People's Revolutionary Government (PRG). The NJM, under Bishop's leadership, had forcefully taken power four years before, on 13 March 1979, from the government of Sir Eric Matthew Gairy, who was widely viewed as corrupt and repressive. The decision to intervene was taken by Jamaica's prime minister Edward Seaga, Barbados's prime minister Tom Adams and others from the Eastern Caribbean, most notably Dame Eugenia Charles, prime minister of Dominica. They sought to justify their action under international law on the basis of the charter of the OECS, specifically Article 8, which, they argued, provided for collective self-defence. The US government also sought to justify their involvement on the basis of humanitarian intervention in order "to protect innocent lives, including up to one thousand Americans".[2] Importantly, the invasion was not sanctioned by the Caribbean Community (CARICOM), the premier regional organization. Moreover, not all the leaders of the OECS, which had just been formed in 1981, had sanctioned the invasion.

In 2009, former prime minister of Jamaica Edward Seaga published a short monograph of eighty-eight pages entitled *The Grenada Intervention: The Inside Story*,[3] in which he seeks to justify his decision to intervene. At first read, I was tempted to dismiss it as a weak, not well-written attempt at historical re-engineering and legacy-building, until a colleague at the University of the West Indies (at Mona) mentioned that it was considered a "bible" on the invasion by her graduate students. Its short length and simplicity, aligned with the name of a person central to the event, no doubt added to its attraction. In addition to setting the record straight, this work allows us to reconsider broader problems relating to the insecurity of small states. In order to assess the veracity of Seaga's account, this essay draws on an interview I conducted on 25 July 1995 with Anthony Abrahams, minister of tourism and information in Seaga's government at the time of the invasion, as well as the account of the then Grenadian governor general, Sir Paul Scoon, of his involvement in the event, which he details in his 2009 book, *Survival for Service: My Experiences as Governor General of Grenada*. It also draws on my 1988 master's thesis, "An Analysis of the Legal Justification for the United States' Invasion of Grenada on the Basis of the Invitation from the OECS", which explored the legality of the invasion under international law.

Summary of *The Grenada Intervention: The Inside Story*

The book presents a brief summary of the events leading up to the 13 March 1979 coup, the period of the revolution and Bishop's death in October 1983. In this book, Seaga notes his refusal to accept the legitimacy of the PRG. His suspicion of the socialist bent of the regime was confirmed with the construction of the airport (since named the Maurice Bishop International Airport) with extensive Cuban assistance which, he argues, was inconsistent with Grenada's developmental needs.[4] Seaga then draws heavily from documents "captured"[5] by Jamaican soldiers to establish a rough chronology of events leading up to Bishop's death and to confirm his suspicions of the subversive and aggressive intent of the Grenada regime towards its Caribbean neighbours.

The book then presents an account of events leading up to the decision to intervene, in particular Seaga's role in the incidents that precipitated the invasion, as well as Governor General Paul Scoon's role in providing "legitimacy" for the intervention. It follows with extensive excerpts from two assessments of the invasion's legitimacy: Christopher C. Joyner,[6] who argues that it was not justifiable under international law; and Aubrey Fraser, who held, among other things, the position of director of the Norman Manley Law School and who, in an editorial in the *West Indian Law Journal* (1983), sought to make a case for its legality. Seaga himself does not intervene in these debates but focuses instead, in his conclusion, on the "rightness" of the action:

> The intervention of October 25, 1983, did not please everyone. Some still believed that Grenada was being moulded in the doctrines of virtuous socialist ideals which should have been allowed to blossom. But few would say that the good derived by the intervention did not exceed the abuses of the civil rights

of the people who had no means of protest, without the imposition of vicious sanctions during forty-two months of PRG control of the country. As polls subsequently showed, the people of Grenada were happy to be free again to choose their own future by democratic means and to remove the blanket of fear under which they were forced to exist. Grenada, by this turn of fortune, became a symbol in the region and elsewhere of the triumph of a greater right.[7]

The book ends with a brief conclusion, which elevates "the rule of law" as the legitimate basis for societal change: "The rule of law, therefore, is still the most balanced and acceptable means for transformation in a society eager for change without chaos. It may be slower but, like the tortoise it will eventually arrive first in the race between development and discontent, while others fall. *Festina lente* – make haste slowly."[8] Appendices containing excerpts of documents and lists of documents removed from Grenada during the invasion form a substantial part of the book (pp. 51–88).

Interrogating Seaga's Account

To the extent that he considers the invasion's legitimacy, Seaga focuses on the role of the OECS and Governor General Paul Scoon in providing the basis for US and Jamaican intervention. Seaga's narrative of the decision to intervene proceeds as follows: He was approached by Barbados's prime minister, Tom Adams, by special emissary, shortly after Bishop's death, to formulate a plan to "rescue the Governor General, who was confined to the state residence". Seaga agreed with this but argued that stronger action was needed, in light of what he viewed as "Austin['s][9] . . . usurping [of] human and civil rights".[10] In his words:

> I told Adams that in the same way that strong force was used to stage the revolution,[11] stronger force should now be used to remove the Revolutionary Military Council. We agreed to get a message to Governor-General Scoon to seek his approval because he had the power to invite external powers to intervene. Scoon agreed, but could not provide a letter approving an intervention until after the event as he was under house arrest.[12]

No date was provided for this chain of events, but one can conclude that it occurred between 19 and 21 October, as, by Seaga's account, he left for Barbados on Friday, 22 October, "to meet with Tom Adams and the leaders of the OECS group led by Eugenia Charles of Dominica".[13] This meeting was set in order to arrive at "decisions" in advance of a CARICOM meeting to be held the following day to discuss the events in Grenada. The meeting decided to invoke Clause 8 of the OECS Treaty, which called for joint action once it had been determined that there was a perceived threat to national security. This threat, they reasoned, was evident in the "execution of Prime Minister Maurice Bishop and the establishment of a Revolutionary Military Council headed by the Marxist-Leninist General Hudson Austin who had Cuban and Soviet backing".[14] St Vincent's prime minister did not agree, proposing instead an investigation of the situation. The meeting agreed to expel Grenada "from OECS international caucuses" and to propose military intervention to CARICOM.

Tom Adams's account suggests that caucuses on Grenada had begun as early as 15 October, when Maurice Bishop was placed under house arrest, and the United States approached Adams with an offer of transportation to assist in freeing Bishop from house arrest.[15] Anthony Abrahams[16] suggests that, certainly by October 19, when Bishop was killed, Adams had approached Seaga to discuss possible action on Grenada. On that day, the Barbados cabinet had taken the decision to collaborate with "Eastern Caribbean countries and larger non-Caribbean countries with the resources necessary to carry out such an intimate operation",[17] an obvious reference to military action. Seaga's narrative above supports this.

Seaga's account suggests that action had been taken to secure an invasion even before the CARICOM meeting. The sequence of events he presents suggests that this initiative might have happened before the meeting on 22 October to which he alluded and, most likely, after his discussion with Barbados on 19 October on the need for the use of force. Indeed, he suggests that a request for US intervention was made even earlier, on 21 October, by Eugenia Charles, then OECS chairperson.[18] He also notes that "[o]n Saturday, October 22, at around 3:00 a.m., President Reagan was awakened and informed that the OECS and the governor general of Grenada had sent a letter to him advising of the decision to intervene in the crisis in Grenada and seeking military support from the United States".[19] This account would suggest that there were two overtures to Reagan to intervene on behalf of the OECS. A more likely explanation is an error in the dates in Seaga's account. The effect of time on his memory is already evident in his reference to Friday, 22 October, leaving us unclear as to whether he was referring to Friday, 21 October, or Saturday, 22 October. In any event, he outlines the sequence following the Barbados meeting that was held after the CARICOM meeting, as follows:

> In Barbados that night on Sunday October 23, the OECS convened an emergency session to discuss ways of ending the anarchy and violence in Grenada. Acting under Clause 8 of the OECS Treaty of 1981, the members had voted previously to ask Barbados, Jamaica and the United States to join them in sending a multinational peacekeeping expedition to Grenada. Hours later, at 2.00 a.m. in the morning of October 22, Sir Paul Scoon, the Governor-General of Grenada, by letter, had asked the OECS, Jamaica, Barbados and the United States to free his country from the Revolutionary Military Council. I had made it clear that Jamaica would not act without a request in writing from the Governor-General, the Constitutional authority. In a letter addressed to me, dated October 24, 1983, Sir Paul Scoon wrote "you are aware that there is a vacuum of authority in Grenada following the killing of the Prime Minister and the subsequent serious violations of human rights and bloodshed. I am, therefore, seriously concerned over the lack of internal security in Grenada. Consequently, I am requesting your help to assist me in stabilizing this grave and dangerous situation. It is my desire that a peace keeping force should be established in Grenada to facilitate a rapid return to peace and tranquility and also a return to democratic rule."[20]

This sequence is muddled, as the references to a 23 October OECS meeting, followed, on the morning of 22 October, by a letter from Scoon requesting intervention, indicate. This could be attributed to the problem of recall so long after the event had taken place or to a clumsy attempt to backdate Scoon's letter. The architects of the invasion did meet on 23 October, after the CARICOM meeting, to finalize the details of the invasion, as per Abrahams. They had also met on 21 October and agreed, formally, to apply non-military sanctions. Grenada was absent from this meeting. In retrospect, it would appear that the OECS, with Barbados's support, had agreed to take military action at that earlier meeting, although this was not disclosed at the time. A meeting of CARICOM heads of government to discuss the regional response was scheduled for the following day, 22 October. The meeting ended on 23 October. The OECS meeting of 21 October was clearly meant to pre-empt the

CARICOM meeting. According to Abrahams, on that very day, a Jamaican delegation, headed for the CARICOM meeting in Trinidad, stopped in Barbados to meet with Adams and some OECS leaders and discuss Grenada.[21] Also, on that day, according to White House spokesman Larry Speakes, "Eastern Caribbean leaders issue an 'informal' appeal to the Reagan administration for help."[22] On 22 October, in the wee hours of the morning (2:45 a.m.), in advance of the CARICOM meeting, US secretary of state George Schultz received a diplomatic cable on behalf of OECS states Jamaica and Barbados requesting US involvement.[23]

Since so much of Seaga's account hinges on the invitation from Scoon, it merits further scrutiny. Seaga's account presents some challenges of sequence. It mentions two letters: one sent to the OECS, Barbados, the United States and Jamaica on October 22 requesting intervention; and another sent to Seaga on October 24, also requesting intervention. It is not clear here whether there were in fact two letters, as the second appears redundant. Further, it is not clear how these letters were communicated as, a few paragraphs earlier, Seaga wrote that, after his talk with Adams and their attempt to secure Scoon's approval for intervention, "Scoon agreed, but could not provide a letter approving an intervention until after the event as he was under house arrest."[24] Under such conditions, it is difficult to see how he could have sent one letter, far less two.

This account of Scoon's involvement is strongly contradicted by Anthony Abrahams, who was then minister of tourism and information in Seaga's government. Abrahams provides an alternative narrative on the role of Scoon's letter and the events leading up to his involvement. His version indicates that Scoon's role was less active than suggested and refutes the claim that Scoon authored the letters of invitation. When asked what Scoon's role was in the invasion, he replied:

> Once the Americans privately indicated to Seaga that they would be prepared to be part of a regional approach, that would be difficult for Jamaica because that now would immediately tie us into the thing. The really ideal solution was if we didn't have to be involved at all. But once we were the middle men to the Americans above the state department.[25] . . . I think the American State Department was very influenced by – I don't remember his name, but he was a coloured ambassador to Trinidad; America had a black ambassador to Trinidad

at the time; . . . as a Black . . . in Trinidad he would have been very sensitive to what he would consider the local climate. And of course the local climate would have been judged not from Barbados or Dominica but from Trinidad . . . the legalities of intervention became very important. Now my recollection is that the lawyer came up with the idea that when the Bishop revolution took place, the constitutional link that Bishop used to legalize his revolution was the governor general. In fact Paul Scoon, as you know, had been governor general from before, and Bishop had appointed and kept him because of some constitutional point that [I] don't remember exactly how the thing was reasoned. The point was that it was agreed or suggested by the lawyers and accepted that if Paul Scoon, during the break down of law and order and the fact that a force was there that had imprisoned the legitimate government, had the legitimate prime minister under house arrest and so forth; if Paul Scoon invited the invasion then that would provide the legal basis for the intervention. So he became very important as the constitutional and legal continuum between the last elected government – Gairy, through Bishop to these new renegades; so Scoon had to be prevailed upon to request the invasion, which he did.[26]

Abrahams sheds further light on the authorship of the letter, which was in question, given the logistical challenges Seaga notes of getting such a letter to the players involved. The following excerpt from the interview substantiates this:

Patsy Lewis: When was this [Scoon's request for the intervention] done?

Anthony Abrahams: Prior to the invasion. The actual letters of invitation, however, were not signed prior to the invasion. The actual letters of invitation were signed on the day of the invasion.[27]

PL: So did he write the letters of invitation or were they written for him?

AA: [*laughter*]

PL: I have information here from an American source that the letters were actually carried in on the American . . .

AA: Well I would confirm that. The letters went into Grenada in the physical possession of two Jamaican ministers of government.

PL: And these were? Yourself and?

AA: The actual letters went in . . .

PL: Yourself and?

AA: Neville Gallimore. Well you should let him tell you that, I don't know . . . the letters went in.

PL: Who wrote the letters?

AA: Well, there were a number of letters,[28] because in the end everybody wanted a letter. Every cat and dog wanted a letter. Every single island that took part in the multinational force had a letter. It wasn't one letter. I don't remember who wrote the letters. I would imagine it would probably have been an American letter, something they would have wanted. I believe the actual letters were composed by a lady here in the prime minister's office here in Jamaica . . .

PL: Are you sure that Paul Scoon was actually contacted before the invasion? And how was he contacted?

AA: I can't tell you that. I really can't tell you when he was first contacted.

PL: Or you don't want to tell me?

AA: I don't know. I don't know. I was, you must remember, I was on this thing . . . I know in Barbados I got instructions that I was to go on an American plane. A young man was coming down from Jamaica, young Gallimore, with some letters. I was to make the arrangements to get us both over there to go and see Paul Scoon and to make sure he signed these letters.

PL: So you can't be sure he actually gave consent before?

AA: No, but the whole context in which the thing, contact . . . you see when I got to Grenada, Paul Scoon . . . I was taken to a house that overlooked Point Saline and Paul Scoon and his wife were already there. They had been brought from the – I don't know what you call it – King's house, the official governor general's house which had by then been, you know . . . part of the intervention strategy, the military strategy was the securing of Paul Scoon alive . . . And that's how that part of this went. I have a picture of myself and Paul Scoon and Neville Gallimore that sits on my dressing table at home.

PL: So you gave him the letters to sign?

AA: Yes, I gave him all the letters to sign.

The Governor General's Account

Scoon's account suggests that he gave tacit approval for the invasion but no written prior consent. In fact, he wrote no letters, but affixed his signature to letters delivered to him after the invasion. Interestingly, Scoon's tacit approval was delivered to British deputy high commissioner David Montgomery, who, along with two colleagues from the US embassy in Barbados, Ken Kurze and Linda Flohr, was allowed by the Revolutionary Military Council (RMC) to enter Grenada by charter plane.[29] While Scoon met with Flohr, in his account, his discussions were limited to the conditions of US citizens, in particular American students studying at St George's University.

It was Montgomery who, in his meeting with Scoon on the morning of 23 October, provided him with "a detailed briefing on the high-powered diplomatic activity taking place in Barbados and elsewhere and also brought [him] up to date on the already substantial and rapidly growing United States military build-up in Barbados".[30] Montgomery declared that "he was unaware of any imminent military action to restore the situation in Grenada, but it could not be ruled out that the outcome of the high level discussions currently taking place between Prime Minister Adams, Prime Minister Seaga and OECS heads of government on the one hand and the United States Government on the other might be agreement to take joint military action".[31] He indicated to Scoon that, in the context of these discussions, he (Scoon) was "widely acknowledged . . . as the sole representative of constitutional authority in Grenada" and proceeded to underscore his importance to any military option. "In a calm, reassuring voice, Montgomery suggested that, in these circumstances, I should perhaps give urgent consideration to the role I would expect to assume if a military operation were to be mounted against the Revolutionary Military Council, adding that, clearly, my views on military action as an option to restore my country to normality would be crucial to any decision on that score."[32]

The fact that it was Montgomery, the British envoy, who briefed Scoon on the possibility of invasion is startling and totally contrary to the British claim that they were ill-informed and unsupportive of the US-led action. This is significant cause for further research on the United Kingdom's involvement in the 1983 chain of events.

Scoon indicated that, given the situation that existed in Grenada at the time, he would support military intervention, but baulked at the suggestion that he put this in writing:

> Montgomery then enquired whether, if requested to do so, I would be prepared to express these sentiments in writing. I temporized by suggesting that since, self evidently, such an undertaking would have to be cloaked in utmost secrecy, this vital factor could not be guaranteed if I were to put such thoughts in writing. . . . That said, I recognized immediately that Montgomery was trying to indicate that while Caribbean political leaders like Tom Adams, Eugenia

Charles, Compton and Seaga might just possibly regard an oral request from me, conveyed via Montgomery, as sufficient justification to initiate military action, it was in the highest degree unlikely that the United States Government would even consider being associated with such action in the absence of an unequivocal, written request from me.[33]

Montgomery queried whether, under these circumstances, Scoon would

authorize him to pass on the gist of my views, to say, Prime Minister Adams, adding that I would not wish military action by friendly states to be inhibited by the absence of a formal request from me. That being so and having regard to the paramount need for secrecy, I would be content for the message being conveyed . . . to be regarded pro tem, as such a request with a formal written request from me to follow as soon as a secure, practicable means of communication became available.[34]

Scoon agreed but commented on the uncomfortable position in which he was placed: "Once again I found myself in the uncomfortable position of having to make a decision of the highest importance with no time for sober reflection."[35] What is clear from this exchange as presented by Scoon is that he was not the initiator of such action; rather, he was petitioned to give his support for a decision that had already been made but needed a rubber stamp.[36]

Further, Scoon's account decisively refutes Seaga's claim that Scoon had written letters on 22 October asking Jamaica and Barbados and the United States to free his country from the Revolutionary Military Council, and on 24 October to Seaga to request his assistance in establishing a "peacekeeping force".[37] Scoon puts the matter to rest in his description of how he came by these letters; an account that substantiates Abrahams's revelations. Scoon received letters "addressed to Tom Adams, Edward Seaga, Eugenia Charles and Ronald Reagan" on 26 October, the day after the invasion, at the Point Salines Great House, the newly established headquarters of the Regional Security System.[38] In his words, he signed these after making one alteration.[39] The Americans were thwarted in their attempt to deliver these to him on the morning of 25 October, when resistance from the People's Revolutionary Army prevented their retrieving him from his official residence.[40] It is unlikely that Seaga had read Scoon's account, which predates his own by six years. Had he done so, he would have offered an explanation for the discrepancies in their accounts. Abrahams's account was published even earlier, in my 1999 article "Revisiting the Grenada Invasion: The OECS' Role, and Its Impact on Regional and International Politics",[41] which would also have been easily accessible to him.

Abrahams's account shows Seaga's role to be more than that of a passive invitee to the invasion but rather that of an active player in bringing about the invasion and the efforts to give it legitimacy. By his own account, Seaga was the first to introduce the idea of a forceful intervention in his conversation with Adams. According to Abrahams, his regime wrote the letters of invitation, having already determined that the governor general would provide the legal cover for the invasion. Further, members of the Jamaican contingent to the CARICOM meeting actively sought to win over Trinidad, Belize and the Bahamas, in favour of intervention. According to Abrahams, the CARICOM meeting was followed by one in Barbados with some OECS leaders and Jamaica in attendance, with Seaga's task being to mobilize US support for the intervention:

> And then what happened out of that meeting, as my recollection goes, is that Tom Adams was mandated to sound out the British, and Seaga was mandated to sound out the Americans to see whether their views on the matter could be ascertained, and to see whether some sort of extra-regional cooperation could be forged to deal with this incident. . . .
>
> My understanding is that the first contact with the State Department was negative in terms of getting involved. And that it was intercession to Reagan directly by Seaga through, I think, Ed Meese, who was Reagan's Chief of Staff – is that what they called it at the time – that brought about the change in the American position. And that change led to a feeling that all of the OECS and Jamaica – and we kept saying we were sorry about Trinidad – along with the Americans and until the last moment, it was hoped, the British.

In the end, Seaga's enthusiasm for invasion was evident from his own account, where he mentions that, concerned that the Americans had made no arrangements for soldiers of the Jamaica Defence Force to be flown to Grenada as part of the invading force, and not wanting to "disappoint" them, he commandeered an Air Jamaica airplane and crew to fly them in. He proclaims proudly that the flight "made history" as it was "the only occasion in which soldiers went to war in an airliner attended by airline hostesses".[42]

CARICOM and the OECS

Seaga, at the end of his brief introduction, points to the significance of the invasion to the CARICOM region:

> It is to be noted that this intervention marked the first time that any CARICOM country was engaged in military action against another. The fact that the intervention restored peace and stability should be considered a red-letter day for CARICOM countries since the alternative would have been exposure of several small and vulnerable islands in the CARICOM group to a similar tyrannical episode in their history. That being the case, the Grenada intervention of October 15, 1983, has established itself as an historical CARICOM day which should not be allowed to pass. Yet the anniversary of this epic event is ignored because history is so easily forgotten.[43]

Yet the organization at the forefront of the invasion was not CARICOM but the OECS. In fact, Seaga's account of CARICOM's role in the invasion decision shows a deliberate marginalization of the organization. It was clear from the start of the crisis that CARICOM was never seriously considered as the appropriate framework for resolving the crisis. Seaga's primary contacts, in his account, were first with Tom Adams,[44] then with OECS leaders. Seaga's account is of a fractured CARICOM meeting, with strong opposition by Guyana to intervention. Abrahams's account suggests even more strongly that the CARICOM meeting was a matter of formality and that the stage for the invasion was already set. Its value lay in their potential ability to convince Trinidad to support intervention. When that was not forthcoming, Seaga lost interest in the meeting. According to Abrahams, Seaga attended a "couple" of sessions but then left him and Gallimore to represent Jamaica.

> AA: Tom Adams had announced that he wasn't going to Trinidad; and I think it was our intention to try and persuade him to come to Trinidad, because [if] Tom didn't come to Trinidad, it was quite clear that it would have been dominated by Burnham and the Trinidadians and so forth. You needed to have everybody there. I remember correctly. . . . I can't remember seeing Eugenia Charles at that conference. She may have been there but I don't remember seeing her in Trinidad. I think the man from St. Lucia, what's his name? [PL: Compton.] Compton; I think Compton looked in on that conference in Trinidad. Seaga came for the opening and one or two sessions but by and large he left myself

and a junior minister from the Ministry of Foreign Affairs, Neville Gallimore, [who] had accompanied us.

PL: So there wasn't a full complement of heads at the CARICOM meeting.

AA: And they didn't seem to ever be there at one time. My impression of the thing is that there was really no discussion at that conference. Everybody came with a quite fixed position. Chambers, as Chairman, seemed to be vacillating. . . . Well, the whole thing was about discussing what to do. But there was not much talk at that meeting, you know. What dominated that meeting was the thinking that this was a domestic matter and that we should not interfere. That was the thinking. I remember this very well. Because Chambers, whom we really tried to move, figuring that if we could get Chambers on the hawkish side . . . and I remember going to see this man called Louis Wiltshire, who was the permanent secretary in the Ministry of Foreign Affairs in Trinidad, who I had been on campus with, and tried to push Louis. I even went to see Wahid Alli, who was the acting president, to try and see if we could push Trinidad in the vicinity of being more interventionist, whatever form the intervention would take, whether it was sanctions; the military thing wasn't on the front burner at that conference. My recollection is that after the conference, well, I returned to Barbados, Seaga returned to Barbados and there was another set of meetings.

PL: So . . . when you went to Barbados on the way to Trinidad initially, you were just trying to persuade Tom Adams to try to come to the meeting. There was no question of alternate action at all?

AA: But of course, there would be discussion as to what really we should be doing, what line should we carry . . .

PL: So what was the discussion then?

AA: Well, the discussion then, I think too, I have a recollection that Compton came in; either Compton or Eugenia, somebody from those islands came into that discussion. I think that was where the sort of action group; that's where they . . . But Trinidad failed to bring about a united Caribbean position, because Guyana's position seemed almost supportive, to me, of what had happened. Price, who had come down on the plane with us from Belize, he said, "Boy, intervention, I have to be a disciple of non-intervention because the Guatemalans are on the other side of the [border], just waiting to hear about intervention." It was an excuse. So out of that meeting, the Trinidad meeting, it was quite clear there was no common action possible between Jamaica, Guyana, Trinidad, Bahamas – so to speak, the bigger peripheral states – to the thing.[45]

The outcome of that CARICOM meeting was the decision to expel Grenada from CARICOM and to support sanctions proposed by the OECS. The prime ministers of Guyana and Trinidad and Tobago, Forbes Burnham and George Chambers respectively, believed that a consensus had been reached that would see the Grenada situation handled without the use of force and outside intervention.[46] If, in fact, a consensus had been reached, it broke down the following day when the meeting resumed. The countries which had already set in motion the events that would lead to military action used the meeting as an occasion for whipping up support for military action behind the scenes, as Abrahams's account suggests.

Seaga's attempt to rewrite the invasion as a positive event for CARICOM reveals an absence of reflection on what it meant for CARICOM, especially given its continued weakness in foreign-policy coordination and security cooperation. The sidelining of CARICOM in the decision to invade was one of the low points of the regional integration process and almost spelled the death of the group. In the end, this was avoided only because the subject of the Grenada invasion was deliberately left off the subsequent Nassau heads of government summit for fear that the tension and bad blood it had generated might tear the organization apart. Ironically, Seaga's government did not show much appreciation for the value of the regional institution. In fact, on two occasions, Seaga acted in a manner that could only have fuelled division. In 1982, at the CARICOM summit, the first to be held for many years and the first with Bishop's government in place, Seaga agitated behind the scenes to whip up support for Grenada's expulsion from the group. The meeting ended with an official CARICOM statement recognizing ideological pluralism within the organization – a repudiation of his more divisive approach. Later, after the invasion, Seaga proposed a CARICOM II that would exclude Guyana and abandon the principle of unanimity in decision-making. Had he succeeded in either of these initiatives, the regional integration process might have been even weaker than it is today, in the unlikely event that it had managed to survive.

The Grenada Invasion and International Law

The decision to evoke Article 8 of the OECS charter to provide legitimate cover for the invasion has been addressed in the literature, including in my own MPhil thesis, which looked specifically at that question. Seaga's account also presents excerpts from Joyner,[47] who assesses then dismisses the various grounds on which its proponents sought to justify the invasion, and from Fraser, who seeks to justify it. I will draw on my own insights to present a brief discussion of the legal case presented.

US president Ronald Reagan presented the rationale for his country's decision to invade, at a joint press conference with Dominica's prime minister Eugenia Charles, on the morning of the invasion. The reasons were: to protect lives, including that of about one thousand US medical students studying at St George's University, to prevent the situation in Grenada from deteriorating and to restore "law and order and governmental institutions".[48] Legal cover was provided by the OECS's invitation "in furtherance of the Purposes and Principles of the Charter of the UN and the Organization of American States".[49] The implicit reference here is to Chapter VII of the United Nations Charter, which recognizes the role of regional organizations in resolving conflicts in their geographical space, and specifically to Article 51, which allows countries to use force in exercising individual and collective self-defence. This was to be differentiated from enforcement, which was prohibited under Article 53.

The Caribbean states added further grounds for their justification. These were expressed in a statement from the OECS to the president of the UN Security Council, and delivered by St Lucia's deputy permanent representative to the United Nations, Donatus St Aimee, on 25 October. These included concern over the "extensive military build-up in Grenada", which gave the island "disproportionate military strength" over its OECS neighbours, and which, under the RMC that had seized control after Bishop's death, presented a "serious threat" to their security and that of neighbouring countries.[50] The specific legal cover for invasion was "pre-emptive self-defence", which is permitted under the UN, Organization of American States[51] and OECS charters.[52] Seaga provided the additional justification of protecting democracy, declaring in an address to the Jamaican House of Representatives that "we will not tolerate subversion and revolution".[53] Adams, in his address to the Barbadian people on October 25, evoked democracy more explicitly, asserting that "we have a view of our future that is democratic, peace-loving, devoted to constitutional and not arbitrary government".[54]

The main justification in respect of the OECS lay in its right to exercise collective self-defence under Article 8 of its charter, and in keeping with Article 51 of the UN charter. It is important to note that the United Nations, which is taken as codifying customary international law, circumscribes the right to a state's use of force to three instances: enforcement authorized by the UN Security Council (Article 42), and the right to individual and collective self-defence in the face of armed attack (Article 51). As stated in Article 51, "[n]othing in the present Charter shall impair the inherent right of individual or collective self-defense if an armed attack occurs against a Member of the United Nations, until the Security Council has taken the measures necessary to maintain international peace and security".[55]

This right is restricted to defence in the face of an armed attack. Article 52 provides some recognition of regional institutions acting to maintain international peace and security, but stipulates that such activities should be "consistent with the Purposes and Principles of the United Nations". Given the limits on the use of force set out in Article 2(4) and the limited scope for its usage in Article 51, it is unlikely that the Grenada intervention, which was in response to internal events, qualified as legitimate action. The majority of UN members supported this perspective. At the thirty-eighth session of the General Assembly, a resolution[56] dismissing the legitimacy of the invasion was adopted by 108 countries, with 9 countries dissenting and 24 abstaining from voting.[57] An earlier resolution before the Security Council on 25 October by Guyana failed to pass, given the veto power of the United States in that body, but the legality of the invasion was passionately challenged in statements from the representatives of seven other countries[58] as well as Grenada's representative.

Even if one were to assume that the General Assembly vote was influenced by political considerations and did not portray an accurate reflection of the state of international law on the matter, the architects of the invasion had to show, given the UN charter's acknowledgement of the legitimacy of collective self-defence in the face of an armed attack, both that they were under attack and that there was a regional arrangement in place that provided for defensive military action. There is no case to be made for self-defence in the face of an armed attack, as there was no attempt to establish that any of the invading states were under attack by Grenadian forces. Even if one were to accept a right of pre-emptive self-defence, then the provisions of Article 8 of the OECS charter, which purportedly provided legal cover for intervention, must be examined. The case for this is weak, as Article 8 limits action, under its remit, to situations where member states are subject to external attack and not to address internal instability. The specific provision is to be found in sub-paragraph 4, which speaks to the functions of the Defence and Security Committee:

> The Defence and Security Committee shall have responsibility for co-ordinating the efforts of Member States for collective defence and the preservation of peace and security against external aggression and for the development of close ties among the Member States of the Organization in matters of defence and security, including measures to combat the activities of mercenaries, operating with or without the support of internal or national elements, in the exercise of the inherent right of individual or collective self-defence recognized by Article 51 of the Charter of the United Nations.

It was particularly important to the government in Grenada at the time, coming to power as it did through extrajudicial means, to differentiate between internal dissent and external aggression. Action in regard to the former was interpreted as interference in the internal affairs of a country, to which Grenada felt itself susceptible, given the hostility towards its revolutionary government that existed in some member states.[59] At the same time, the PRG's concern about the possibility of US-backed mercenary intervention, along with the insecurity of other governments who had already experienced similar instances, and concern as to the vulnerability of small states with no army to repel other sources of external intervention, provided a common basis for security cooperation as envisaged under Article 8. The dissatisfaction with the limited purview of Article 8 led a number of OECS countries[60] to enter into a broader security arrangement with Barbados, under a 1982 memorandum of understanding.[61] This gave rise to the Regional Security System, which was headquartered in Barbados and anchored by the Barbados Defence Force, with the Barbadian government bearing 49 per cent of its operating costs. The provisions of this agreement went beyond the stipulations in Article 8 of the OECS charter and provided for support in the event of "national emergencies" and "threats to national security".[62]

It is clear that Article 8 of the OECS charter was never intended to provide justification for intervention in domestic situations. Further, Article 8 presented the additional hurdle of requiring unanimous consent to justify action. This was hardly forthcoming from the Grenadian authorities at the time – that is, from the RMC, which had taken control after Bishop's death. Consequently, it was necessary to involve Governor General Scoon on the basis that he provided legal continuity across the various regimes (Grenada United Labour Party, PRG and RMC). Even if this argument could be justified, then the lack of unanimity among the remaining states undermines the use of Article 8 as permission for intervention. As Seaga notes, St Vincent's prime minister Milton Cato was not in favour of intervention, and Montserrat, a full member of the OECS, was not constitutionally able to authorize any such action without the consent of the British government, given its status as a British dependency. As we know, this consent was never forthcoming. Thus, the unanimity criterion under Article 8 was not fulfilled.[63] Therefore, under international law, the OECS could not be seen to be legitimately exercising a right to collective self-defence. The matter is further complicated by the fact that they were relying on the military capability of governments that were not party to the treaty to exercise that right.

Fraser presents a more involved case for justification under Article 8. In an apparent recognition of the limitations of the collective self-defence claim, he sought instead to rationalize the OECS action in the context of "external aggression, including mercenary aggression" within the provisions of the charter. To justify this, he had to identify said external aggression and mercenary elements. He points his finger at the Cuban construction workers in Grenada, who, he declared, were not only "available, but the clear evidence is that they actually took a direct part in the hostilities".[64] He declares that they "undertook the brunt of the fighting", even appealing to Castro for military reinforcements, which he refused. Fraser thus concludes that by their action in Grenada without the approval of their government, and as non-nationals of Grenada who were "paid by Grenada", they were "therefore, employed for personal gain".[65]

This perspective hinges on the fictional US account that Cubans provided the main resistance to the invasion and that they were in the pay of the Grenadian government. Even if the first is true, that the Cubans were the main force engaging with the invading forces – and this is debatable[66] – and even if Fraser's definition of a mercenary is accepted, then he would have to prove that their involvement in the events that led to Bishop's death a full week before the invasion was such that their reclassification from construction workers to mercenaries is justified. Their resistance to the invading forces cannot be retroactively applied to justify intervention based on the fact that they provided some resistance during the invasion. The argument is clearly without merit. In addition, Fraser's attempt to justify the intervention under Articles 51 and 52 of the UN charter, on the basis that an armed attack had occurred in Grenada and that OECS leaders "reasonably apprehended 'an armed attack' against any of the other countries in the OECS", can just as easily be dismissed. Fraser notes: "Consequently, the other members of the OECS, confronted by the armed resistance of the Cuban workers, supported as they were by the massive arsenal of weaponry and ammunition provided . . . by Marxist/Leninist regimes, the Soviet Union and North Korea . . . were reasonably justified in the belief that the security of the member states of the OECS, including Grenada, was greatly endangered by aggression from external forces."[67]

He has provided no evidence to substantiate his claim that an armed attack had occurred prior to the invasion, which would have then triggered intervention under Article 8. Simply put, Cuban construction workers were not involved in any way in the events leading up to Bishop's death on 19 October, which precipitated the invasion. They became active, and then only in self-defence, when attacked by US forces on 25 October. Fraser's argument, at best, obfuscates this reality under a general veil of fear of Cuban "involvement" as justification for invasion.

Grenada as a Credible Threat

To sustain the credibility of the right to collective defence acknowledged under the UN charter, it is left to be shown that the OECS countries were either under attack or had reasonable fear to expect an attack from Grenada. The latter scenario speaks to pre-emptive self-defence, which is controversial in international law. The concern that Grenada presented a threat to its neighbours, apparently validated by the stockpile of arms uncovered after the invasion, was proffered as justification. Seaga sets the stage for this by speaking of secret agreements between Grenada and communist countries such as Cuba, the Soviet Union and North Korea, which included the supply of military weaponry:

> The intent was clearly to use Grenada as a central point for rallying the leftist forces of the other six small islands of the Commonwealth Caribbean in the Organization of Eastern Caribbean States (OECS). Most islands had small cells of Marxist leaders capable of expanding support with a potential of repeating the Grenada experience. Arms would be needed. The Grenadian stockpile that included used and surplus Soviet World War II weapons would be the source.[68]

Abrahams's account also sets much store on the insecurity of small OECS countries, occasioned by the build-up of armaments in Grenada, as underlying their support for military action. He suggests that Jamaica was unsure of proceeding without Trinidad's support but was convinced by Eugenia Charles of the urgency of action:

> It was very, very important to Jamaica that Trinidad be part of whatever we agreed to do; we wanted to see that Trinidad would also do the same. And a feeling even that if Trinidad wasn't going to get involved, we shouldn't get involved. But then I think Eugenia Charles really reached Seaga. And I think the way she reached him was what I was telling you earlier about this idea that twelve or thirteen people could land in one of these islands and take it over overnight. Now let me tell you another thing. Somebody had landed in Barbados – go back and check this – some little coot out of England, not even a political motive, had landed in Barbados and almost took it over in one night. . . . So there was this feeling that you really couldn't continue to allow this kind of instability where people just float in, twelve men float in or twelve men go abroad and sit down in a room up in London and decide to plan a revolution and land and catch everybody by surprise because in most of these countries, armed men knowing their way around the country can take it over.[69]

Needless to say, the RMC, which was desperately trying to prevent a civil war, had little internal support and no external allies, even among these "small cells of Marxist leaders", so it was hardly in a position to "export revolution" anywhere.

To substantiate his position of Grenada as threat, Seaga presents a detailed list of what he calls "military materiel" given to Grenada under secret agreements with Cuba, North Korea and the Soviet Union. His extensive listing of the armaments promised by the Soviet Union between 1981 and 1983 includes eight armoured personnel carriers, two armoured reconnaissance and patrol vehicles, a universal excavator, a crane, a bulldozer, thirty military trucks, five jeeps, five ambulances, one thousand used and reconditioned AK submarine guns, three hundred pistols, ammunition, spare parts, and uniforms, inter alia.[70] This is hardly the arsenal of a "regional super power", as Seaga categorized Grenada. These weapons, which were in keeping with the government's resolve to defend itself against mercenary intervention, a concern it shared with its fellow OECS governments, could hardly be used to launch a military attack against its neighbours. Nowhere in this list is there any means of getting such arms to neighbouring island states. Notably lacking are boats, landing craft, airplanes or assault weapons. Even if an attack could be launched using the country's ailing coast guard vessel, the other OECS countries already had defensive mechanisms in place through the Regional Security System they had created with Barbados, which relied heavily on Barbados's military. It is hardly likely that the arms in Grenada's possession could compete with the US and British arms supplied to the Barbadian and Jamaican defence forces. If the possession of weaponry equates to an intent to intervene, then Barbados and Jamaica presented a greater threat to their neighbouring territories.

Myths and Inaccuracies

I now turn to some of the myths generated to set the ground for intervention, which Seaga repeats in his monograph. He asserts that the Point Salines airport runway under construction, for which Cuba provided technical input and equipment and which was funded by grants from a large number of countries, including the European Community, was longer than Jamaica's and could not be justified on the basis of expanding the tourist sector.[71] Rather, he argues, the airport was a means of securing Cuba's strategic interests, such as refuelling of troop carriers en route to Angola. He does not repeat the US charges, which were given media prominence while the airport was under construction, of its potential use as a Soviet base, probably because the credibility of this blatant piece of Cold War propaganda could not be sustained in the saner ethos of the post–Cold War era. What he fails to mention, though, is that, after the invasion, the Americans completed construction of the runway.

Abrahams noted his disgust when he realized that the US charges of a military base being constructed had no credibility:

> The interesting thing is, I know the Americans had spread a lot of propaganda about a base being there . . . and to some extent that propaganda would have influenced our decision as well. Because I would tell you that one of the things that upset me very deeply was when I got to Grenada, going one day on tour with the American military, and hearing them talk about the airport . . . and I turned to the man and asked, where was the submarine base? And he looked at me and laughed, you know. So there was a lot of mis-information and so forth.[72]

To support the Grenada-as-a-threat claim, Seaga speaks of a veil of secrecy surrounding the revolution, which was lifted only when Bishop was killed. As a young journalist in Grenada, I can attest that the revolution sparked widespread media attention and visits from journalists from the West as well as the East. Seaga also claims that Radio Free Grenada was the most powerful broadcaster in the English-speaking Caribbean, with its aim being "the broadcast of radical socialism".[73] Further research will have to be done to establish whether Radio Free Grenada had, in fact, the most powerful range, but even if this were the case, it hardly justifies intervention. He charges that Radio Free Grenada was staffed by "some of the most committed leftists of the Jamaica Broadcasting Corporation (JBC) who were openly criticized for their biased presentations and linkages with the communist Workers Party of Jamaica, led by Trevor Munroe in the 1970s. The employment of these radio and television journalists, who had been ideologically smeared and widely condemned in Jamaica, was terminated at JBC by the new Board of Directors after 1980."[74] He fails to note his role in the dismissal of the entire news-and-current-affairs department of the JBC, after his party won elections in 1980, and the subsequent court ruling that found that they were wrongfully dismissed and that awarded damages.

Seaga's account is marred by many inaccuracies and a clear lack of knowledge about Grenada before, during or after the revolution. His brief attempt at setting the stage for understanding the advent of the revolution is sketchy and replete with inaccuracies. The NJM did not hold six seats in parliament to Gairy's nine.[75] It was the alliance – comprising the NJM and the traditional opposition, the Grenada National Party, put together in an attempt to oust

Gairy politically – that constituted the parliamentary opposition. Despite his access to documents stolen from Grenada by the Jamaica Defence Force, Seaga shows little understanding of or interest in understanding the events leading up to Bishop's arrest, preferring instead to quote an excerpt from a message from Jamaica's high commissioner in Trinidad and Tobago describing the events leading to Bishop's death. He refers to the "Communist Party of Grenada and the New Jewel Movement" as "corresponding with countries to seek assistance and treaties with other socialist fraternal countries for the supply of war materiel".[76] There was no such body as the Communist Party of Grenada.

Seaga claims that the revolution ran out of steam because external aid was used "to [arm] the country as a superpower in the region" and not so much for social programmes. Rather than continuing to fund social and economic programmes as had been done at the start of the revolution, he argues that money was diverted to "fund ideological ventures" which "created a basis for mass dissension which soon enveloped the political programme with dire result".[77] Seaga seems unaware of the global recession occurring at the time, the falling commodity prices that adversely affected small states heavily dependent on an undiversified primary agricultural export sector, and of the natural hazards – two floods – which Grenada experienced during the first year of the revolution, which affected production. Even then, the economy experienced the highest rate of economic growth among OECS countries (1979–1983) and growth rates significantly higher than those achieved since its independence in 1974. It was against this background of an undiversified economy and attempts to expand the tourism sector that the construction of the Point Salines International Airport must be placed.

Seaga's account is a shallow, even contemptuous, failure to understand Grenada. His abysmal ignorance of the country and insensitivity are revealed in his reference to the capital, St George's, as "Point George".[78] Even more embarrassingly, and with apparent ignorance of the country's sovereign status, in his statement to Jamaica's parliament the day after the invasion, he assured the people of Grenada that "the action in which we joined was intended to free them from being pawns in a power play which had converted their lovely *spice colony* to a fearsome camp. From this action we hoped they will derive a new freedom and a new opportunity to build new futures."[79]

This contempt is most evident in what he does not say in his monograph: that his government imposed visa restrictions on Grenadians, fellow CAR-ICOM members, which they kept in place throughout his term in office. Those were lifted only when the People's National Party regained office in Jamaica in 1989. Added to this is his admission that the documents he used to help inform his book were illegally removed from Grenada by members of the Jamaica Defence Force.

An Absence of Reflection

Seaga, in justifying his writing of this account, says, "I felt compelled to write this book *The Grenada Intervention: The Inside Story*, because of the wealth of inaccuracies and misunderstanding which were being treated as concretized facts in the arguments pro and con on the intervention. This book seeks to shed much light to clarify the confusion and assist in settling the international controversy for many interested parties."[80]

In reality, the book does not do this. Instead, it is written through the lens of the Cold War and as if the literal and figurative Berlin Wall had not collapsed. It provides no attempt by one of the main architects of the invasion to better understand the time, the developmental concerns and challenges facing small states, or to reflect on alternative responses to the crisis. More importantly, he fails to reflect on the undermining of the already tenuous and compromised sovereignty of small states through the invasion by the world's most powerful state, on the invitation of neighbouring countries. Instead, Seaga continues to be a Cold War warrior, long after the Cold War has ended. The events in Grenada that gave rise to the revolution and its downfall, tragic as they were, provide a rich opportunity for analysing some of the enduring challenges that small states face as they seek to maintain a place among sovereign nations. Foremost among these are challenges of resources, democracy and security. But Grenada suggests another story, of a people with resilience to overcome the trauma and divisions of the past and with the capacity to forgive and move on. Unfortunately, none of these complexities and textures of the real Grenada appear in Seaga's flawed morality tale of good and evil.[81]

NOTES

1.   Patsy Lewis-Meeks, "An Analysis of the Legal Justification for the United States' Invasion of Grenada on the Basis of the Invitation from the OECS" (MPhil thesis, Cambridge University, 1988), 6.

2.   Sybil Farrell Lewis and Dale T. Mathews, eds., "Documents on the Invasion of Grenada", *Caribbean Monthly Bulletin* 17, nos. 11–12 (November–December 1983), supplement no. 1 (Institute of Caribbean Studies, University of Puerto Rico, Rio Piedras, Puerto Rico).

3.   Edward Seaga, *The Grenada Intervention: The Inside Story* (Kingston: n.p., 2009).

4.   Ibid., 18.

5.   Ibid., 11.

6.   Christopher C. Joyner, "Reflections on the Lawfulness of Invasion", *American Journal of International Law* 78, no. 1 (1984): 131–44.

7.   Seaga, *Grenada Intervention*, 51.

8.   Ibid.

9.   Hudson Austin, who was the commander of the People's Revolutionary Army, became the head of the Revolutionary Military Council that sought to take control of the government after Maurice Bishop's death.

10.   Seaga, *Grenada Intervention*, 19.

11.   It is not clear whether Seaga was referring to the 1979 revolution which brought Bishop to power or to the events of October 19, which ended Bishop's life and that of his government.

12.   Seaga, *Grenada Intervention*, 19.

13.   Ibid.

14.   Ibid., 20.

15.   See Gary Williams, "The Tail That Wagged the Dog: The OECS' Role in the 1983 Intervention in Grenada", *European Review of Latin American and Caribbean Studies* 61 (1997): 95–116.

16.   Anthony Abrahams (former Jamaican minister of tourism and information), interview by the author, 25 July 1995.

17.   William Gilmore, *The Grenada Intervention: Analysis and Documentation* (London: Mansell, 1984), 102.

18.   Seaga, *Grenada Intervention*, 24.

19.   Ibid., 22.

20.   Ibid., 21.

21.   Abrahams, interview.

22.   Lewis, "Revisiting the Grenada Invasion", 95.

23. Patrick E. Tyler and David Hoffman, "US Says Aim Is to Restore Order", *Washington Post*, 26 October 1983, A1–A2.

24. Seaga, *Grenada Intervention*, 19.

25. Abrahams claims that the US State Department was not in favour of intervention, so Seaga appealed directly to President Reagan through his national security advisor, Ed Meese.

26. Abrahams, interview.

27. This account differs somewhat from Scoon's, which is discussed below. While the intent was for Scoon to have signed the letter on the day of the invasion, difficulties in effecting his safe "rescue" from his home delayed the signing until the following day.

28. That there were multiple letters was corroborated by a senior official at the OECS at the time, who does not wish to be identified.

29. Paul Scoon, *Survival for Service: My Experiences as Governor General of Grenada* (Oxford: Macmillan Caribbean, 2003), 133.

30. Ibid., 134.

31. Ibid., 134.

32. Ibid., 134–35.

33. Ibid., 135.

34. Ibid., 136–37.

35. Ibid., 136.

36. There is the further legal question of whether, even if he had been the initiator of intervention, Scoon was legally authorized to do so as ceremonial head of state. In the event that he did have this authority, the question then arises of to whom he should have made this appeal for intervention. His position as Her Majesty's representative would suggest that his appeal should have been made to the British government.

37. Seaga, *Grenada Intervention*, 21.

38. The Regional Security System emerged from a memorandum of understanding between the governments of Antigua and Barbuda, Barbados, Dominica, St Lucia, and St Vincent and the Grenadines, which was signed on 29 October 1982. Grenada, wary of the possibility of intervention in its internal affairs by its neighbours, was not party to this agreement.

39. Scoon, *Survival for Service*, 145.

40. Ibid., 142–44.

41. Lewis, "Revisiting the Grenada Invasion", 85–120.

42. Seaga, *Grenada Intervention*, 25.

43. Ibid., iv.

44. According to Abrahams's account, discussions between Seaga and Adams first

took place when Bishop was placed under house arrest and not, as in Seaga's account, after he was killed. It seems likely that forceful intervention was considered from then.

45. Abrahams, interview.
46. Lewis and Matthews, "Documents on the Invasion", "Address to the Nation on October 25, 1983 by His Excellency L.F.S. Burnham, O.E., S.C., President of the Co-operative Republic of Guyana on Guyana's Position in Relation to the Events in Grenada", 63–65, and "Statement by the Honourable Prime Minister George Chambers to the House of Representatives of the Parliament of Trinidad and Tobago on October 26, 1983 on the Grenada Crisis", 75–78.
47. Seaga, *Grenada Intervention*, 33–40.
48. Tyler and Hoffman, "US Says Aim Is to Restore Order", A1.
49. Permanent Representative of the United States of America to the Security Council, United Nations, 25 October 1983, UN Security Council Official Records, UN Doc. S/160/76.
50. Organization of Eastern Caribbean States, Statement on the Grenada Situation, 25 October 1983, in Gilmore, *Grenada Intervention*, 97–98.
51. Article 18 of the Organization of American States charter prohibits the use of force, while Article 21 acknowledges its use only in self-defence.
52. Statement by St Lucia's representative before the UN General Assembly.
53. "PM Tells Why Our Men Are Fighting", *Gleaner*, 26 October 1983, 19.
54. Gilmore, *Grenada Intervention*, 105.
55. "Charter of the United Nations", chapter VII, article 51, in William W. Bishop Jr, *International Law: Cases and Materials*, 3rd ed. (Boston: Little Brown, 1971), appendix A, 1067.
56. UN General Assembly Resolution 38/7, "The Situation in Grenada", 43rd plenary meeting, 2 November 1983, in United Nations, "Resolutions and Decisions Adopted by the General Assembly during Its Thirty-Eight Session, 20 September–20 December 1983 and 26 June 1984". General Assembly Official Records: Thirty-Eighth Session. Supplement No. 47 (A/38/47), http://www.un.org/ga/search/view_doc.asp?symbol=a/38/47(SUPP), 19.
57. For details of the vote on UN resolution A/RES/38/7, see UNBISNET, Dag Hammarskjold Library. http://unbisnet.un.org:8080/ipac20/ipac.jsp?session=O431450T09693.31556&profile=voting&uri=full=3100023~!476574~!0&ri=1&aspect=power&menu=search&source=~!horizon.
58. These were Cuba, Nicaragua, Guyana, Mexico, Libya, the Soviet Union and the Democratic Republic of Yemen.
59. The Declaration of St George, which the PRG signed in 1979 with the governments of Dominica and St Lucia in place then, gives a better barometer of its view

on the matter, as it spoke directly to the question of intervention, reaffirming adherence to principles of sovereignty and non-interference and specifically noting that any regional military force established should be "limited to the countering of external aggression, including the threat of invasion by mercenaries". "The Declaration of St George", paragraph 7 (mimeo, St George's, Grenada, 16 July 1979).

60. The countries represented were Antigua and Barbuda, Dominica, St Lucia, and St Vincent and the Grenadines. Grenada and Montserrat, a British dependency, were not signatories.

61. "Declaration of St George".

62. Ibid.

63. For a detailed treatment of OECS voting provisions and the issue of Grenada's representation at the meeting of the OECS's decision to intervene, see Lewis-Meeks, "Analysis", 14–16.

64. Seaga, *Grenada Intervention*, 43.

65. Ibid., 44.

66. For an eyewitness account of the invasion that establishes the role of Grenadians in resisting the US invasion, see Hugh O'Shaughnessy, *Grenada Revolution, Invasion and Aftermath* (London: Sphere Books, 1984). See also Scoon's account in chapter 9 of *Survival for Service*, 137–57.

67. Seaga, *Grenada Intervention*, 46.

68. Ibid., 17.

69. Abrahams, interview.

70. Ibid., appendix 4.

71. Ibid., 8.

72. Abrahams, interview.

73. Seaga, *Grenada Intervention*, 6.

74. Ibid., 7.

75. Ibid., 2.

76. Ibid., 11.

77. Ibid., 18.

78. Ibid., 31.

79. Ibid., 29; my italics.

80. Ibid, iii.

81. Some of these questions are being explored in a study that I am conducting with Heather Ricketts, which seeks to understand Grenadians' responses to the 1983 events and to Hurricane Ivan in 2004.

7.

The Grenada Invasion, International Law and the Scoon Invitation

A Thirty-Year Retrospective

ROBERT J. BECK

ABSTRACT

All the international legal rationales for the US–OECS invasion of Grenada in October 1983 arguably depend, at least in part, on the nature, substance and circumstances of the request for external assistance that was made by Grenadian governor general Sir Paul Scoon. Of all the factual circumstances surrounding the Grenada episode, perhaps the least well known in the 1980s were those related to the so-called Scoon invitation. More than thirty years later, this chapter identifies the politically and legally consequential details of the Scoon invitation to which we are now privy, drawing upon the memoir accounts of key participants, scholarly interviews with crucial Grenadian decision-makers, and declassified US government documents. Situating the Grenada case within post-1983 state practice on "interventions by invitation", it concludes that Sir Paul did not initiate his informal, oral invitation or author his formal, written one and that even though he genuinely supported "Operation Urgent Fury", the governor general's invitation did not legally justify the operation.

Introduction

The US-led invasion of Grenada, because of its special circumstances, its many and inconsistent public rationales proposed by the Reagan administration, and its multiple state participants, was variously characterized by international legal scholars in the 1980s as a "regional peacekeeping" action,[1] an "intervention in response to lawful invitation",[2] an "intervention to protect nationals",[3] a "humanitarian intervention",[4] and later, as one of the "two major examples" of unilateral "pro-democratic intervention".[5] The cogency of each of these legal rationales arguably depends, at least in part, on the nature, substance and circumstances of the request for external assistance that was made by Grenadian governor general Sir Paul Scoon. Justification of the operation as an "intervention in response to lawful invitation" was directly dependent, of course, on the Scoon invitation. For most international lawyers, justification as "regional peacekeeping" also relied upon, or was very substantially strengthened by, Sir Paul's request. Moreover, insofar as Scoon's written invitation referred to "serious violations of human rights and bloodshed", the "lack of internal security in Grenada", the "grave and dangerous situation", and the desire for a "return to democratic rule", his request could plausibly be invoked to bolster the "intervention to protect nationals", the "humanitarian intervention", and the "pro-democratic intervention" justifications.

Of all the factual circumstances surrounding the Grenada episode, though, perhaps the least well known in the 1980s were those related to this "Scoon invitation". The UK House of Commons Foreign Affairs Committee, for example, concluded in its 1984 report, after interviewing Scoon, that "[b]oth the timing and nature" of Sir Paul's request remained "shrouded in mystery" and the "parties directly involved [evidently intended] that the mystery should not be dispelled".[6] Similarly, the *Economist* judged, in 1984, that the request had been "almost certainly a fabrication concocted between the Organisation of Eastern Caribbean States (OECS) and Washington to calm the post-invasion diplomatic storm. As concoctions go, it was flimsy."[7] But thirty years after the Grenada invasion, to what politically and legally consequential details are we now privy that international legal scholars and other observers in the 1980s were not? What are the implications of these details? The following discussion will be informed by, and draw upon, the following vital sources: published memoir accounts by key participants, scholarly interviews with Grenadian decision-makers conducted primarily in the late 1980s and 1990s, and declassified US government documents.

The Grenadian Governor General and His Invitation

In 1978, Sir Paul Scoon was appointed as the Commonwealth member state's second governor general by Queen Elizabeth II, Grenada's head of state. Five years later, what were the scope and legal standing of his role? Under the 1967 Constitution, which Grenada formally adopted in 1974 on gaining its independence from Great Britain, the governor general had enjoyed certain broad executive powers. In March 1979, however, the People's Revolutionary Government of Maurice Bishop suspended the 1967 Constitution, proclaiming instead a series of "People's Laws". The second law vested "all executive and legislative power" in the People's Revolutionary Government, while the third relegated the governor general's role to that of being merely the queen's "representative", with the capacity to "perform such functions as the [People's Revolutionary Government] may from time to time advise". Having been delegated only limited minor powers of removal and appointment, the office of governor general was, in October 1983, constitutionally regarded as principally advisory and ceremonial.[8] The governor general certainly did not "govern" Grenada, nor was he even a formal representative of Her Majesty's Government. Even so, Sir Paul took his role seriously, as did the queen[9] and the government leaders of many of Grenada's neighbouring states. Alluding to Jamaica and the member states of the OECS, Scoon would address the prime minister of Barbados in his formal invitation letter of 24 October 1983:

> You are aware that there is a vacuum of authority in Grenada following the killing of the Prime Minister and the subsequent serious violations of human rights and bloodshed.
>
> I am therefore seriously concerned over the lack of internal security in Grenada. Consequently I am requesting your help to assist me in stabilizing this grave and dangerous situation. It is my desire that a peacekeeping force should be established in Grenada to facilitate a rapid return to peace and tranquillity and also a return to democratic rule.
>
> In this connection I am also seeking assistance from the United States, from

Jamaica, and from the Organization of Eastern Caribbean States through its current chairman the Hon. Eugenia Charles [prime minister of Dominica] in the spirit of the treaty establishing that organization to which my country is a signatory.[10]

From where, however, did this letter of invitation originate?

After 19 October

On "Bloody Wednesday", 19 October 1983, Bishop and scores of his countrymen were killed in the violent aftermath of an abortive attempt to restore Bishop's premiership – from which the charismatic and popular leader had been ousted on 13 October 1983 by a coup within his own Marxist-Leninist party. After 19 October, Governor General Scoon would communicate with a wide range of personalities in Grenada, including citizens and foreign nationals, both in and out of formal government service.

On the morning of 21 October, Scoon met with General Hudson Austin. On Radio Free Grenada, on the evening of 19 October, Austin had announced the establishment of the Revolutionary Military Council (RMC) and a four-day, round-the-clock, shoot-to-kill curfew.[11] Scoon now felt that Grenada was "without a Government".[12] Nevertheless, Austin would describe to him the RMC's plans to form a mixed civilian-military government and would ask Scoon to remain in office and to help establish it.[13] Sir Paul wondered, though, "to what extent could I trust the RMC in a seemingly deteriorating situation".[14] The next day, Scoon received a visit from the RMC's Major Leon Cornwall, who sought Scoon's "advice and comments" on a draft RMC announcement, but the governor general "wanted no part in that exercise".[15]

The governor general also met on three consecutive days with John Kelly, Britain's permanent representative to Grenada.[16] Kelly had been "concerned about [Scoon's] personal welfare" and, at Scoon's request, would prove "instrumental in putting [him] in touch with London".[17] Sir Paul was also in contact by telephone with the secretary general of the Commonwealth Shridath Ramphal, the Trinidad and Tobago president Ellis Clarke, and Buckingham Palace.[18] According to Scoon, however, his "telephone conversations [with Ramphal, Clarke and Her Majesty's assistant private secretary Robert Fellowes] had nothing to do with subsequent events in Grenada that were to take place within three days or so". Scoon "did not solicit advice from these individuals", he submits, "nor did they proffer any".[19]

Sir Paul would also meet with one US official before the invasion. After declining her repeated requests, for diplomatic protocol reasons, he spoke briefly on the afternoon of Monday, 24 October, with the "relentless" Linda Flohr,[20] ostensibly third secretary of the US embassy in Bridgetown, Barbados, but actually an experienced CIA case officer.[21] According to Scoon, his meeting with Flohr "was quite brief. She heard nothing from me about the events which were unfolding in Grenada, nor did she get my personal assessment on the state of affairs in Grenada."[22] In fact, Flohr was primarily conducting reconnaissance, as Scoon remained "under house arrest and the area was ringed with armoured personnel carriers and antiaircraft guns. . . . Noting no proper landing site for our helicopter within two miles of the governor general's residence, except perhaps for its tennis court, [Flohr] said goodbye to Sir Paul, adding that she was sure the United States would do everything to free his country."[23]

Notably, on no occasion before 23 October did Scoon request help from his Caribbean neighbours. Neither did he directly request military assistance from US government officials before 25 October, when Operation Urgent Fury was launched, nor did he seek Britain's armed help. Even so, Scoon did confide to President Ellis Clarke that "I would prefer not to have a military solution even though in the back of my mind I thought this was perhaps the best option".[24] Scoon admitted in a 2006 interview that he had "also felt that the United States was the only one who could help; the British would prevaricate and were too far away to act quickly".[25]

On Sunday morning, 23 October, Sir Paul met privately for an hour, in the garden of his residence, with David Montgomery, the British deputy high commissioner to Barbados.[26] Montgomery would describe Scoon then as having been in "an extremely isolated, difficult and even dangerous position" and therefore "really frightened".[27]

The governor general now received "the first reliable report of what was happening outside Grenada".[28] He had been unaware of the advanced state of military planning until Montgomery transmitted a message from Barbadian prime minister Tom Adams that the OECS had decided to seek assistance from the United States and that Jamaica and Barbados would be participants.[29] Montgomery advised Scoon that "some sort of military action" could "not be ruled out" and that Scoon should therefore prepare himself for such a contingency, underscoring that, as governor general, Scoon represented the sole constitutional authority on Grenada: "if the United States intervened they could not run Grenada, only he could; consequently, Scoon should plan the appropriate political measures".[30]

Scholar Gary Williams, who interviewed Sir Paul in 2006, concludes that "Scoon certainly did not request help of his own volition and it was only when Montgomery directly asked him, 'Would you welcome intervention?' that Scoon admitted that he saw it as the only thing that could save Grenada, otherwise there was the possibility of sliding into civil war".[31] John Kelly reinforced this account of Scoon's thinking in a 1995 interview, reporting that Scoon had replied to Montgomery that intervention was the "only solution".[32] According to Scoon's own memoir:

> [C]learly my views on military action as an option to restore my country to normality . . . would be crucial to any decision on that score [as per Montgomery]. The awesome significance of these disturbing words caused me to ponder for some time before commenting that while military intervention into one's territory was not the sort of thing I would normally advocate, the current potentially explosive situation in Grenada was such that it was difficult to avoid the conclusion that only the presence of friendly, foreign troops could rescue Grenadians from the abyss into which they had fallen and bring stability and order back into our daily lives. Therefore, if a military operation to achieve that was to be undertaken by our sister states – if necessary with assistance from the United States, I would give such an initiative my fullest support.[33]

Scoon viewed the prospective intervention as not "American, [but rather] one by Caribbean states supported by the United States".[34]

Montgomery then asked whether Sir Paul might be willing to issue a *written* request for assistance; because Scoon was concerned for his personal safety, he agreed then to simply issue an oral request. This Montgomery could convey in turn to the Barbadian prime minister "to be regarded *pro tem*, as such a request with a formal written request from [Scoon] to follow as soon as a secure, practicable means of communication became available".[35] In reflecting on Montgomery's enquiry regarding a written request, Scoon had begun "to have the uneasy feeling that the fate of [his] country and [his] fellow Grenadians might well depend on the relatively simple act of [his] signing a piece of paper".[36] As Montgomery would note in 2009, "Anyone who knows Sir Paul Scoon knows that he is a very careful man."[37] Still, "faced with the information" provided by Montgomery and "because he knew the people who were advocating it – Tom Adams, [Edward] Seaga, Miss [Eugenia] Charles and [John] Compton – he was prepared to give tacit approval to an armed intervention".[38]

Only word of Sir Paul's meeting with Montgomery,[39] but not of Scoon's decision, would reach London's senior decision-makers on 24 October. As Margaret Thatcher, prime minister in 1983, recalled in her memoir: "the Deputy High Commissioner in Bridgetown reported after a day visit to Grenada that British citizens were safe, that the new regime in Grenada was willing to allow arrangements to be made for them to leave if they wished and that Sir Paul Scoon . . . was well and in reasonably good heart. He did not request our military intervention, either directly or indirectly."[40]

US Decision-Making

On Sunday, 23 October, in the Cabinet Room of Government House in Bridgetown, Barbados, American diplomats were meeting with Caribbean leaders to discuss, among other matters, the nature and implications of the 21 October OECS decision to issue a request for US intervention in Grenada,[41] a request as yet not formally drafted by them but nevertheless under "active consideration" in Washington. In fact, a formal OECS request would be drafted then at Government House.[42] According to US ambassador Frank McNeil, who had been specially dispatched to the Caribbean,[43] the fact of Montgomery's morning meeting with Governor General Scoon was known. However, neither the substance nor the outcome of that meeting was then known.[44]

At some point that Sunday, Ambassador McNeil received a cable instructing him to "ask OECS military representatives if it would be possible to communicate with Governor-General Scoon in advance of military operations to elicit a request for military assistance from Scoon".[45] Charles Gillespie, deputy assistant secretary of state for inter-american affairs at the time, revealed in a 1995 interview that Washington had "believed it might make things easier if

Scoon characterized the situation as an emergency and his request as a cry for help".[46] In his 2007 book, Williams would characterize the Sunday-afternoon attitude of Washington and Caribbean leaders this way: "There was a feeling that Scoon's request would be important at some stage but Washington was not going to hold its breath waiting for it. The Caribbean leaders probably reasoned that if Washington had an invitation from a head of state it might make their final decision easier and quicker."[47]

Later on Sunday, President Reagan signed the formal National Security Decision directive that authorized Operation Urgent Fury to proceed.[48] Reagan had now given his "go" order,[49] and the invasion decision was essentially "set in concrete".[50] Word of Scoon's request would not be received by the US government, however, until around twelve-thirty a.m. on 24 October.[51] At that very early hour on Monday, the Barbadian prime minister called the US embassy in Bridgetown and conveyed some very important news: in a meeting at the governor general's residence on Sunday, Sir Paul Scoon had asked Deputy High Commissioner Montgomery to relay a request for outside assistance.[53] Scoon would have sought help through official channels, Adams explained, but Sir Paul had feared that he would have been killed had he done so.[53] In addition, Adams reported that Scoon was prepared "fully [to] co-operate in an intervention and would do whatever was necessary to form an interim administration afterwards".[54]

The US embassy promptly relayed this essential intelligence to Washington, where it was already too late to affect the invasion decision to any significant extent but not too late to bolster invasion justification. A legal team went to work. Among other issues, the legal status of the governor general had to be ascertained accurately.[55] Presumably informed by the legal team's efforts, on 24 October, the State Department provided the text of a draft letter that the OECS might wish to transmit to Scoon to elicit a request for assistance. The draft contained an "assurance that any request received from the Governor General would be kept private until he is safe" and promised "assistance as long as necessary to permit the people of Grenada to reconstitute governmental institutions".[56]

Sir Paul's invitation made doubly clear the necessity of his rescue from virtual house arrest. Already, on Friday, 21 October, the governor general's role in helping to establish a provisional government had been recognized by the

State Department,[57] the role having been highlighted a day earlier by prime minister of St Lucia John Compton in a private conversation with Charles Gillespie.[58] Now, there were two compelling reasons to rescue Scoon. A special operations unit, SEAL Team 6, supported by a brave foreign service officer, Larry Rossin, was ultimately assigned the essential task.[59]

The Written Invitation

When Rossin's heli-borne team arrived at Government House on 25 October, the team encountered fierce anti-aircraft fire, and Rossin could therefore not rendezvous as planned with Scoon and deliver a draft letter of invitation to him.[60] The next day, however, Sir Paul Scoon was successfully evacuated to the carrier USS *Guam*. Later on 26 October, Scoon was flown from the *Guam* to Grenada's Point Salines Great House.

> It was here that [Barbadian] Brigadier [Rudyard] Lewis handed me the draft letters which I should have received from Prime Minister Tom Adams two days earlier. Lewis apologized for the late delivery but explained that it was not practicable to get them to me earlier in view of the delicate nature of the preparedness for the military exercise. In fact, an attempt was made to get the letters to me at Governor General's House on the morning of October 25 with the arrival of the Seals, but the risk was too great. I perused the letters carefully and made one alteration before signing them. These letters were addressed to Tom Adams, Edward Seaga, Eugenia Charles and Ronald Reagan.[61]

Larry Rossin was apparently among the various officials assembled at the Great House. According to Rossin, "I together with . . . Rudyard Lewis received a written request from Sir Paul Scoon for intervention."[62] Rossin also recalls that, very early on Wednesday morning, 26 October, perhaps around three a.m., he had managed to contact Scoon by radio from the *Guam*. The two then discussed Sir Paul's "invitation to US and Caribbean forces to restore order in Grenada, which [Scoon] confirmed".[63]

In witnessing Scoon's signature of a written request, which would not actually arrive at the US embassy in Barbados until 27 October when Prime Minister Adams had it delivered there, Rossin was able at last to address Washington's concern that it had requests for American assistance *in writing*. As Charles Gillespie would recall, "the word I was getting which helped me set my priorities was that we simply, absolutely, positively must have a request for assistance from Sir Paul Scoon . . . in writing. If we didn't have that, we would have to accept the possibility that we would have major problems around the world, politically . . . but especially in Washington."[64] According to the CIA's Duane Clarridge, as a "legal nicety for the lawyers", the Reagan administration "needed to have Sir Paul Scoon . . . sign a document requesting US intervention".[65] Hence, "although we had access to him, for security reasons we didn't want his signing in advance of hostilities", and thus we decided "a helicopter with [US] officers bearing the document would go to his residence shortly after hostilities commenced". Despite the mission's dangers, "[t]here was little choice. Sir Paul's signature and above all his safety were paramount political considerations".[66]

Just like the formal OECS request for US intervention,[67] Scoon's letter had been drafted in Barbados, most probably by the Barbadians. Intriguingly, when the letter's text was transmitted from the US embassy in Bridgetown to Washington, very early on the morning of 25 October, the telegram noted that the "authors [of the Scoon letter] here in Barbados inform us that it has been cleaared [*sic*] by all the participating countries as well as the British",[68] though it seems unlikely that David Montgomery or anyone at the high commission would have seen the letter or cleared it.

Conclusion

In the end, despite what Reagan administration officials would formally assert, the governor general's request could have exerted virtually no significant influence on the US-invasion decision. Moreover, given its timing, Scoon's invitation could have had no impact whatsoever on the OECS decision to take action.[69] Almost certainly, Scoon's informal, oral invitation was elicited by British deputy high commissioner David Montgomery. Moreover, Scoon's formal, written one was drafted by others, on Barbados – albeit reviewed, edited and signed by Scoon on Grenada a day after the military operation was launched.

Even so, Sir Paul was no pawn of the United States or of his Caribbean neighbours, and he genuinely endorsed Montgomery's "sensible and justifiable compromise" of initially transmitting secretly Scoon's oral request for external assistance to Prime Minister Adams.[70] Furthermore, Scoon was authentically supportive of the October 1983 operation by the OECS and the United States, as he would continue to be. As Sir Paul averred in a 2004 interview with the BBC, "the intervention was right", and he was "prepared to defend former President Reagan's decision to the very end".[71]

Scoon's own views notwithstanding, many international legal scholars will probably continue to judge his invitation as insufficient to have justified Operation Urgent Fury. The 1984 assessment of international-law scholar Christopher Joyner therefore still seems appropriate:

> Whether Governor-General Scoon in fact "remained the sole source of govern-mental legitimacy" on Grenada after October 24, 1983 is both arguable and unclear. That he alone possessed sufficient legal and constitutional authority at that time to legitimate an official invitation for the US and OECS military forces to intervene also seems polemical. What appears beyond dispute is simply that the Governor-General did issue a private appeal for action and that his personal safety may have been in jeopardy. Yet, though hardly inconsequential, these con-siderations in and of themselves fall short of legally validating external military intervention into the domestic affairs of a sovereign state.[72]

Of course, even the State Department conceded in a confidential memoran-dum to National Security Adviser Robert McFarlane on 2 November 1983 – a document only declassified in 2002 – that the US government had been "vulnerable on the international legal justifications of the invasion".[73]

Since the 1983 Grenada operation, states have continued to engage in puta-tive "interventions by invitation". From an international legal standpoint, what patterns may be discerned in post-Grenada state practice? After the 1989 US intervention in Panama, many observers contended that consent by a "lesser official" – one argument that had been proffered by the Reagan administration to justify its Grenada action[74] – could *only* serve as "one of several factors which could conceivably justify an intervention".[75] As a more general matter, states have mostly *not* criticized post-1983 "interventions by invitation" against either secessionist groups or military coups, such as that by Grenada's RMC. By contrast, interventions "against popular uprisings" or entailing "conflicts about who controls the central government" have "pro-voked resistance".[76]

During the Cold War, the intervention cases of Sri Lanka (1987–90) and Lebanon (1976–90) "indicate that international recognition of the *internal character* of a conflict (secessionist; inter-communal) and the *legitimacy of the government* (democratically elected; proportionally constituted) played an important role . . . in the acceptance by other States of interventions at the invitation of a government".[77] Since the Cold War's end, jurist Georg Nolte concludes, states have increasingly used governmental invitation as a basis for multilateral interventions. They have done so "either in addition to, or in combination with, an authorization or commendation of the UN Security Council (e.g. Macedonia 2001, Afghanistan 2001, Iraq 2004, Sudan 2004–07, Chad after 2006, Timor-Leste 2006, Kosovo 2008), or as an independent justification (Solomon Islands 2003, Tonga 2006)".[78] In assessing the international legality of these ostensibly government invitation–inspired interventions, as well as of future ones, a nuanced appreciation of the details of the 1983 Grenada case – and especially of Sir Paul Scoon's invitation – is most valuable.

Acknowledgements

The author wishes to acknowledge the invaluable editorial assistance of Gary Williams. He is most grateful, too, for Dr Williams's most generous sharing of declassified US government documents and the transcript of the 2009 Centre for Contemporary British History/LSE IDEAS Witness Seminar, "Britain and the Grenada Crisis, 1983: Cold War in the Caribbean".

NOTES

1.   J. Moore, "Grenada and the International Double Standard", *American Journal of International Law* 78 (1984): 153–56.

2.   Ibid., 145, 159–61.

3.   A.C. Arend and R. Beck, *International Law and the Use of Force: Beyond the UN Charter Paradigm* (London: Routledge, 1993), 101.

4.   F. Tesón, *Humanitarian Intervention: An Inquiry into Law and Morality* (Dobbs Ferry: Transnational, 1988), 188–200.

5. S. Chesterman, *Just War or Just Peace? Humanitarian Intervention and International Law* (Oxford: Oxford University Press, 2001), 90, 99–102.

6. UK Parliament, House of Commons, *Foreign Affairs Committee, Second Report, Grenada Session 1983–84* (London: HMSO, 1984), xvi.

7. "Britain's Grenada Shut-Out: Say Something, If Only Goodbye", *Economist*, 10 March 1984, 34.

8. C. Joyner, "Reflections on the Lawfulness of Invasion", *American Journal of International Law* 78 (1984): 139.

9. G. Williams, "A Matter of Regret: Britain, the 1983 Grenada Crisis, and the Special Relationship", *Twentieth Century British History* 12 (2001): 221.

10. W. Gilmore, *The Grenada Intervention: Analysis and Documentation* (London: Mansell, 1984), 95.

11. R. Beck, *The Grenada Invasion: Politics, Law and Foreign Policy Decision-Making* (Boulder: Westview, 1993), 16.

12. P. Scoon, *Survival for Service: My Experiences as Governor General of Grenada* (London: Macmillan, 2003), 121, 125.

13. Ibid., 123.

14. Ibid., 125.

15. Ibid., 126.

16. Ibid., 125.

17. Ibid.; see also CCBH, "Britain and the Grenada Crisis, 1983: Cold War in the Caribbean" (Centre for Contemporary British History/LSE IDEAS Witness Seminar, 29 May 2009), 42.

18. G. Williams, *US–Grenada Relations: Revolution and Intervention in the Backyard* (New York: Palgrave Macmillan, 2007), 133.

19. Scoon, *Survival for Service*, 126.

20. Ibid., 134.

21. D. Clarridge, *A Spy for All Seasons: My Life in the CIA*, with Digby Diehl (New York: Scribner, 1997), 250.

22. Scoon, *Survival for Service*, 134.

23. Clarridge, *Spy for All Seasons*, 256.

24. Scoon, *Survival for Service*, 126.

25. Williams, *US–Grenada Relations*, 240.

26. Beck, *Grenada Invasion*, 156; Scoon, *Survival for Service*, 134–36.

27. CCBH, "Britain and the Grenada Crisis", 44.

28. Scoon, *Survival for Service*, 135.

29. Williams, *US–Grenada Relations*, 133; CCBH, "Britain and the Grenada Crisis", 45.

30. Williams, *US–Grenada Relations*, 133; Scoon, *Survival for Service*, 134.

31. Williams, *US–Grenada Relations*, 133–34.

32. G. Williams, "The Tail That Wagged the Dog: The Organization of Eastern Caribbean States' Role in the 1983 Intervention in Grenada", *European Review of Latin American and Caribbean Studies* 61 (1996): 112.

33. Scoon, *Survival for Service*, 135.

34. CCBH, "Britain and the Grenada Crisis", 46.

35. Scoon, *Survival for Service*, 136.

36. Ibid., 135–36.

37. CCBH, "Britain and the Grenada Crisis", 44.

38. Ibid., 59.

39. Williams, "Matter of Regret", 218.

40. M. Thatcher, *The Downing Street Years* (London: Harper Collins, 1995), 330; see also UK Parliament, *Foreign Affairs Report*, 81.

41. Beck, *Grenada Invasion*, 111–12; Williams, *US–Grenada Relations*, 113–15.

42. Beck, *Grenada Invasion*, 154.

43. F. McNeil, *War and Peace in Central America: Reality and Illusion* (New York: Charles Scribner's Sons, 1988), 172–74; R. Beck, "The 'McNeil Mission' and the Decision to Invade Grenada", *Naval War College Review* 44 (1991): 93–114.

44. Williams, *US–Grenada Relations*, 141.

45. Ibid.

46. Ibid.

47. Ibid.

48. National Security Council, "Response to Caribbean Governments' Request to Restore Democracy on Grenada", National Security Decision Directive 110A, 23 October 1983, declassified 6 February 1996, http://www.fas.org/irp/offdocs /nsdd/nsdd-110a.htm (accessed 27 August 2012).

49. Beck, *Grenada Invasion*, 150.

50. Ibid.

51. Williams, *US–Grenada Relations*, 147.

52. Beck, *Grenada Invasion*, 156.

53. Ibid., 197.

54. Williams, *US–Grenada Relations*, 147.

55. Beck, *Grenada Invasion*, 157.

56. Williams, *US–Grenada Relations*, 244.

57. Beck, *Grenada Invasion*, 109.

58. Williams, *US–Grenada Relations*, 103.

59. Beck, *Grenada Invasion*, 19–20; G. Shultz, *Turmoil and Triumph: My Years as Secretary of State* (New York: Charles Scribner's Sons, 1993), 334; Clarridge, *Spy for All Seasons*, 257.

60. Beck, *Grenada Invasion*, 19–20; Clarridge, *Spy for All Seasons*, 252, 257.

61. Scoon, *Survival for Service*, 145.

62. Beck, *Grenada Invasion*, 43.

63. Ibid., 20; see also CCBH, "Britain and the Grenada Crisis", 46.

64. Charles Gillespie, interviewed by Charles Stuart Kennedy, 19 September 1995, Frontline Diplomacy, Manuscript Division, Library of Congress, Washington, DC. Available from http://memory.loc.gov/ammem/collections/diplomacy/ (accessed 27 May 2015).

65. Clarridge, *Spy for All Seasons*, 252.

66. Ibid., 257.

67. Beck, *Grenada Invasion*, 154.

68. US Embassy, Bridgetown, "Letter from Governor General Requesting Help", secret telegram to Secretary of State, 250745Z, 25 October 1983, Bridgetown 06631; Milan Bish, US Embassy, Bridgetown, "Uncleared Informal Minutes of Meeting between Ambassadors Bish and McNeil with West Indian Heads of Government to Discuss Grenada Situation", secret telegram to Secretary of State, 252203Z, 25 October 1983, Bridgetown 06654.

69. Beck, *Grenada Invasion*, 205.

70. Scoon, *Survival for Service*, 136.

71. "Reagan 'Saved Grenada'", BBC Caribbean, 7 June 2004, http://www.bbc.co.uk/caribbean/news/story/2004/06/040607_scoon-on-reagan.shtml (accessed 27 August 2012).

72. Joyner, "Reflections", 139.

73. Charles Hill, Executive Secretary, US Department of State, confidential memorandum to Robert C. McFarlane, White House, 2 November 1983, declassified 12 June 2002, http://www.margaretthatcher.org/document/5DC19A39A1FF43A49E21DABE09F25572.pdf (accessed 27 August 2012).

74. Beck, *Grenada Invasion*, 49–90.

75. G. Nolte, "Intervention by Invitation", *Max Planck Encyclopaedia of Public International Law* (Heidelberg and Oxford: Max Planck Institute for Comparative Public Law and International Law and Oxford University Press, 2011), 3.

76. Ibid.

77. Ibid., 4 (emphasis added); see also C. Le Mon, "Unilateral Intervention by Invitation in Civil Wars: The Effective Control Test Tested", *New York University Journal of International Law and Politics* 35 (2003): 741–93.

78. Nolte, "Intervention by Invitation", 4.

8.

Journalism and the Invasion of Grenada Thirty Years On

A Retrospective

HOWARD TUMBER

ABSTRACT

The 1983 US-led invasion of Grenada represents an important case study of journalism in the front line because it marked a changing point in the relationship between journalists and the US administration. The exclusion of news organizations and independent journalists at the time can be conceived of as a test in trying new forms of information management. The tensions experienced between journalists, government and military officers signalled the need to design alternative solutions to the problem of information coverage in wartime.

Introduction

In 2013, the thirtieth anniversary of the October 1983 United States military invasion of Grenada provided an opportunity to examine the role of the media in covering these events. Far from contemporary forms of embedded journalism where reporters are attached to the armed forces, gaining unique access to information and benefiting from special protection, reporters in Grenada were neither authorized nor welcomed to accompany the armed forces in their military adventure in the Caribbean. On the contrary, the Pentagon ordered that journalists should not be allowed to enter the island for two days following the US invasion. Even those who attempted to reach Grenada by boat were taken off the island, held for forty-eight hours and then released.[1] The US government excluded the press from the battlefield through an access denial that imposed a prior restraint based on the national security exception. In other words, the government placed a restriction on expression (reporting), which is meant to be protected by the First Amendment, because of national security concerns.[2]

Grenada's invasion represents an important case study of journalism in the front line because it marked a changing point in the relationship between journalists and the US administration. The exclusion of news organizations and independent journalists at the time can be conceived of as a test in trying new forms of information management. The tensions experienced between journalists, government and military officers signalled the need to design alternative solutions to the problem of information coverage in wartime.

Historical Context

About thirty years ago, the US invasion of Grenada was a major international news story. The *New York Times* headline of 26 October 1983 read "1,900 US Troops, with Caribbean Allies, Invade Grenada and Fight Leftist Units; Moscow Protests; British Are Critical".[3] In retrospect, the rhetoric used by US president Ronald Reagan and his administration in dubbing Grenada, Cuba and Nicaragua as the "Caribbean red triangle", to justify the military actions of 1983, bears strong similarities to the "axis of evil" pronouncements of President George W. Bush: "They imply a crucial connection without having to articulate or defend accusations that influential economic or political ties exist and have resulted in significant threat."[4]

Why Did the Media Blackout Happen?

For the invasion of Grenada, or "Operation Urgent Fury", as it was titled, there was a clear and organized plan to control the information about events involving US forces.[5] Following an order from the US Department of Defense, reporters were not allowed to work from the island, on the grounds of alleged safety reasons.[6] The *New York Times* reported: "President Reagan said through a spokesman that reporters would be allowed onto the island when American military commanders determined that conditions were safe *for them*."[7] The extent to which this was a legitimate statement became controversial: "The argument about reporter safety is a weak one. Prior to Grenada, military conflicts were never considered too dangerous for the press to cover first-hand; members of the media have taken their chances on the battlefield numerous times and were prepared to do so again in Grenada without the guarantees of government protection."[8]

The chronology of the events can be summarized as follows: on 25 October, Operation Urgent Fury began; the following day, reporters were prevented from going to Grenada, so news came only from ham radio operators on the island; on 27 October, fifteen pool reporters were allowed access for several hours and escorted to the island by military officers; on the following day, a larger number of reporters were allowed on to the island; and finally, on 30 October, permission was granted to all media.[9] Driving the two-day exclusion of the press from Grenada was the US government's anticipation of press coverage perceived as potentially threatening, together with their logistic needs to achieve military surprise, to concentrate on military objectives with no distraction from the press, and to have all troops available for the operation – that is, not have some occupied in protecting reporters.[10]

The *Financial Times* reported, "[T]he 300 journalists covering the events in Grenada are having to do so from the neighbouring island of Barbados."[11] Members of major news magazines, newspapers and television channels were held captive by US forces at the Grantley Adams airport until the military forces enabled journalists, five days after the beginning of the invasion, to gain access to the island.[12]

Despite the US administration's and commanders' argument that secrecy was required in order to minimize risk for the military operation and for American lives, there was a clear objective to manipulate and manage the news by allowing only Pentagon press agents to work from the island.[13] There were allegations that the authorities disseminated inaccurate, misleading and distorted information, such as misinformation about the whereabouts of navy ships, that they failed to disclose details about the bombing of a civilian mental hospital and hid the true nature of the invading force.[14] "Because the Grenadian government had expelled virtually all Western reporters from the island one week before the invasion, the United States decision to exclude the press was a highly effective way of barring coverage of the operation."[15]

The media blackout imposed during the Grenada invasion cannot be understood without considering the impact of the Vietnam War media coverage on the successive military actions during the decades that followed.[16] Under the shadow of the memories of the Vietnam coverage, the Reagan administration was determined to apply strict information control. This was directly connected with the perception of a media bias against official policies and US interventions in other countries. According to politicians and commanders, a direct cause of audience demoralization and opposition to foreign policies in Vietnam was the uncensored reporting and unrestricted access to information by the media. For governments and military, the lesson of the Vietnam War was that the media, and television in particular, was to blame for the US defeat in South East Asia. Commanders and politicians were convinced that the years of uncensored reporting, unrestricted access and the mismanagement of military briefings in Saigon were directly responsible for providing information and succour to the enemy, for lowering morale at home and for losing the battle for public opinion. It was a scenario that they believed must not be repeated in future conflicts. Since then the United States has experimented with different methods of "controlling" and "managing" the media, with stricter controls imposed in order to contain information and ultimately win the battle for the hearts and minds of the public.[17]

The Reagan administration was determined to avoid the Saigon experience by imposing strict control on information that they perceived could change the minds of the public. Military and defence officials in the United States noted the experience of the British in managing the media coverage of the Falklands conflict. The uses of both military and civilian minders, the stationing of reporters in military units and the use of pooling arrangements were all adopted by the US government and military in various guises in future conflicts. However, the information policy adopted by the British government and the military during the Falklands conflict was poorly organized and lacked planning. There was an absence of agreed procedure or criteria, of a centralized system of control and of coordination between departments. But whatever seemingly "on the hoof" measures the British introduced, they were based on the "myth" of Vietnam.

The *New York Times* was clear about the media management link with the Falklands war. As a former public relations officer working for the government told the paper, "the Falkland business gave us a useful pointer" on how a limited war operation might be handled: "the British kept the number of correspondents with the task force down to a minimum and were discreet about the information they passed out. They actively censored pictures and dispatches going back to London."[18]

The blackout of press coverage of Operation Urgent Fury in October 1983 was part of a plan to evade the likely negative impact of military actions that may not have ended as initially expected.[19] The use of tourist rather than military maps, the lack of information about the location of the US medical students on the island who were supposedly a main priority in the operation, the uncertainty about the enemy's identities, the killing of hospital patients by mistaking civilians for military targets and the inadequate military equipment of troops on the ground reinforced the application of the plan to control the flow of information.

By excluding journalists and any other avenue for recording independent film and television footage, the US administration secured the management and release of pictures, which thereby constituted the only evidence of the first two days of the Urgent Fury operation. The US audience could receive only what the Pentagon camera crews supplied; for example, a video of warehouses appearing to be stacked with automatic weapons was used to verify claims of imminent terrorist threats coming from Grenada.[20] While hundreds of reporters were waiting in Barbados to gain access, no independent journalists were present in Grenada to corroborate the "official" information. The US administration was so concerned with secrecy that Larry Speakes, the then White House press secretary, was not informed about the invasion until shortly after it began.[21] By contrast, local radio operators in Grenada had already warned about an imminent invasion of the island.[22] When Speakes and other White House press officers were asked by journalists about this rumour, they promptly denied it. As a result, press officers were furious that they had not been informed and consequently may have misled journalists. The deputy White House press secretary for foreign affairs, Les Janka, resigned just after the Urgent Fury operation, arguing that the credibility of White House press officials had been compromised. There were rumours that Speakes had discussed resigning over the matter, but he denied this.[23]

The media blackout in Grenada created a clear distrust among journalists. A *New York Times* article of 26 October 1983, titled "Reporting the News in a Communiqué War", wrote: "Journalists, many sent recently to Bridgetown, Barbados, 150 miles from Grenada, have been unable to get firsthand confirmation of information on such matters as the extent of casualties in the invasion or the situation of United States students and tourists caught in the upheaval." Newspaper editors were not unfamiliar with this "communiqué war" situation – the Falklands conflict in 1982, the fighting between Iran and Iraq that started in 1980, and the Soviet invasion of Afghanistan in 1979 were all examples of this. They said "those experiences made them particularly wary of efforts by a government to minimize reports of its casualties and maximize accounts of damage to enemy forces".[24]

The criticism continued the next day, 27 October, with the *New York Times* reporting "US Bars Coverage of Grenada Action; News Groups Protest":

> Howard Simons, managing editor of the *Washington Post*, said: "I'm screaming about it because writing letters takes too long. I think a secret war, like secret government, is antithetical to an open society. It's absolutely outrageous." . . . Seymour Topping, managing editor of the *New York Times*, said, "We have strenuously protested to the White House and the Defense Department about the lack of access to the story in Grenada by our correspondents who are waiting on Barbados. We also are disturbed by the paucity of details about the operation released by the Pentagon at a time when the American people require all the facts to make judgments about the actions of our Government."[25]

The press criticism of the Reagan administration's policy continued. On 28 October, the *New York Times* stated: "The Reagan Administration permitted a pool of reporters to go to Grenada for the afternoon yesterday as a furore continued over the limitations imposed on news coverage of the invasion of the Caribbean island. . . . The Administration's assertion that it had not permitted reporters to go to the island . . . until military commanders had determined that it was safe for them, was sharply criticized in both Congress and the media."[26]

Unsurprisingly, the exclusion of the media and the lack of response to journalists' logistic needs provoked an outcry from news organizations. As a result, an open conflict with these organizations and a controversy about the media blackout were installed in the public domain.[27] The official decision to bar reporters, affecting media coverage, was contested by news organizations, which severely criticized the government using editorial complaints and a lawsuit.[28] The former appeared in the *New York Times* and *The Times* of London, among others, during the week that followed the invasion, emphasizing the right to free speech and public access to information.

The American Society of Newspaper Editors stated that the restrictions on coverage imposed by the Reagan administration "go beyond the normal limits of military censorship".[29] Jerry Freidheim, executive vice president of the American Newspaper Publishers Association, said the limitations were "unprecedented and intolerable", and asked that Congress investigate what he called a "policy of secret wars hidden from the American people. . . . The Reagan Administration's policy on coverage has caused considerable consternation and suspicion among editorial writers and commentators."[30] John Chancellor of NBC News said, "the Reagan Administration has produced a bureaucrat's dream. . . . Do anything, no one is watching."[31]

A lawsuit (*Flynt v. Weinberger*, 1994) claimed violation of the First Amendment in the exclusion of reporters from Grenada, but was finally dismissed by the court for being considered "moot".[32] The general public seemed to back the official decision of denial of press access, as the letters to NBC running ten-to-one against admitting the press showed.[33] However, the US commanders and politicians had to respond to the fundamental right of the public to be informed, while the mistrust of the administration by the media was sealed despite reporting access eventually being established.

How Was the Blackout Possible?

The geographical location of Grenada played an important role in the media blackout. In the 1980s, the existing media technologies required an infrastructure that was restricted by its cost, accessibility and scope. Grenada was not as remote as the Falklands, in which case the difficulties of transporting and accessing means for broadcasting information generated important barriers for war correspondents.

Today, the Internet and mobile personal satellite communications systems enormously increase the possibilities of accessing information. "Technology shapes the tone and substance of the military–press relationship. Technology is at the root of many of the military's security concerns about news coverage."[34] The 2011 Arab Spring showed that today it is possible to access alternative sources of information without being in the front line.[35] If we consider these new technologies, a complete media blackout as occurred in Grenada is much more difficult to imagine. However, in 1983, the only chance that journalists had to access information independently was by being on the island. The transportation requirements and the American navy's capacity to monitor a couple of relatively small islands made access to Grenada impossible without military authorization. Similarly, the use of digital technologies eliminates the duration of the conflict as a variable to be considered in the possibility of broadcasting relevant information. Back in 1983, a very short military intervention could create a challenge for news organizations lacking military support. Today, the widespread "real-time communication capabilities have made war a far more transparent enterprise than military officials have been accustomed to".[36] In view of high-tech weaponry and global communication, the conflict between the opposing interests of the press and the military – that is, between the press's need to inform the public and the military's obligation to conduct war effectively – is likely to persist.[37]

The Sidle Panel and Report

The establishment of a media-military relations panel appointed by the Pentagon and chaired by General Winant Sidle (between 6 and 10 February 1984 in Washington, DC)[38] was the government's response to the intense criticism of the reporting restrictions and the tension that developed between the media and the US authorities during the Grenada conflict. The main goal of the commission was to find a way to manage media operations and establish relations with news organizations in future military interventions. Sidle was asked to look at how the United States should conduct military operations in a manner that safeguards the lives of its military and protects the security of the operation while keeping the American public informed through the media.[39]

The major news organizations decided that, although they would cooperate fully with the panel, they would not provide members to the commission, as it was not deemed appropriate for media personnel to serve on a government panel. Instead, the non-military membership of the panel was composed of experienced, retired media personnel and representatives of schools of journalism who were experts in military-media relations. The Department of Defense organizations involved also agreed to provide members.[40]

In preparation for the hearings, news media organizations and professional journalists were sent a letter asking for their views. "The letter included nine questions to be used by the commission. Formulated by General Sidle, the questionnaire asked media organizations their views on censorship, the First Amendment, the use of press pools to cover military operations, accreditation of report for media pools, and logistical needs of the different media."[41]

The majority of the nineteen media representatives who testified before the committee requested a return to the procedures that existed prior to the Grenada invasion, whereas the military members of the panel were looking to develop more formal procedures for media coverage of combat operations. The main issue that emerged from the various testimonies of both military and media personnel was one of trust, with some military officers questioning the media's ethics and patriotism, and some members of the press suspecting the military of censorship not only for security considerations but also for political purposes.

The Sidle panel recommended the following: integration between the military, public affairs and operational planning; a large pooling system; an assessment of the need to pre-establish accredited journalists in the case of military operations; journalists' compliance with security guidelines; adequate equipment and training for military staff to help media coverage; provision of communication facilities and transportation when these do not compromise military operations; and better communication and understanding between military and media workers.[42] Journalists and their access to the front line, then, would be coordinated in accordance with the military activities supervised by the US commanders. "Media representatives that appeared before the Sidle panel were against the pooling arrangements in general, but they agreed that such arrangements could be necessary for them to obtain early access to an event. This sort of arrangement would be used only when the number of media personnel allowed on an operation was limited because of security of logistics."[43]

The US military involvement in Panama (1989) provided the first opportunity to test the implementation of the Sidle panel's recommendations.[44] However, this operation proved a disaster for the "new" pooling system because Dick Cheney, then Secretary of Defense, obstructed the mobilization of the pool and journalists were unable to cover the engagement. Local commanders demanded changes in stories and caused delays in passing dispatches through military channels.[45] The sixteen-member press pool arrived in Panama four hours after US troops invaded and were only allowed to send their first reports after ten hours.

A delay in the media's ability to gain access and report independently – in the case of Grenada, for days rather than hours – enables governments and military to set the terms not only of the initial coverage and debate but also of all subsequent treatment of the story. These administration spokesmen become the primary definers of topics, enabling them to establish the initial definition or primary interpretation of the conflict in question. The interpretation then "commands the field" in all subsequent treatment, setting the terms of reference within which all further coverage takes place. Although the strength of this "effect" is disputed, news source analysis would suggest that prior to the advent of user-generated content, it had a strong degree of efficacy.[46]

General Sidle was critical of the exercise and of the manner in which his recommendations were implemented. Further discussions between military commanders and news organizations followed the Panama fiasco and eventually led to all future battle plans containing a section on dealing with the media. To some extent, this worked reasonably well in the military engagements in Somalia in the early 1990s and in Haiti in 1994, although the pool system remained unpopular with news organizations.[47]

During the first Gulf War (1991), organized pools and formal briefings were the order of the day. Journalists were restricted in their travel movements and had to subject their copy to formal security review. To overcome the problem of how to cope with hundreds of journalists reporting from the region, the military organized ad hoc press pools. However, many journalists decided to ignore these pools, preferring to move about independently. The outcome was frustration for news organizations and continuing bewilderment for the military about how journalists operate.[48]

Military-media relations went through a further downturn during the Kosovo campaign in 1999, a conflict where journalists had little access to the province and relied on the military for information about the bombing campaign. For the invasion in Afghanistan (2001), many editors, bureau chiefs and correspondents regarded the Pentagon's reporting rules as some of the toughest ever.[49] The main grievances consisted of the lack of reasonable access to land and sea bases from which air attacks on Taliban positions were launched, and the restrictions on access and information emanating from the Pentagon.

The mythical legacy of Vietnam was still alive in the recent Iraq War (2003), with apprehension on the part of the military and government that the public would react badly to pictures of casualties.

> Commanders and politicians were anxious about the effects of displays of bloodied bodies of civilians rather than ones of 'precision strikes on legitimate targets', or the media reproduction of photographs showing Iraqi prisoners in Abu Ghraib being abused by American guards as occurred in April 2004. In the US, there remains a particular fear that body bags containing dead servicemen from Iraq or Afghanistan can sap domestic support for the war. This explains why the US military transported home in secrecy the bodies of those killed while on duty, with no photographs allowed throughout 2003–4, and also explains the military's acute embarrassment when pictures were obtained by newspapers of flag-draped coffins in a cargo plane.[50]

The Sidle commission can be viewed as influential because it was an attempt not only to placate the press but also to develop a blueprint for working relationships between the military and the media, enabling both parties to achieve their relative aims. Media-coverage plans and procedures in the Iraq War can be seen as a development initiated by the Sidle commission.[51] Journalists need to be accredited and assembled by the military. This creates a mechanism to facilitate the relationship with the military forces, but it can also exclude unfriendly journalists from areas considered inappropriate by these forces.[52] Safety and training courses in preparation for the impending invasion and the embedded journalism experience may also create greater sympathy with US troops.

Conclusion

The Grenada intervention was the zenith of US media-control operations following the lessons of the Falklands conflict. These types of operations are not possible any longer because of the multiple channels allowing users to generate and distribute content. Although journalists and news organizations may still find different obstacles in accessing information (as they are, in the current conflict in Syria), digital technologies have generated new possibilities for producing and broadcasting information that can overcome some of these barriers. From mobile phones with cameras to very popular blogs and real-time devices, Internet connections have enabled myriad possibilities for information to be produced and circulated to journalists' and non-journalists' networked connections.

Despite the changes in technology, the management of domestic public opinion compels governments and military into careful planning, rehearsal and management of information from and about any war or conflict. They have to use various methods of ensuring a continuous stream of positive media coverage that is ostensibly freely gathered by independent journalists and news organizations. The media policies adopted during the invasion of Grenada failed to do this, showing that censorship and the denial of access diminished the "free media" claim of the United States. Further, as illustrated by the media's coverage and comments, and confirmed by the Sidle panel, media restrictions undermined the persuasiveness of what the government and military reported.

NOTES

1. P.G. Cassell, "Restrictions on Press Coverage of Military Operations: The Right of Access, Grenada 'Off-the-Record' Wars", *Georgetown Law Journal* 73 (1985): 944.
2. R.W. Pincus, "Press Access to Military Operations: Grenada and the Need for a New Analytical Framework", *University of Pennsylvania Law Review* 135, no. 3 (1987): 813–50.
3. C. Worrill, "African People Should Not Forget Grenada", *Final Call*, 2003, http://

www.finalcall.com/artman/publish/article_1090.shtml (accessed 18 November 2012); C. Worrill, "African People Should Not Forget the US Invasion of Grenada", *Final Call,* 2003, http://www.finalcall.com/artman/publish/Perspectives_1 /article_8354.shtml (accessed 17 May 2015).

4.   R. Andersen, *A Century of Media, A Century of War* (New York: Peter Lang, 2007), 123.

5.   M. Schoenfeld, "Military and the Media: Resolving the Conflict" (Operations Department report, Naval War College, Newport, 19 June 1992), http://www.dtic .mil/dtic/tr/fulltext/u2/a253110.pdf (accessed 18 November 2012); A. Naparstek, "Partners in Conflict: The Media and the Military in Grenada, Panama and the Persian Gulf Wars" (BA thesis, Washington University, St Louis, Missouri, 15 May 1993), http://www.naparstek.com/thetortoise/thesis/chap2.htm (accessed 18 November 2012).

6.   Cassell, "Restrictions on Press Coverage", 943.

7.   "Military vs. Press: Troubled History", *New York Times,* 29 October 1983, 1. http:// www.nytimes.com/1983/10/29/world/military-vs-press-troubled-history.html (accessed 18 May 2015).

8.   Pincus, "Press Access to Military Operations", 848.

9.   Cassell, "Restrictions on Press Coverage", 944.

10. Pincus, "Press Access to Military Operations", 841–42.

11. "The Invasion of Grenada: Press Coverage Curbed", *Financial Times,* 28 October 1983, 6.

12. Cassell, "Restrictions on Press Coverage", 944.

13. Ibid.

14. Ibid.

15. Pincus, "Press Access to Military Operations", 846.

16. Naparstek, "Partners in Conflict"; H. Tumber, "Covering War and Peace", in *Handbook of Journalism Studies,* ed. K. Wahl-Jorgensen and T. Hanitzsch (Oxford: Routledge, 2009), 386–97.

17. Tumber, "Covering War and Peace".

18. "Military vs. Press", *New York Times,* 1.

19. J. Sharkey, "Will Truth Again Be First Casualty?" (paper, Institute of Communications Studies, University of Leeds, 2001), http://media.leeds.ac.uk /papers/vp018b90.html (accessed 17 May 2015).

20. Andersen, Century of Media, 123.

21. M. Campbell, "Media Access to United States Military Operations: Grenada and Beyond" (thesis submitted to Kansas State University, School of Journalism and Mass Communications, 1989), 28.

22. Ibid.

23. Ibid., 30.

24. J. Friendly, "Reporting the News in a Communiqué War", *New York Times*, 26 October 1983, http://www.nytimes.com/1983/10/26/world/reporting-the-news -in-a-communique-war.html (17 May 2015).

25. P. Gailey, "US Bars Coverage of Grenada Action: News Groups Protest", *New York Times*, 27 October 1983, http://www.nytimes.com/1983/10/27/world/us-bars -coverage-of-grenada-action-news-groups-protest.html (accessed 18 November 2012).

26. "US Allows 15 Reporters to Go to Grenada for Day", *New York Times*, 28 October 1983, http://www.nytimes.com/1983/10/28/world/us-allows-15-reporters-to-go -to-grenada-for-day.html (accessed 17 May 2015).

27. Schoenfeld, "Military and the Media", 9–10.

28. S.D. Cooper, "Press Controls in Wartime: The Legal, Historical, and Institutional Context", *American Communication Journal* 6, no. 4 (2003).

29. "US Allows 15 Reporters to Go to Grenada".

30. Ibid.

31. "Grenada Invasion", *New York Times*.

32. Cassell, "Restrictions on Press Coverage", 948; Cooper, "Press Controls in Wartime".

33. Cassell, "Restrictions on Press Coverage", 945.

34. P. Seib, *Beyond the Front Lines: How the News Media Cover a World Shaped by War* (New York: Palgrave, 2004), 47.

35. B. Zimmer, "Twitterology: A New Science?" *New York Times*, 30 October 2011, http://www.nytimes.com/2011/10/30/ opinion/sunday/twitterology-a-new-science. html?_r=1 (accessed 18 November 2012).

36. Seib, *Beyond the Front Lines*, 48.

37. Cooper, "Press Controls in Wartime".

38. Office of Assistant Secretary of Defense, News Release Reference Number 2030, 1984, Washington, DC; General Winant Sidle, Report by the Chairman of the Joint Chiefs of Staff Military-Media Relations Panel (Chairman of the Joint Chiefs of Staff, Washington, DC, 1984), 3.

39. Ibid., 6.

40. Ibid.

41. Campbell, "Media Access", 65.

42. Sidle Panel Report, as cited in G.C. Woodward, "The Rules of the Game: The Military and the Press in the Persian Gulf War", in *The Media and the Persian Gulf War*, ed. R.E. Denton Jr (Westport, CT: Praeger, 1993), 9; see also Cassell, "Restrictions on Press Coverage", 931–73.

43. Campbell, "Media Access", 67.

44. K.T. Olson, "The Constitutionality of Department of Defense Press Restrictions on Wartime Correspondents Covering the Persian Gulf War", *Drake Law Review* 41 (1992): 522.

45. Woodward, "Rules of the Game", 9–10.

46. See S. Hall et al., *Policing the Crisis* (London: Macmillan, 1978), 58–59; see also P. Schlesinger and H. Tumber, *Reporting Crime: The Media Politics of Criminal Justice* (Oxford: Clarendon, 1994), 17.

47. Tumber, "Covering War and Peace", 391.

48. Ibid.

49. N. Hickey, "Access Denied: The Pentagon's War Reporting Rules Are the Toughest Ever", *Columbia Journalism Review* (January–February 2002), 27.

50. Tumber, "Covering War and Peace", 392.

51. See H. Tumber and J. Palmer, *Media at War: The Iraq Crisis* (London: Sage, 2004), 2.

52. Andersen, *A Century of Media*, 123.

9.

The United States in the Caribbean

Thirty Years after American Fury

SHRIDATH RAMPHAL

ABSTRACT

This chapter traces the origins of the military invasion launched by the United States of America in Grenada in 1983, and describes the efforts made by the author as secretary general of the Commonwealth to restore the country to constitutional government and the rule of law. The author believes that Caribbean governments had let themselves down through a majority of them siding with the American invasion. He underlines the need for global society to make the world a safer place for small states such as Grenada.

Introduction

The Caribbean generally has had a long record of free elections and acceptable democratic governance, but, from time to time, it threw up unorthodox prime ministers, and none more quixotic than Eric Gairy, first elected premier in Grenada in 1967, then becoming prime minister, on independence, in 1974. He was essentially fascist by disposition, given to cult and occult activities and repressive governance. He was an ardent believer in UFOs, on which topic he once addressed the UN General Assembly. At his first Commonwealth Heads of Government meeting (in 1977, in London), he embarrassed everyone (save himself) by rising before the chairman (Britain's prime minister,

James Callaghan) could start the plenary session, saying "Let us pray" and, in the stunned silence that followed, proceeding to do just that. It was his first meeting and I suppose it was his gauche way of announcing himself. Many leaders from politics, the private sector, trade unions and other facets of Caribbean society despised but tolerated him. In a real sense, he started it all.

The coup by the New JEWEL Movement (NJM) was on 13 March 1979. It was popular in the sense of getting rid of Gairy, but many had misgivings about the method. Contributing to both popularity and misgiving was the proclamation of the NJM as a Marxist Socialist party and its development of especially close ties with Cuba. Importantly, the People's Revolutionary Government, into which the NJM was converted, did not sever its links with the West Indies Associated States Council of Ministers, with the Caribbean Community (CARICOM), or with the Commonwealth, and, although it had suspended the constitution, it left Sir Paul Scoon, the governor general and queen's representative, in place. When the member governments of the West Indies Associated States decided, in 1981, to replace the loose grouping with a formal treaty organization, the Organisation of Eastern Caribbean States (OECS), none of the governments objected to the membership of Grenada, and, indeed, one of the signatories to the treaty was Maurice Bishop as prime minister.

I was in London as Commonwealth secretary general, at the time of the NJM coup. I contacted Bishop immediately and, within days, flew to Grenada with a small delegation from the secretariat. What do you do in the face of a popular coup? My instinct was to get Bishop to regularize the situation as quickly as possible by announcing his intention to call early general elections (which he would have won at a canter) and restore the constitutionality of governance and a return to the rule of law.

Support from Commonwealth Countries

I met Bishop on the balcony of a small house. He had not yet occupied government headquarters. He had Bernard Coard with him, and they were heavily and obviously body-guarded, though there was no general air of militarization. They were glad to see me; it was a mark of recognition. But their pleasure was more material. They wished help from the Commonwealth: project funding from the Caribbean Development Bank, technical assistance from the secretariat and general support from Commonwealth countries. Maurice Bishop was clearly the political leader, Bernard Coard more the technocrat, but with heavy socialist overtones.

I came quickly to the point. Caribbean countries and Commonwealth countries generally could not be comfortable with a coup as a basis for recognition, however unworthy the government it replaced, without some promise or indication of regularization of the situation on democratic lines. There was a general air of relief that Gairy was gone, but they should not expect congratulation for bringing it about by force. I said that, obviously, the NJM was riding a wave of popularity. An early general election would confirm their legitimacy and make assistance of all kinds available. It soon became clear that I was talking to the deaf.

There was no issue of legitimacy, I was told. The revolution was their election; it needed no confirmation. Their power derived directly from the people; all the world's great revolutions were like that. To talk of elections was to question the legitimacy of the revolution. In all this, Coard was the more ideological and uncompromising of the two. I argued that however strongly they felt about their domestic situation, other countries with whom they have to deal would not share their passion and therefore their conclusion. This was the realpolitik; they needed to acknowledge it as a practical reality and make it possible for others not merely to recognize them but to help. I believed that my appeal to pragmatism may have made a small dent in Bishop's revolutionary armour; I was sure it bounced off of Coard's without a mark.

In the end, Coard's resistance prevailed with the People's Revolutionary Government, including Bishop, who as late as two years afterwards asserted (to an American interviewer):

> [T]he revolution came on 13th March 1979. That is just two years ago. Under the system we inherited, elections were held once in five years. After you had your revolution in America, it took you thirteen years to call your elections. After the British had their revolution in the 17th century, it took them over 150 years to call their elections. So what is the problem? What is the reason for the pressure? We are going to call our elections. But we will do it at the appropriate time. Meanwhile we are going to get down to some serious business of building the country and dealing with the priorities that our people have set for Grenada.[1]

And that they did – at least in the beginning – with programmes in health, education, welfare and agriculture. Unemployment and illiteracy were reduced, and growth in the economy was evident. Plans for tourism were being put in place, centred on the airport that the Cubans were helping them to build.

Meanwhile, in our discussion on the balcony, I persisted, aiming to continue the effort at another level. I proposed that a group of eminent persons from the region might be constituted by the Commonwealth as a Caribbean Advisory Group to assist the government in the process of transition ahead. Bishop agreed with this, and Coard concurred without enthusiasm. It was chaired by an eminent Dominican, Justice Telford Georges (later the first chief justice of Zimbabwe), and included William Demas (chairman of the Caribbean Development Bank and former secretary general of CARICOM). It was serviced by the CARICOM secretariat.

The group held meetings with Bishop and his colleagues and advised them strongly that the holding of elections was the sine qua non of progress. This was just as strongly resisted by the People's Revolutionary Government. In the face of this obduracy, the group concluded that they could make no progress and disbanded. With Caribbean advice spurned, the Bishop government turned to Cuba, which was an ideological soulmate in any event, but it did not turn its back on CARICOM. In the community, however, it lived an uneasy life, as it sought to inject its Marxist philosophies into regional policy. Its closest friend was Guyana, whose socialism was more pragmatic, but who defended Grenada's right to pursue its chosen path. So too, with less intensity, did Trinidad and Tobago, Belize and the Bahamas, hence the emergence of the notion of "ideological pluralism" within the community – and its grudging acceptance by more rightist, pro-American governments.

The political flag-bearer of this latter group was Edward Seaga in Jamaica, who had, in a recent general election, ousted Michael Manley, an avowed social democrat – whose socialism, however, was more rhetorical than practical. Seaga, by comparison, was a Cold War ideologue with close personal links to the new right wing of the Republican Party in Washington. President Reagan was elected only three weeks after Seaga's own victory in Jamaica – with his doctrinaire right wing in the ascendancy. Seaga was the first head of government that Reagan met after his election. This political conjuncture was to provide a propitious environment for the invasion of Grenada nine months later.

I shall not go over the factual events, which have been well canvassed:

1. the People's Revolutionary Government turning in on itself as the Coard faction denounced Bishop's group as "right opportunists" and "petty bourgeois" and physically detained him;
2. the people intervening to free him;
3. the violent counter-attack by the Coard/Austin coup-makers and the brutal execution of Bishop and his ministers;
4. the chance this provided the Americans to do what they had long wanted to do – namely, invade Grenada to teach left-wing aspirants a lesson and act out their doctrine of "pre-emptive strike";
5. the US/Seaga/Adams–inspired invitation from the OECS members to invade Grenada for them;
6. the duplicitous exercise in Trinidad as Prime Minister Chambers sought a non-violent response from CARICOM even as Jamaican troops were flying into Barbados to await word from the United States that the invasion was on;
7. Dame Eugenia Charles giving Reagan cover on global television for the landings in Grenada;
8. the ex post facto invitation from Governor General Scoon to bolster legitimacy for the invasion;
9. and so much more, forever to the shame of the Caribbean.

Seven months before the US invasion, before any question of Bishop's demise or of threats to the safety of American students had arisen, Ronald Reagan had already set the stage for military action. In a speech at the Washington Hilton to the National Association of Manufacturers on 10 March 1983, he said:

> [T]hat tiny little island is building now, or having built for it, on its soil and shores, a naval base, a superior air base, storage bases and facilities for the storage of munitions, barracks, and training grounds for the military. I'm sure all of that is not simply to encourage the export of nutmeg. . . . It isn't nutmeg that's at stake in the Caribbean and Central America; it is the United States national security. Soviet military theorists want to destroy our capacity to re-supply

Western Europe in case of an emergency. We've been slow to understand that the defence of the Caribbean and Central America against Marxist-Leninist takeover is vital to our national security in ways we're not accustomed to thinking about.[2]

In his own election campaign in 1981, Seaga had pledged to break diplomatic relations with Cuba and to draw Jamaica close to the US – direct reversals of the policies pursued by Michael Manley, who had been in charge of the country's affairs for the previous decade. True to his word, Seaga broke diplomatic relations with Cuba and established close relations with insiders in the Reagan camp, who were later to become key players not only in the Reagan government but also, later, in the administration of George W. Bush. Prominent among them were Richard Perle ("The Prince of Darkness") and Paul Wolfowitz, antecedents of Bush's "Vulcans" and of "The Project for the New American Century" – early architects of American unilateralism and the doctrine of "pre-emption".

Most of the governments of the OECS were acting out of fear, and their fears were not fanciful. Leaders of their left-wing groups, including Maurice Bishop, had met on Union Island in the Grenadines prior to the March 1979 coup in Grenada and had declared their intention to remove their governments from office by whatever means necessary – a threat that the governments of these small states did not take lightly.

Commonwealth Engagement

From the outset, my own influence in London was deployed in support of continued Commonwealth engagement with Grenada. In 1979, OECS (then the West Indies Associated States) leaders hoped that the British government would intervene or at least sever relationships with the Bishop regime, but the British government argued that Britain recognized states, not governments, and, as Sir Paul Scoon had been retained as the governor general and the representative of the queen, diplomatic links would continue. Bishop himself attended both the 1979 and the 1981 Commonwealth summits in Lusaka and Melbourne, respectively, and became something of a spokesman for the cause of small and disadvantaged states. He was articulate and persuasive and was well liked by the majority of his Commonwealth peers. Over time, even the

West Indies Associated States/OECS countries were beginning to recognize that he was a moderating influence in the regime in Grenada. But the fact that he was, was his undoing.

In London, I followed these events with horror and alarm. On 20 October, the day after Bishop's death, I issued the following statement from Marlborough House:

> I share the deep sense of horror which is widespread throughout the Commonwealth at the tragic loss of life in Grenada, including that of the Prime Minister and Ministers of the Government. I feel sure that Commonwealth Caribbean Governments, in particular, will wish to use every influence through co-ordinated responses to ensure that the will and the interests of the people of Grenada are respected and the integrity of the island state preserved.

I had begun to learn what was unfolding among the Caribbean countries and was both shocked and troubled. There seemed to be three lines of action: one led by Dominica (only slightly bigger than Grenada), whose president, Dame Eugenia Charles, was chairperson of the OECS, acting prominently with John Compton, the prime minister of St Lucia (which housed the secretariat of the OECS), and "Tom" Adams, the prime minister of Barbados (which was not a member of the OECS). Another was led by the prime minister of Trinidad and Tobago (George Chambers), who was the chairman-in-office of CARICOM. The third, more clandestine, was the Jamaica-US cabal, which had been long-established. In the end, the first and the third were to merge, and the second, perhaps the most legitimate actor, was to be discarded.

In Seaga's monograph of 2009, *The Grenada Intervention: The Inside Story*, he says: "I told Adams that in the same way that strong force was used to stage the revolution, stronger force should now be used to remove the Revolutionary Military Council."[3] Of course, that "stronger force" was at hand.

Six months before all this, on 21 April 1983, Maurice Bishop had written formally to me (as secretary general), asking me to forward his letter to all Commonwealth governments. I did so, to all fifty countries. It was a global cri de cœur:

> The US is continuing its acts of economic aggression against our small country. Attempts have been made to prevent us from receiving assistance from regional and international financial institutions . . . [examples].

We are now increasingly concerned because these attacks on our economy have also been given political impetus in the form of adverse pronouncements by top United States personnel . . . [examples of hostile statements followed, ending with President Reagan's "nutmeg" speech of 10 March 1983: "it is not nutmeg that is at stake in the Caribbean, it is the United States National Security"].

Given the historic record of US military interventionism, it is our opinion that the pronouncement of the President of the United States that Grenada constitutes a threat to the national security of the United States of America is an indication of hostile designs. This is for us cause for grave concern . . .

In our concern, we draw these matters to your attention for your information and close consideration and for whatever assistance you can provide to prevent this ominous threat of aggression against our country from materialising.[4]

It is intriguing that when Thatcher received her copy of this letter, she scribbled in the margin: "I really don't think we can ignore it. Why did Mr Ramphal *circulate* it? We really must ask." She had overlooked that Bishop had asked for general circulation. But was she being more protective of Reagan's image than Grenada's security? In any event, Britain did ignore the warning – and the plea. It is ironic that when the "ominous threat of aggression" did materialize, Bishop's own death would provide the pretext for it.

When, in the early morning of 25 October, without notice, the Dominican prime minister and chairperson of the OECS Dame Eugenia was awakened and flown by the United States to Washington to appear on global television at President Reagan's side as he announced the Grenada invasion, that announcement was the first inkling the OECS and other CARICOM countries had that the invasion was on. CARICOM was officially notified when the US ambassador in Trinidad and Tobago called the Foreign Ministry. Not even Margaret Thatcher, the British prime minister and close friend of Reagan, had been told that the invasion would take place. The Thatcher episode is a story all of its own but too long to tell fully here.

Aggravation

Suffice it to say that, on the day of the invasion and in subsequent media statements, Thatcher and her ministers did not conceal their aggravation that the United States had invaded a Commonwealth country and one of which the queen was still head of state. Thatcher was genuinely annoyed on at least three grounds: she believed the invasion was wrong in principle; it made problems for her in the cruise-missile debate going on in Britain; and she was irritated that her "close and special friend" Ron should have gone ahead with the invasion without telling her he was doing so and despite her advice that he should not. On a phone-in programme on the BBC World Service on the morning of 30 October, she said: "If you are going to pronounce a new law that wherever communism reigns against the will of the people, even though it has happened internally there, the United States shall enter, then we are going to have really terrible wars in the world."

She was right, but her public hostility abated in private conversations with Reagan – the "special relationship" had to come first. The record of Thatcher's telephone conversation with Reagan indicated little more than formal affront at being blindsided – and her advice ignored. Perhaps her basic attitude to the invasion was reflected in her own words to him on the telephone: "I just hope, Ron, that the restoration of constitutional government in Grenada will be very soon and that they will manage to put together a government which can get back to democracy." Thereafter, it was pleasantries between two good friends.

On the morning of this conversation between Reagan and Thatcher, I was interviewed by the BBC's *Today* programme about the invasion. I was in a far more sombre mood than the prime minister. Questioned about whether I was asked for advice prior to the invasion, I said:

> No I was not. I wish indeed I was. I would not have had any difficulty in saying that there were other ways that must be pursued . . . that we don't in fact help Grenada or help the Caribbean by taking the law into our own hands, or worse still inviting external powers to take the law into their hands on behalf of the region.
>
> [I went on to make it clear that I was against the US invasion.] In the wake of what obviously was a divided region, a divided Caribbean on the question of intervention of any kind, I would have thought that the United States, in this situation, as a friend of the region – and it has been a friend of the region in many respects – would have been counselling calm and wisdom, would have been counselling negotiation, would have been helping the region to put great pressure on the quite grotesque regime that killed Maurice Bishop and seized power, before resorting to this kind of armed intervention.

I issued a separate statement from Marlborough House, which went to all Commonwealth governments and to the CARICOM and OECS secretariats, to this effect:

> I have already condemned unreservedly the killing of Prime Minister Bishop and some of his colleagues. Now the tragedy is deepening. Today's external intervention will occasion further disquiet within the Commonwealth.
>
> If there is a lesson in these events, it must surely be in the chain of tragedy that begins with the overthrow of constitutional government, and the deep passions and anxieties that are aroused when the contests of super powers are brought within regions of small developing countries.
>
> But nothing must obscure the urgent need to provide the people of Grenada with the earliest possible opportunity to determine their own future free of pressures or constraints of any kind.
>
> [And I offered the thought that] [t]here may be a role for the Commonwealth to play in contributing to the restoration of constitutional government in Grenada.

The OECS, meanwhile, had formally notified me of their decision to "take appropriate action" and that "bearing in mind the relative lack of military resources in the possession of the OECS countries, the member governments have sought assistance for this purpose from friendly countries within the region and subsequently from outside". Then followed the important words: "Three Governments have responded to the OECS member governments' request to form a multi-national force for the purpose of undertaking a pre-emptive defensive strike in order to remove this dangerous threat to peace and security to their sub-region and to establish a situation of normality in Grenada. These Governments are Barbados, Jamaica and the United States."

OECS and International Reaction

"A pre-emptive defensive strike" – the language of Washington's hard right that was to resonate worldwide in conflicts beyond Grenada, from Iraq to Afghanistan, over years to come. Late that first night of the invasion, as the world was beginning to react to the news, I received a message from the director general of the OECS, Dr Vaughan Lewis, to the following effect: "Member States of the Organisation are of the view that the necessity now is for the Caribbean and Commonwealth countries to put themselves in a position to speedily arrange for peacekeeping forces to be put in place to create a situation that will allow the non-CARICOM personnel to withdraw from Grenada." This was heartening, but, of course, by then matters were out of the hands of the small OECS countries for whom the director general spoke.

Recently declassified US military information confirms that "nearly eight thousand soldiers, sailors, airmen and marines had participated in URGENT FURY along with 353 Caribbean allies" – over 93 per cent were American forces. Of the eighty-eight Americans and Grenadians (military and civilian) killed, 79 per cent were Grenadian. Major General Norman Schwarzkopf, who later led the Iraq attack, coordinated the ground operation in Grenada.

International reaction was so immediate that, late that same day, the United Nations Security Council took up the situation in Grenada as an emergency matter and met for ten hours into the night, in debate on a draft resolution calling "for an immediate cessation of the armed intervention in Grenada and for the immediate withdrawal of the foreign forces from that country". Under other provisions of the text, the council would have deeply deplored "the armed intervention in Grenada" as "a flagrant violation of international law and of the independence, sovereignty and territorial integrity of that State". The vote on the draft resolution was eleven in favour to one against (United States), with three abstentions (Britain, Togo and Zaire). Of the five permanent members, three were in favour, including France; and Britain was not against. The single American vote against was a veto, and so the resolution failed.

On 2 November, the General Assembly, whose decisions are not enforceable, debated a similar resolution, which was adopted by 108 votes to 9. The nine countries voting against were Barbados, Jamaica, four OECS countries, Israel, El Salvador and the United States. Britain did not vote against; it abstained – as in the Security Council.

These were resounding condemnations by the international community of the invasion of Grenada, and unambiguous demands for the withdrawal of the American and Caribbean military. The voting was not on East-West lines; nor on North-South. It was not the "non-aligned" against the West. It was a global rejection of the notion of a "pre-emptive defensive strike". It was an unusual coming together of an outraged international community. I felt humiliated that some Caribbean Commonwealth countries, whose international standing as a region was so high, stood indicted. I took comfort in the fact that it was only some.

The OECS secretariat had said in their formal announcement of the invasion: "It is the intention of the member governments of the OECS that once the threat has been removed, they will invite the Governor-General of Grenada to assume executive authority of the country under the provisions of the Grenada constitution of 1973 and to appoint a broad-based interim government to administer the country pending the holding of general elections."[5]

I knew this was conditioned on "once the threat has been removed", but I would make the assumption that it had been. Seized with the notions of constitutionality and an interim administration, I immediately began to work on assembling such a team. Concurrently, I sought out constitutional lawyers known to the Caribbean, who could advise the Governor-General. I needed to talk to Scoon, but there was no normal service. Fortunately, facilitated by an American satellite link, he rang me on 28 October.

Sir Paul confirmed that he was in authority and would make a radio broadcast that night, principally to confirm that he was in authority. He volunteered that he would not touch on the withdrawal of the forces in Grenada, but would thank them for their assistance. I asked whether he wished to discuss the question of a Commonwealth security presence in the light of indications I had had from OECS countries, including Dame Eugenia Charles. He said it was too early for that, but he would talk to me later. I told him I had begun to think of it, but that I wanted him to know that the Commonwealth would move only in response to a request from Grenada and only in the context of the withdrawal of foreign forces.

He referred to "a caretaker administration" and asked whether I could contact Alister McIntyre and enquire whether he would head it. Alister was an excellent choice – an eminent Grenadian, at the time assistant secretary general of the United Nations at the United Nations Conference on Trade and Development in Geneva. I assured him I would do so immediately.

That was the beginning of a series of telephone communications between us over these logistical matters. In them, I had the impression that Scoon either could not or did not wish to discuss the issue of troop withdrawal. As it turned out, Scoon eventually rejected the idea of withdrawal of US troops, and Alister McIntyre could not take up the task for reasons of ill health. But, I had laid the foundation with Scoon – and, behind the scenes, with Seaga and the leaders of the OECS, through Tom Adams – for an interim administration whose priority task would be the holding of general elections.

Avoiding Fracturing the Commonwealth

We were now into November and looming (on 23 November) was the Commonwealth summit in New Delhi under Indira Gandhi's chairmanship.

I had a twofold task: to ensure that the Commonwealth stood resolutely by its principles of internationalism, and yet to contrive that the Caribbean participation with the United States in the invasion of Grenada did not fracture the Commonwealth. I also had a third goal, mainly personal, to rebuild a relationship among the heads of Commonwealth Caribbean governments, who remained bitterly divided on all that had transpired.

Grenada was not specifically on the agenda of the Commonwealth meeting as representatives of forty-one countries came together, but Indira Gandhi set the scene with a biting comment in her statement at the opening ceremony. It was a comment directed as much at the Caribbean countries that had participated in the invasion as it was at the United States. She said: "In the wider interest of peace, all powers should accept and strictly observe the principles of peaceful coexistence, non-intervention and non-interference. We cannot acquiesce in the reasons being advanced to justify the use of force by one state against another, to install regimes of particular persuasion or to destabilise regimes deemed to be inconvenient. Recent unfortunate events in Grenada have caused profound disquiet."

On the second day, the seething anger of the African countries was unleashed over what they considered to be the cover that Caribbean countries had given to the United States to invade Grenada.

First, Zambia's Kenneth Kaunda, and then Robert Mugabe of Zimbabwe, spoke of the issue. They both claimed that a precedent had been set for powerful neighbours such as South Africa (still, then, under the apartheid regime) to invade them. Kaunda declared that "those of his colleagues in the Caribbean who had acted with the United States had created a real nightmare for him personally and for his country". Mugabe was even more direct. He stated:

If their colleagues in the Commonwealth could sanction this kind of thinking

by sanctioning the invasion of Grenada, the African member states were entitled
to regard them as acting against African interests . . .

Powerful states, which wanted to promote their own ideological systems
through-out the world, were trying to use their might to manipulate small states,
even by way of invasion if this was considered necessary, and to seek to establish
within such states regimes which they could manipulate as puppets.

Later in the debate, Tanzania's president, Julius Nyerere, practically
accused the leaders of the Caribbean countries that participated in the invasion of lying. He said:

[I]t was in the nature of man to try to justify and find good reasons for what he
had done. Those in the Eastern Caribbean had given their good reasons for join-
ing the Americans in the invasion. Frankly, he thought they were overdoing it.
. . . The Americans had invaded a small Caribbean country. It was not possible
for the Commonwealth to keep quiet about it, and he hoped the Commonwealth
would find some appropriate way of expressing its anger.

Edward Seaga, the Jamaican prime minister and architect of the Grenada
invasion, had chosen not to attend the Commonwealth meeting. Therefore,
it was left to Tom Adams, the Barbados prime minister, and the leaders of
the OECS countries to justify their position. They did so with reasonable
success, garnering sympathy from the leaders of other small island states
and Australia's prime minister, Bob Hawke. Their defence, wisely, was not
avowal of a new doctrine of "pre-emption", but an assertion of their sense of
helplessness – of their smallness.

I had so orchestrated the debate, with Mrs Gandhi's help, that the OECS
and Barbados leaders were given free rein by the chair to speak, while encouraging the Caribbean leaders who had opposed the invasion not to speak.
Thus, Belize and the Bahamas remained silent and the only brief interventions by Chambers (Trinidad and Tobago) and Burnham (Guyana) were to
draw attention to a statement circulated by Chambers of his remarks to his
parliament in which he described the CARICOM meeting he had chaired
prior to the invasion. My purpose, of course, was to ensure that the Caribbean
countries did not set upon themselves in the councils of the Commonwealth.
Apart from the Africans, there was no overwhelming mood in the meeting
to condemn the Caribbean countries.

In summing up the session, I made no mention of the differences between the African leaders and the leaders of the Caribbean countries that had participated in the invasion. Instead, I focused on what I called "a forward looking approach, particularly one concerned with the recuperation of Grenada and a return to constitutional government". The discussion ended on a uniquely Commonwealth note: an invitation to the heads to attend the pending India–West Indies cricket test match in Bombay.

The heads of government went off to a "retreat" weekend on 26 and 27 November in Goa. Unlike other "retreats", my plan was that there should be no more debate on Grenada. Instead, I drafted and circulated three paragraphs for the communiqué reflecting the nuances of the plenary debate. I ensured that all the Caribbean countries were content with it and then persuaded the leading African countries not to object to it. This process was successful; when the entire draft communiqué of the meeting came before the heads of government (who had insisted on seeing it and amending it as they saw fit), the three paragraphs on Grenada were accepted without comment.

The section of the communiqué on Grenada did four important things:

1. It agreed that the emphasis should be on reconstruction not recrimination and affirmed the Commonwealth's readiness to help.
2. In welcoming an interim administration, it did so with the expectation that it would function free of external interference, pressure, or the presence of foreign military forces.
3. It emphasized that the Commonwealth leaders attached great importance to the early return by Commonwealth Caribbean countries to the spirit of fraternity and cooperation that had been characteristic of the region.
4. It required the secretary general to undertake a study of the special needs of small states consonant with the right to sovereignty and territorial integrity.

As to the Commonwealth's readiness to help in the absence of foreign military forces, suffice it to say that, although by then the OECS and Barbados were for the replacement of American troops by a Caribbean police presence (which I had organized), the Americans and Jamaica were not – nor, by then, were Scoon and his interim administration. There was no place for the Commonwealth – and the OECS had lost control of Grenada. It was an American conquest.

General Elections

The Americans were still there when, nine months later, in September 1984, I had a request from the interim administration in Grenada for the Commonwealth to witness general elections set down for 3 December. I duly circulated the request to Commonwealth governments. The communication from Kenneth Kaunda, the president of Zambia, summed up the Commonwealth response. In a letter to me, he said: "As long as foreign military forces continue to be deployed in Grenada up to the election time and after, Zambia cannot support the presence of a Commonwealth Observer Team, because to support such a suggestion would be contrary to the Commonwealth Summit decision of last year in New Delhi on the matter." I informed the Grenada administration of the Commonwealth's position.

Conclusion

More than thirty years later, I continue to believe that Caribbean governments let themselves down through the majority who sided with an American invasion of their region – and those among them who participated actively in engineering it. The vote in the UN General Assembly negated credits that the Caribbean had worked hard to build up in the years since Jamaica's and Trinidad and Tobago's independence in 1962. It was especially harrowing for me as a Caribbean person, but I took comfort in the robustness with which the Commonwealth stood on the side of principle.

But the Grenada episode was not all a dark spot for the Caribbean and the Commonwealth. Aware that small countries would continue to be susceptible to the internal conditions that caused the coup d'état in Grenada in 1979 and again in 1983 and to the risk of invasion by larger powers intent upon procuring their own interests, I ensured that I received a mandate from the New Delhi summit for a study of the special needs of small states, including their security needs.

In 1984, I appointed a distinguished group drawn from small and large states of the Commonwealth to produce the study. It was chaired by the same jurist from Dominica whose Caribbean Advisory Group had tried to persuade Maurice Bishop five years earlier to hold elections. The study was ready by August 1985. It was entitled "Vulnerability: Small States in the Global Society". It became a seminal document on the problems of small states, informing the work not only of the Commonwealth, but also of the United Nations, the World Bank and the International Monetary Fund. It led to the Commonwealth Secretariat being today the lead institution on small states.

Small states are not scaled-down models of larger states; they are unique, and so are their needs and the challenges they pose for themselves, their regions and the world community. Twice on my Commonwealth watch – in the Falklands and in Grenada – smallness was a factor in a major threat to world order. After the Falklands, I had warned the Commonwealth: "tomorrow it could be another small country – this time with no capacity to provide or invoke a response – that is the victim of aggression". It was to be Grenada. Global society has to make the world a safer place for small states and to make them safe for the world.

NOTES

1.   *Class*, September 1984, 19, published by Class Promotions Inc., New York. Quoted in M. Shahabudeen, *The Conquest of Grenada: Sovereignty in the Periphery* (Georgetown, Guyana: University of Guyana, 1986), 7.

2.   Ronald Reagan, "Remarks on Central America and El Salvador at the Annual Meeting of the National Association of Manufacturers" (Ronald Reagan Presidential Library, 1983).

3.   Edward Seaga, *The Grenada Intervention: The Inside Story* (Kingston: n.p., 2009), 19.

4.   Letter from Prime Minister Maurice Bishop, Grenada, to Commonwealth Secretary General Shridath Ramphal, 21 April 1983 (Ramphal private archive).

5.   Organisation of the Eastern Caribbean States, statement on the situation in Grenada of 25 October 1983 (Secretariat of the Organisation of the Eastern Caribbean States, Castries, St Lucia), in William C. Gilmore, *The Grenada Intervention: Analysis and Documentation* (London: Mansell, 1984), 97–98.

Part 3.

GRENADA REDUX

10.

Written Into Amnesia?

*The Truth and Reconciliation
Commission of Grenada*

JERMAINE O. McCALPIN

ABSTRACT

*The experience of the South African Truth and Reconciliation Com-
mission has served as inspiration to the world, especially to countries
grappling with the critical question of how to deal with the past in the
aftermath of violence and trauma. The Truth and Reconciliation Commission of Grenada was founded within this context. Diverging from the
ideal state of a successful truth commission, the reality of the Truth and
Reconciliation Commission of Grenada is that it was an underpublicized,
undersupported mechanism. The concomitant goals of truth and reconciliation are noble but difficult to achieve, and the Truth and Reconciliation
Commission of Grenada epitomized this. Ultimately, each traumatized
society has to decide whether a truth commission will break the silence
on the past or will help to write the past into amnesia.*

We must remember what happened in order to keep it from happening again.
. . . But we must forget the feelings, the emotions that go with it. It is only by
forgetting that we are able to go on.[1]
—Rwandan official

Drawing Inspiration from South Africa

The South African Truth and Reconciliation Commission (TRC) was established in 1995 in an attempt to help South Africans heal from their deeply
divisive and violently racist past and move towards a more inclusive future.[2]
The strategy was based on the idea of embracing the truth of what happened
during apartheid, with the intent of encouraging reconciliation. While their
TRC was not the first truth commission, it has been the most researched and
copied one. Its work revealed the painful difficulty of truth-telling. The belief
that truth-telling is painful but cathartic is critical to the work of truth commissions, which are based on the premise that "truth hurts but silence kills".

Several truth commissions have drawn explicit inspiration from the South
African TRC, including that of Grenada, which was founded in 2001 as a
direct descendant of the South African TRC model: reconciliation of erstwhile divided and broken relationships is the by-product of truth-telling and
an effective way to make peace with the past. Truth and reconciliation must,
however, be properly understood and not treated as automatic in societies
that have been heavily traumatized by past events. It is this trauma that often
induces amnesia, shaped by a desire to forget the past, almost in the manner
that one "forgets" a few pieces of furniture in a move to a new house. Grenada continues to struggle with this complex: wanting to move on, wanting
to forget, wanting justice.

The central argument of this chapter is that, while there are positive lessons and influences to be observed from the South African TRC, many truth
commissions, including the Truth and Reconciliation Commission of Grenada (TRCG), have attempted to adapt unique features of the South African experiences and, in the end, made some of the same mistakes as the
South African TRC. The earnest desire to pattern the umbilical relationship
between truth and reconciliation is a critical failure of the TRCG. The secondary argument here is that we have not properly learned the lesson that truth
does not inevitably lead to reconciliation in deeply divided societies such as
South Africa. Third, that truth is highly contested and never the automatic
result of official excavation as in the work of truth commissions. The TRCG
did not properly address the reality that even though truth is indispensable
to reconciliation, justice is also required for reconciliation to occur. In the

end, the TRCG became more of a symbolic rather than a practical approach to dealing with the pain of Grenada's political past. The result is that its work has been "written into amnesia".

Nonetheless, truth commissions are potent transitional mechanisms that are critical to societies who want to "look back in order to go forward". I conclude by outlining the successes and failures of the TRCG as a truth commission experiment. The chapter focuses on assessing the value of the TRCG to Grenada's resolve to move on from the deep divisions caused by the revolution and the consequent US invasion. The report of the TRCG, as well as reactions to it, will be critically discussed. In the end, all truth commissions must be judged on the impact of their reports and not sentimentally on the fact that they were established to "exhume the past", as painful as this exercise often is.

Truth Commissions and Reckoning

In terms of a definition, a truth commission may be defined as an "official but non-judicial body that is established often by an act of government to probe a pattern of violence, human rights violations and atrocities in a country within a specific time frame with an end to suggest ways to deal with the past that places emphasis on non-repetition, justice and historical accuracy".[3] In essence, truth commissions are remembrance projects. They are geared towards documenting and, sometimes, developing a collective memory of a nation's past. This development of a collective remembrance is painful and potentially divisive. As Priscilla Hayner argues, "remembering is not easy, but forgetting may be impossible".[4]

Truth commissions do not occur or operate in a vacuum. They are often considered a critical part of transitional justice efforts in many societies. Transitional justice is essentially "how societies reckon with their past".[5] This reckoning is part of how a society addresses the atrocities of the past in such a way as to render justice in the present and lay the foundations for future justice. Most truth commissions have operated within this larger "reckoning" framework. Dealing with the past is always important if societies are to move on. Truth commissions, therefore, provide the documentary evidence of the past that needs to be reckoned with.

There have been more than forty truth commissions since the first one was inaugurated in Uganda in 1974.[6] The most recent truth commission, the *Comissão Nacional da Verdade,* was convened in Brazil in November 2011 and became operational in May 2012. It was established to investigate rights abuses, including those committed during military rule from 1964 to 1985. Its mandate period is, however, from 1946 to 1988.

Despite their extensive usage, truth commissions are grossly misunderstood and misappropriated. They have so often become victims of hyperbolic expectations viewing them like a magic pill or a panacea to cure all societies of all kinds of maladies. It is important to note that, while the mechanism of a truth commission is universal, the experiences and details of truth commissions differ from society to society. Truth commissions have to be translated into the specific reality of a country in order to be successful.

Background on the Grenada Conflict

Grenada and Haiti are the two Caribbean countries to have employed truth commissions. Both also share the distinction of being sites of US invasion in the latter decades of the twentieth century. The presumption of restoring order and democracy was used to "justify" both interventions, though they were conducted in radically different circumstances. Nonetheless, since its independence from British rule in 1974, Grenada has been a relatively stable society. The exception is, however, the revolutionary period from 1979 to October 1983 under the New JEWEL Movement (NJM), the revolutionary party that wrested power from Eric Gairy. Internal divisions fractured the NJM irreparably, and, on 19 October 1983, Prime Minister Maurice Bishop and members of his cabinet were murdered. This resulted in martial law and general uncertainty and confusion. The apparent external unity of the revolution had internally warped into disagreements about leadership structure; the initial agreement at the party's congress regarding joint leadership (between Bishop and Bernard Coard) and Bishop's subsequent withdrawal of this agreement were a trigger mechanism for the ruling party crisis. In his first interview since being freed in September 2009, Coard contended that "the seeds of what happened on October 19, 1983 were sown by some of the things we [NJM] did when we took power. People look on it as a 'split', but there were many, many dimensions involved."[7] Whatever the dimensions involved, the revolution appeared to have imploded. Derrick James, a secretary to Prime Minister Bishop on the Workers' Committee, candidly stated, "you have to understand that because the revolution was born out of weapons it should not be surprising that the revolution closed with this type of violence because it had ruled by the guns".[8] More than thirty years later, that era continues to be among the most contested and controversial not only in Grenada but across the wider Caribbean.

On 25 October 1983, the United States and several Caribbean countries invaded Grenada. There are as many versions of what happened as there are Grenadians. The reality, however, is that, while Grenada has maintained democratic stability since then, there is an internal insecurity about what happened in October 1983 or even since 1979. The question is even more lingering largely because the Grenada 17, Coard and others who were held responsible for the deaths of the prime minister and his cabinet, are still there. Their presence is a constant reminder that October 1983 happened. Their subsequent release in September 2009 has not led to the closure of this chapter of Grenadian history, even if the last page appears to be turning.[9] The return of the remaining seven of the incarcerated Grenada 17 to freedom in September 2009 points to the need for closure but has certainly brought the past once again into scrutiny. While there has been no threat to Grenada's democracy, the sense of resolution is absent. Grenadians still speak passionately, though guardedly, about the events of 1983.

The need to "move on from the past" is always enunciated as the best way to deal with it. But what does it mean to move on from the past? Does it mean to collectively forget that these events occurred? How does a society or an individual do that? In 2001, the Keith Mitchell government decided that a truth commission would be a meaningful way to excavate and exhume the truth of 1983.

Origins and Composition of the TRCG

The TRCG was founded on 4 September 2001, in accordance with the Commission of Inquiry Act. The commission was appointed by the governor general, Sir Daniel Williams, and was directed "to inquire into and record certain political events which occurred in Grenada during the period 1 January 1976 to 31 December 1991".[10] While the mandate period is more than fifteen years, most of the commission's work, and certainly Grenadians' preoccupation, was with October 1983. The TRCG subdivided its mandate into three historical periods: 1976–79 (the pre-revolutionary years), 1979–83 (the revolutionary experiment), and 1983–91 (the demise of the revolution, the assassination of Prime Minister Bishop and the conviction of the Grenada 17).

The commission comprised three commissioners and one secretary. The Honourable Donald A.B. Trotman of Guyana, a former judge of the Supreme Court of Guyana, was chosen as chairman. The other two commissioners were Bishop Sehon Goodridge of Barbados, Anglican bishop of the Windward Islands, and Father Mark Haynes of Grenada, a Roman Catholic priest. Claudette Joseph, an attorney-at-law practising in Grenada, was appointed as secretary.

Terms of Reference

The commission stated that, within six months from the date of the first sitting of the commission, or within a reasonable period thereafter, it would inquire into and record certain political events which occurred in Grenada during the period of 1 January 1976 to 31 December 1991, with particular reference to the following:

1. the events leading up to and including those of 13 March 1979 and repercussions;
2. the shooting deaths of various persons at Plains, Mount Rose and Mount Rich in St Patrick's during the period 13 March [1979] to 31 December 1983;
3. the events leading up to and including those of 19 October 1983 with particular reference to the following:
    i.   the root causes of the general political turmoil in the State;
    ii.   the circumstances surrounding the deaths of various persons, including the Prime Minister and other Ministers of Government, on what was then referred to as Fort Rupert (now Fort George);
    iii. to ascertain as far as it is practicable the identities and total number of persons who lost their lives on Fort Rupert;
    iv.   the disposal of the bodies of those who lost their lives on Fort Rupert;

4. foreign intervention by armed forces of the United States and the Caribbean in October 1983.[11]

Based on the above time frame and the additional time to write up the report, it was to have been submitted in 2004; however, it was not handed in until 2006. The full title of the report was *The Truth and Reconciliation Commission Grenada Report, Redeeming the Past: A Time for Healing*. When we consider the terms of reference of the TRCG, as spelled out in the Commission of Inquiry Act, we begin to realize that the prospects for a successful truth commission were dim. To paraphrase, the specific terms of reference stipulate that the findings of the TRCG are not binding or judgmental in a judicial sense; it is a legal structure that is to act as a fact-finding and advisory body. The TRCG set itself four objectives:[12]

1. To seek to uncover the truth behind certain political events which occurred in Grenada during the specified period;
2. To provide the nation with a comprehensive understanding of those political events as referred to above, so that any mistakes made in the past may not be repeated;
3. To provide the nation with an opportunity to become genuinely reconciled and be permanently healed [later, the TRCG calls for permanent healing and permanent reconciliation];
4. Generally to make such recommendations as the Commission may find fit in all the circumstances.

As I will discuss later, these objectives (especially the second and third), with the exception of the last, were too impractical and imprecise to be tenable. Ultimately, while Grenadians had long sought after the truth (or truths) of what happened in their political past, I argue that justice would always be the logical extension and telos of the exercise. In other words, truth, while multifaceted and complex, is never the end of any "national excavation project"; justice is. The reality that confronted Grenada and Grenadians, however, is that there is no one vision of justice. I will return to this discussion towards the end of the chapter.

Report of the TRCG

The report is divided into three volumes: volume 1 contains the substance of the commission's work. Volume 2 primarily consists of appendices which include memoranda, other relevant documents and newspaper clippings. Volume 3 is made up of letters received and sent by the TRCG during the inquiry. Speaking on the TRCG, the then attorney general Raymond Anthony argued that the "process is meant to clear the soul and get to the truth". However, this process is fraught with complications, especially when one is speaking of a nation and not just an individual. The TRCG, while having an extensive time mandate, was always mindful that it was not just "certain political events" but, in particular, one series of political events that had left a deep chasm in Grenadian society. And while Grenada has not been prone to violence, the silence surrounding October 1983 dominates everything about its politics. The need to know the truth, however painful it is, can always justify the excavation project called a truth commission.

In an uncharacteristic confession, in the first few pages of the report, the TRCG admits that "during its extensive and intensive inquiry, it unearthed little more knowledge of the truth of facts and events pertaining to the periods under inquiry than that which was already known".[13] If the inquiry was so intensive and extensive, why did it not yield anything new? What is the relevance or necessity of a truth commission if it fails to unearth new details? The question that lingers on in Grenada, nine years since the report has been submitted, is what was the value of the exhumation of that painful chapter in Grenada's history? The TRCG seemed to have an excuse for all its failures to expand the reach of reconciliation and to prompt justice and closure for Grenada's divided history. The introduction continues to outline factors that pre-empted the search for truth. It lists five factors:[14]

1. *The wide gap in time between the occurrence of these events, causing memories to fade; some people who knew some of the truth had died or emigrated; and evidence was lost or suppressed.*

Memories, like other traditions, are passed down. The South African TRC, from which the TRCG draws its lineage and inspiration, investigated happenings from 1960 to 1994, a period of thirty-four years, compared to the fifteen years being looked at by the TRCG. While it is understandable that events might not be in the forefront of the society's collective memory, it is unlikely that everyone who knows of these dramatic events is dead, amnesiac or an émigré.

2. Fear of victimization and repercussions for those who know the truth.

No one can discount these fears. However, this is not unique to the Grenadian commission, and all truth commissions have to face this difficulty. There will always be those who want the truth to remain hidden. However, when a truth commission confesses that some truths may have been left unearthed because of possible repercussions, it has not dug deep enough. Drawing from the lessons of more than forty truth commissions, we see that the most successful ones (under more political duress than the TRCG encountered) have had to be brave and defiant in the face of political difficulty. Victimization and re-traumatization are very possible side effects of unearthing the past. However, the South African TRC's mantra – "truth hurts but silence kills" – captures the need to look beyond the pain of truth.

3. Lack of provisions for amnesty, witness protection or undertakings not to prosecute persons who gave evidence or information.

The barter of amnesty for truth has only been negotiated by the South African TRC. This Faustian bargain was not entirely successful in South Africa because, while it increased the volume of "truth", there is no way of measuring the quality of truth that emerged from this quid pro quo exercise. Amnesty provisions are neither necessary nor sufficient conditions for successful truth commissions, so its absence is not convincing enough to account for the failure of the TRCG.

4. Many persons have long purged these sordid portions of history from their minds and do not want to revisit them.

The TRCG argues that many Grenadians have decided to use amnesia to erase these painful and traumatic experiences, and therefore it would be difficult to ask them to reopen old wounds. While the individual revisiting of a painful past may not be desired, a collective reopening is necessary if the past is to be adequately dealt with. As a remembrance project, a truth commission always has to confront the reality that any exhumation, physical or otherwise, will mean confronting painful memories. In the end, it is the TRCG that helps to write this part of Grenada's history into amnesia.

5. Many persons who have already reconciled their differences and grievances do not want to hear anything more about what has already been done.

If one has truly reconciled differences rather than suppressed them, then speaking of the past will not be as disruptive as the TRCG contends. Reconciliation is not an act or a moment; it is a process. Certainly, it often starts with an act or a moment. We know we are on our way to reconciliation when X or Y does or does not occur. This obsession with reconciliation as a "first order" principle and primary goal of a truth commission weakens the necessary focus on justice, which I believe has to precede reconciliation.

The report then moves on to claim that

> whereas in the past much of the known truth was used or intended to be used for condemnation and blame-casting, the truth uncovered or examined by the TRC is to be examined and applied for the purpose of encouraging a process of healing and reconciliation. It is a call to all concerned to see the truth in a new light and for a new and different purpose – a positive purpose.[15]
>
> [It further states that] truth and reconciliation are concomitant virtues. They must coexist to reinforce each other. We wish to urge, of course, that reconciliation would take place more easily when the truth is told and known, and when, however painful, it is accepted by both the aggrieved and their perceived wrongdoers.[16]

No mention is made here or elsewhere of how truth leads to reconciliation, and no examination of their relationship with or impact on justice is discussed. The most egregious misstep of the TRCG and many South African–inspired truth commissions is that they confuse the enunciation of a desire for reconciliation with the actual achievement of it. The achievement of truth, reconciliation and, I would argue, even more so, justice, cannot be a haphazard exercise. Justice is the link that holds together truth and the possibility for reconciliation. Without justice, reconciliation is a fool's paradise. It is clear that justice is not one thing or one outcome; what is rendered may not satisfy the demands of all who clamour for justice, but the obligation is to satisfy some, to remediate some injustice. Yet, the argument is often made that, at a minimum, a truth commission, by virtue of unearthing and probing the past, has rendered justice. That approach to justice is like calling four correctly positioned tyres a car; it meets the basic requirements but would not satisfy the standards of functionality or reliability. As I will discuss later, both truth and reconciliation are risks, and if they are not properly calculated, they may end up too risky for fragile societies that have taken a "vow of silence" on their past.

I have examined the South African TRC process in detail in other research,[17] and the question has to be asked as to whether a truth commission was the best way to achieve reconciliation in Grenada, given the TRCG's overabundance of self-doubt and pre-emption of failure. A truth commission has to be a carefully considered project. It must not be embarked on because it seems to be in vogue or because other societies have used and benefited from it.[18] Each society has unique characteristics that can never be adapted.

Motivations are very important in understanding truth commissions. Why they are created will partly explain their likelihood of success. What is clear is that the TRCG was not the result of any serious and sustained call by civil society to find out the truth of the period 1976–91. It was created by the Keith Mitchell government under the guise of putting the past to rest. While this was commendable, there was no popular support or understanding of the mechanism of a truth commission. The Grenada 17, who were imprisoned for the assassination of Prime Minister Bishop and others, at times thought it was created to free them; at other times, they argued it was initiated to frustrate their efforts at appeal by giving them a false hope of being freed.[19]

The TRCG's field work yielded scepticism regarding the necessity or true purpose of the truth commission. In a very candid submission, "Field Officers' Report February 10, 2002–April 10, 2002",[20] sentiments "on the ground" regarding the commission are expressed. According to the field officer, "it was evident from the onset that the nation was not ready for a T&R commission. Widespread ignorance of the purpose, intent and mission of the Commission manifested itself in the various communities with which the Field Officers interacted."[21] It is clear that proper consultation, sensitization or public education was not done before deciding to establish a truth commission. Additionally, the truth commission was greeted as a political instrument or ploy by many of the persons interviewed by the field officers: "An unprecedented level of suspicion and distrust was directed towards the current political administration. Almost without exception, every individual approached prefaced his/her verbal response to the Commission's work by asking 'Is this political?' . . . in some cases, defending the integrity of the Commission and staff who were perceived as 'doing Keith Mitchell's dirty work'."[22]

The field officers' recommendations are very important. However, there is no evidence that the TRCG (even after the nearly two-year delay of its report) ever seriously addressed them as a precursor to strengthening the commission. In any event, the recommendations are actions that should have preceded the establishment of the commission. I will examine three of them. The first states, "[T]here is an URGENT need for public education to reduce current anti-TRC climate."[23] No truth commission can be considered effective without adequate public education regarding its work and mission. The profound sense of ignorance surrounding the TRCG's work critically impacted its effectiveness in many ways, both as a remembrance project and as a practical approach to resolving the past. As recently as June 2013, the author asked several Grenadians in Grenada if they had ever heard of the TRCG and the report it submitted in 2006. A few indicated that they had heard mention of a truth commission; however, none of them had seen a copy of the report or ever heard what had happened regarding its recommendations. In an interview with former TRCG commissioner Father Mark Haynes, he lamented the fact that there was no official launch of the report and public sensitization, and, once the report was submitted, that was the end of it.[24]

The field officers' report also argued that "the media should be more forceful in the process of public education".[25] While this was certainly part of the problem, the TRCG was obligated to promote its own work and to use the media to educate the public. It was not the principal responsibility of the media to promote the TRCG; that is the explicit job of the commission itself. The South African TRC highlighted its own work, and the media did assist in increasing publicity. However, the marked difference is that the TRC conducted its work in a public manner that incorporated the entire country. The

TRCG, in comparison, operated like a "secret commission". Even in the nine years since its report was submitted, many Grenadians have neither seen nor heard of the report and its contents.

Finally, the field officers recommended that "the life of the TRC should be extended by approximately six months as the nation is now beginning to get a feel of and to appreciate the TRC".[26] The TRCG certainly accepted this recommendation. It is, however, not clear if the extension reduced the anti-TRCG climate, increased public knowledge of the TRCG mandate or incorporated Grenadians into its work.

The Grenada 17

This is the most intriguing section of the TRCG's report; not for the details it reveals, but rather because of what one would have expected to see discussed. The lingering question is why the commission would not have seen it as mandatory to have an audience with the Grenada 17, especially seeing that, as I would argue, its biggest prospect for fostering or sowing the seeds of national reconciliation lay in hearing from these imprisoned leaders as to their roles and responsibilities in the events leading up to the assassination of Maurice Bishop and his colleagues. There can be no excuse given by the TRCG that "efforts were made to contact the Grenada 17 but it did not materialize".[27] That is tantamount to saying that the TRCG decided that reconciliation could occur without the single most important part of the exercise. Documents included in the report's appendices indicate some measure of responsibility and contrition expressed by some of the Grenada 17 regarding their role in the happenings of the period 1979 to 1983, but especially of October 1983.[28] What is not obvious is what specific wrongs the apologies are expected to extirpate.

The TRCG was, however, quick to point out that the "Grenada 17 are not on trial before the Commission and in any event the Commission cannot lawfully presume, nor does it want to embark upon any excursion into, the deeds or misdeeds of the Grenada 17".[29] This appears almost dismissive of the necessity of interviewing the Grenada 17 to get to the truth of what happened in October 1983. It sounds as if the TRCG is saying that we can write up and document the truth without this piece of the puzzle. I do not believe there is, was or can be any supplementary source that can replace hearing from the principal participants in the assassination of Bishop and members of his cabinet.

Many Grenadians also misunderstood the work and purpose of the TRCG. They thought that the commission was created as a mechanism by the then prime minister Keith Mitchell as a means to eventually freeing the Grenada 17, who seemed like relics in a modern era; one never knows how to treat or regard them. (A concurrent Amnesty International report, aptly titled "The Grenada 17: The Last of the Cold War Prisoners?",[30] addresses the issue of their continued incarceration.) The TRCG was forced to clarify the matter by insisting that the seventeen's freedom was not its raison d'être. In the years since all of the Grenada 17 have been freed, nothing much has occurred that has concretely indicated that Grenadians have come to terms with what happened in their country between 1979 and 1983. We eagerly await the stories of the men and woman who were incarcerated for the assassination of Bishop and his colleagues. A forum held in June 2013 with several of the Grenada 17 was a step in the direction of national reconciliation and justice. It is, to my knowledge, the first time there was any such forum, at which they spoke candidly about the past, the mistakes made, their reintegration into Grenadian society and the need to have their stories told.[31] At this forum, they spoke candidly and sadly about the context within which the party and the revolution imploded; their burden of responsibility; and the reality that, thirty years later, wounds had still not healed. There was the general sentiment that a larger forum needed to be created for them to publicly share their roles, experiences and lessons. Bernard Coard wrote a paper in 1997 titled "Reflections and Apologies", in which he stated that the Grenada 17 apologized unreservedly to the Grenadian people. An apology is certainly a first step towards reconciliation; the second has to be taking responsibility. Coard contends that "we took moral and political responsibility for what happened . . . we take collective responsibility for everything that went wrong".[32] The third step of the process to reconciliation has to be what concrete measures have been taken to indicate that one is truly sorry – because saying sorry is never enough.[33] Several commentators have criticized Coard and the others for their willingness to take political and moral responsibility without taking personal or criminal responsibility.

This question of responsibility is one that faces all transitional societies. In East Germany, South Africa and many other societies, the conundrum of responsibility is inescapable. The issue becomes whether one can take responsibility without being subject to sanctions, punishment and reparation/compensation claims. Further, should not a hierarchy of responsibility be created? In the Grenadian case, is there equal responsibility among the Grenada 17 for the occurrences of October 1983? Who should be punished or found liable – those who gave the orders, those who communicated them or those who executed them? The question of responsibility always brings along what I call the "big fish–small fish dilemma" – that is, should the architects or guardians of the commandment (to kill, to imprison and so on) be punished or only the enforcer and executor of the order? As Elster[34] posited, it is often difficult to separate levels and types of responsibility when atrocities and human rights violations occur. The idea of architects/guardians versus enforcers/executors is one I developed from examining the South African TRC process. Jon Elster examines this complexity in *Closing the Books: Transitional Justice in Comparative Perspective*. Are we, as citizens of a society who stand (or stood) by while these atrocities occurred, absolved of blame? The cadre of the complicit is quite large.

Obstacles to Healing and Reconciliation in Grenada

The TRCG provides measured reflection on some of the obstacles to reconciliation. One noticeable omission is that the TRCG itself may have hindered the prospects for reconciliation because it failed to provide us with a meaningful understanding of how to foster reconciliation, anywhere in its report or research. Some of the general obstacles to reconciliation, in the TRCG's estimation, are:

1. the execution of Maurice Bishop and others being an inexcusable, almost unforgivable act, according to many;
2. the acrimony surrounding the few days of the "reign of terror" by the Revolutionary Military Council;
3. the division over the significance of particular events, such as 13 March 1979, the day of the overthrow of Eric Gairy's regime by Bishop; 19 October 1983, the day of the assassination of Bishop and others; and

25 October 1983, the day of the invasion; and the issue of monuments, memorials and dates for public holidays;

4. the issue of renaming the airport – if it ought to be called Maurice Bishop International Airport;

5. the lack of concrete evidence about the disposal of the remains of Bishop and others who were executed on 19 October 1983;

6. the continued incarceration of the Grenada 17;

7. the lack of personal and political responsibility; and

8. the unwillingness to reconcile.[35]

The obstacles to reconciliation are definitely significant and would, if left unaddressed, frustrate any prospects. It is rather unfortunate that the report of the TRCG fails to provide Grenadians with a blueprint or even a guide as to how these obstacles can be mitigated. Rather, the TRCG puts on a pageantry that rivals that of the South African TRC's parading of forgiveness and reconciliation. The marked difference is that the South African TRC went to great lengths to explain the categories of truth, reconciliation and justice. While the TRCG report is correct in arguing that "people must freely reconcile, they must want to do it",[36] reconciliation is not an automatic consequence of a desire to "move on from the past". Reconciliation is more complex and complicated than the TRCG's examination reveals. This trite characterization of the frustrating and reversible process to reconciliation is disappointing. Even in South Africa, for all the admiration its TRC and transition have received, reconciliation is still a far way off. Rajeev Bhargava argues that what South Africa has really achieved in the present is a "minimally decent society".[37] He argues that a minimally decent society is one governed by minimally moral rules, which are moral not because they promote a comprehensive conception of the good life but because they prevent excessive wrongdoing or evil. The TRCG has gone beyond that to proclaim permanent healing and reconciliation without articulating what they mean, how these are to be achieved and in what time frame.

The report introduces the term "true reconciliation", which "means, among other things, accepting the fact that I have done something wrong, or something wrong has been done to me, and having the heart and desire not just to say sorry, but also to show in tangible ways the genuineness of my words and the acceptance of forgiveness".[38] In the TRCG's words, "there are some preconditions for true reconciliation: an admission of guilt; sorrow on the part of the wrongdoers; and forgiveness on the part of the victims".[39] (I would imagine this extends to the family of the dead and to the entire society.)

It is rather curious that the commission would say that "Grenada has a history to remember but also a history to forget."[40] What are the rules of remembering and forgetting in such a conundrum? How does a truth commission, or anyone, for that matter, determine what must be remembered or memorialized and what is to be forgotten? Ugor Ungor[41] calls this process of writing into amnesia one of "organizing oblivion" – a systematic approach to pushing the past into not just the realm of fiction but that of abeyance. The reality of writing into amnesia is that it removes from memory, and to remove from memory is to remove from history.

Recommendations and Projections of the TRCG[42]

The report continues in a consistently vague fashion. The recommendations are a melange of confessions of failure, missteps and some sincere reflections on how to move beyond the past. For instance:

1. "The TRC recommends that those in authority should persistently make serious public appeals, and take some seriously relevant actions nationally, regionally, and internationally to ascertain from those who may know where those remains [of Bishop and the others] are, or what may have happened to them."[43]

    The still-missing remains of Bishop and his cabinet colleagues continue to frustrate efforts to literally and figuratively put the past to rest. After all their research and fact-finding, the commission was still inconclusive as to the location of the remains. The irony is that, without conclusive forensic evidence, many Grenadians have drawn their own conclusions as to the whereabouts of the victims as well as those responsible for their deaths.

2. "The TRC recommends that the relevant authorities should revisit this question of compensation and find some ways of compensating those persons who suffered serious physical disability; those who have lost arms and limbs. . . . Monetary compensation may not be possible for everyone, but some form of reparation could be considered in order to give satisfac-

tion to restore some form of dignity to the victims and families of those who suffered or died."

While it is commendable to advise the relevant authorities to revisit the issue of compensation and reparation, this should have been a part of the TRCG's own work and recommendations. If the TRCG was indeed made "in the image and likeness of the South African TRC", then a reparations committee should have been carefully planned and established. In other words, they should have developed or outlined a programme of reparations and compensation rather than passing it on to some other body to do so. A significant dimension of and, in some cases, a model of justice is compensation. The past cannot be undone; in a literal sense, nothing can compensate for the suffering caused. However, that is not to say that nothing should be done to provide compensation for victims and survivors. Most of the persons who appeared before or wrote to the TRCG requested reparation or compensation for lost wages, false imprisonment, improper termination of employment, detention and abuse by the state. There is no reconciliation until people can feel that the injustices they or others suffered are properly regarded or compensated. The South African TRC awarded, in 2003, approximately thirty thousand rand (9.8 rand equals US$1) to nearly twenty thousand victims (defined by the TRC) as a one-time reparation payment. This did not and could not capture all the victims of apartheid and racism, but it was demonstrative of the fact that unless victims feel justice has been served, talk about reconciliation is just that – talk. It is in light of this fact that the TRCG's reneging on a critical dimension of truth commissions and the justice they desire to achieve – compensation – is so obviously a grand failure.

3. "The TRC recommends, however, that as far as possible and in the interest of national healing and reconciliation, arrangements could be made and proper security structures be put in place so that the families of those who died at Fort Rupert can confront the Grenada 17 in an open hearing."

I find this to be one of the most curious recommendations. It is the TRCG that should have provided that forum and not some other body. These "confrontations" fall under the ambit of truth commissions. Public hearings or testimonies of perpetrators and the victims or their families are to be provided by truth commissions. The TRCG's attempt to pass on its responsibilities means that it ultimately failed to discover the truths surrounding the events under its mandate. One very positive development was the meeting of Bishop's daughter, Nadia Bishop, with some of the incarcerated seventeen between 2007 and 2008. While it was not an open hearing and she did not stand as representative of other victims or their families, it was a meaningful demonstration of the need to let acrimony recede and healing and reconciliation take its place.

Nadia Bishop articulated the reality that there were no unaffected parties to the divisions in Grenadian politics and society. She said: "I want forgiveness to be a full circle. I am not only offering forgiveness, but I ask for forgiveness as well."[44] Bishop sought proxy forgiveness on behalf of her father and was extending forgiveness on his and her family's behalf. And this is what has to take place in Grenada on a national scale for the nation to really move on from the past. The TRCG did not initiate this meeting, but credit has to be given to it for introducing the need for truth and reconciliation. The June 2013 forum at which members of the Grenada 17 spoke has to be expanded to a national dialogue about how, once and for all, Grenadians can stop speaking in hushed tones about the revolution, its demise and aftermath. The national conversation is the only way reconciliation is possible; the truth that the TRCG expressed has not satisfied the need for closure.

4. "The Commission recommends that those who have in any way participated in or contributed to such atrocities, crimes, violence, etc [and] who are still alive should come forward and take responsibility for their wrong doings, and apologize to the victims and families of victims. Furthermore, the present political authority could apologize to the nation for the sins, mistakes and wrong doings of the political authorities of the past."

    What incentives would wrongdoers have to voluntarily appear to confess their participation in past atrocities? What are the legal ramifications for such actions? So the issue of responsibility and culpability in such a small society may extend wider than one would imagine.

5. "[T]hat this Report be made available for public information."[45]

    This recommendation is almost tragic, given that all indicators suggest that a proper public education campaign was not embarked on. Drawing on the experiences of previous truth commissions, especially the South African TRC, no truth commission can be successful unless its work is made public and accessible. It is a necessary condition that a successful truth commission has to be public in a dual sense: in terms of the manner in which its work is conducted and also in terms of how available and accessible its final report is.

5. "[T]hat the curriculum of school includes matters contained in the report, so that students of today and for generations to come may have knowledge of that aspect of their history."

This is a powerful recommendation. However, it lacks sincerity, primarily because the TRC fails to adequately provide an "official truth" for its mandate period in such a way that incorporates all elements of Grenada's past. What will be included in this curriculum? Will this inclusion only increase the likelihood of "ancestral bitterness" towards the descendants of persons who were critical actors? Teaching the past in deeply divided societies is always a difficult endeavour because it involves two risks. The first is that it may sanitize the past in such a way that the atrocities and pain it caused are glossed over. The other possibility is that it may evoke painful memories of the past and actually result in a reversion into acrimony and bitterness. Teaching the past, or more appropriately, learning from the past, requires a balancing between remembering and "selective" amnesia. In one of my interviews, I asked Wendy Grenade, a political scientist, about the power of amnesia and she replied, "There is a lot of amnesia. There are even the ghosts of the revolution, and one of the ghosts that haunts Grenada is the ghost of induced amnesia. This ghost of induced amnesia haunts our school system. Our school curriculum is silent on the past, especially the revolution. Yet, ironically, the scars of the revolution are ever-present in the Grenadian soul. The ghost is also within our culture."[46]

6. "That before setting up any Commission of Inquiry – such as that of the TRC – the relevant authority should ensure greater public awareness of such Commission, and all appropriate machinery be put in place so that the commission's work may be effectively done."

Without a doubt, this final recommendation provides great justification for calling the TRCG a weak truth commission. While this lack of awareness may not exclusively be the TRCG's fault, truth commissions generally are self-promoters. So the task of making the public aware of its works should be left up to the truth commission. It is inexcusable to contend that some other constituted body should have promoted the TRCG. This confession of failure is particularly dramatic because it appears that only a few persons have ever seen the actual truth commission report. It is important to create a truth commission as a means of digging through the past and providing a way to move on from it. It is, however, more important to do it well so that it is not only that the excavation takes place, but also the foundations for moving on are laid. Additionally, this recommendation points to the reality that the TRCG suffered from an identity crisis. It was a truth commission that was created by commission of inquiry legislation that emulated the South African truth commission, but, in the end, calls itself a commission of inquiry.[47]

Assessing the TRCG

The truth of the TRCG can be succinctly stated: you cannot expect to achieve reconciliation in a society with such deep divisions if the truth has not been properly unearthed and engaged. The lack of participation by the Grenada 17 is no small part of the ultimate failure of the TRCG. No final closure can be brought to that chapter of Grenadian history if this group is not heard from. While another truth commission is not necessary in Grenada, some other forum has to be created for there to be a national dialogue, one that is initiated by civil society, especially religious organizations.

The missing remains of Prime Minister Bishop and members of his cabinet are indicative of the "absent presence" of that tragic October day in 1983. Until these remains are located and receive a proper burial, this chapter of Grenada's history will always be contentious. While the culpability of Bernard Coard and the other members of the NJM/Revolutionary Military Council is not in doubt, the obvious omission is their own confession that they bear some personal responsibility in the happenings of October 1983 that culminated in the assassination of Bishop and the others and in the US-led invasion. One critic of the TRCG asks, "How come he [Coard] wants us to believe after 23 years that he is such an innocent man and only wants to take 'moral responsibility' and not 'criminal responsibility' for the heinous killings?"[48] The wounds are still fresh in Grenada, largely because not only did the TRCG reveal no new truths, but also many who really know what happened are keeping their silence.[49] It is my belief that the TRCG ends up as a signatory to this "vow of silence" by not properly handling the risks both of truth-telling and of reconciliation. Its clandestine ethos made it difficult for Grenadians to really measure its significance, given the reality that many did not know of its existence and few have seen or heard of its report. Nonetheless, there were some encouraging signs from the TRCG.

Successes

The TRCG's ultimate value is in what it symbolized – that societies deeply divided or traumatized by their past do not have to take a vow of silence. While truth commissions have been utilized across the world, each is as unique as the society from which it emerges. Symbols are important because they stand for something even deeper. For one, the TRCG opened up a deeply contentious past to public scrutiny. Even under the most auspicious of circumstances, a truth commission's desire to excavate and reopen the past in order to properly inter it is painfully difficult. The TRCG was established to confront this part of Grenada's history that has been unmistakably hard to avoid. It gave victims and survivors a critical opportunity to share their private stories in such a way that these stories could become part of the story of the TRCG. What made the South African TRC so admirable is the fact that the truth and reconciliation process, including the public hearings, provided an audience for and gave voice to many persons and their stories of pain, anger, loss, redemption, justice and so on. Truth commission hearings are fundamentally important to national catharsis; they are forums in which a plethora of often contradictory emotions and sentiments are aired. However, for a society so deeply wounded as Grenada, symbols are not enough.

Failures of the TRCG

It failed to add any new truths about the most contested episodes of Grenada's post-independent history. Beyond the report having "a commendable aura of humanity and sobriety, it offers precious little of any substantial truths by which to guide the prospect for reconciliation. . . . The TRC has given us no clearer picture of the past, no better understanding of the nature of events. . . it is the silence people keeping."[50]

The commission failed to interview the Grenada 17. They claimed that they made several attempts to do so. The letter of the Grenada 17 to the TRC on 5 February 2000 suggests that they welcomed the idea of a truth commission. One argument to explain this is that they felt it was established to free them. As the letter highlighted, "We wish to state that we stand willing and ready to fully participate in the proceedings of a Truth and Reconciliation Commission, including giving full evidence and facing cross-examination once it is clear that truth and reconciliation are indeed the objectives of the exercise."[51] While the commission was established in 2001, it appears no contact was made with the seventeen until February 2002, when indirect communication was achieved through the commissioner of corrections. Furthermore, the TRCG used the standard vocabulary of truth commissions without telling us how they conceptualized these terms. As we are all well aware, forgiveness, reconciliation, truth, justice, compensation (especially the former three) are not self-explanatory. The TRCG's emphasis on reconciliation is belied by its lack of contextualization and conceptualization. Reconciliation is not willed into being; it has to be worked on, if it is to be achieved. Reconciliation is deeply indeterminate; according to Rajeev Bhargava: "Societies cannot bring about reconciliation through the process of collective acknowledgement of grave wrongs-cum-forgiveness, because reconciliation requires a profound change in people – a deep and drawn-out process . . . such reconciliation, if and when it happens, can only be a fortunate by-product of the whole TRC process, and not intentionally brought about by it."[52]

The truth commission proceedings and hearings were not well publicized and the final report not very accessible. Any successful truth commission must conduct its work publicly and publicize its findings. The publicity/ accessibility criterion is fundamental to the very raison d'être of a truth commission. The very existence of a truth commission is so that the truth is not only unearthed but that it is done publicly and publicized. If only a few know of its work, then it is an exercise in discovering private truths; but public truths must be held up to the scrutiny of the public. The truth aspect of truth commissions must not be taken for granted. The South African experience revealed the complexity of truth and its many dimensions.[53]

Judging the Past and Making the Future?

Ultimately, the TRCG was a monumental undertaking, especially given the deafening silence surrounding what took place in the fairly recent past. Once the past was exhumed, the TRCG was faced with the Sisyphean task of moving Grenada to closure, having reopened old, unhealed wounds. Arguably, it had very limited success primarily because the TRCG was prematurely born and never gathered enough strength or support institutionally and publicly. One may wonder as to the necessity of a truth commission for a state such as Grenada that, since the October 1983 invasion, had remained a stable democracy. The TRCG was important in making the conscious effort to not let the past just fade into obscurity without attempting to heal the lingering wounds which it had left on Grenadian society. Nonetheless, a truth commission is not guaranteed success simply because it is better for societies to remember than to forget. As a remembrance project, the TRCG invoked the past but failed to properly address some of the lingering issues it unearthed. The lack of a concrete framework for justice for those who were victims of human rights violations and for the families of those killed in October 1983, and for the country at large, weakened the effectiveness of the TRCG. This is not to say that justice has a singular definition. Justice in Grenada as it relates to the post-revolution period and onwards will certainly mean different things to different people. In my conversations with a few Grenadians, they expressed the view that those who were imprisoned have served time and so that was some justice done. Others felt that they did not do enough time and should have paid with their lives in the same way Bishop and his cabinet members did. Others still felt that excavating the past was justice enough. Many others argued that some kind of compensation to victims and their families was necessary. However, no one that I spoke with expressed the view that it would be justice to leave things as they were. Justice in deeply wounded societies has to be a delicate balancing act between leaving the wound to heal and reopening it and placing some salve on it. In other words, justice may not follow an "either/or" pattern in a society like Grenada. It is not mandatory that we either leave the past and let bygones be bygones or reopen it and deal with the consequences. In the end, justice demands that we both open the past to scrutiny and remedy as well as commit other aspects of the past to oblivion.

The South African experience was painfully unique, and any effort to mirror or copy it would ultimately fail. To get to reconciliation, one always has to traverse the road of truth and justice. The South African TRC, as commendable as its work has been, took the "shortcut" by thinking reconciliation would happen once truth was exhumed. Truth commissions, for all their potential for success, are often burdened with the weight of expectations that they will "become all things to all men". They are always expected to do more than is ever possible. The TRCG needed to pattern the South African TRC's accessibility and "publicness". Instead, it copied their weakness by making reconciliation the twin of truth.

The concluding statement of the report provides added justification for the need to properly understand and examine truth commission experiments across the world. The report proclaims, "[S]everal countries around the world have recognized the need to establish appropriate agencies to stimulate a process of healing and reconciliation in their troubled fragmented societies . . . but it is to the unique credit of the Grenadian people that the TRC of Grenada is the first and so far only of its kind in the Caribbean."[54] There is absolutely no excuse for this kind of misplaced claim of victory, given that the Haitian Truth Commission preceded Grenada's by more than five years in its founding and ten years in its report and that both are members of the Caribbean Community. South Africa provided the world with the first "real-time" truth commission – many of its hearings were broadcast around the world. It has inspired many countries to confront their pasts in order to lay the foundations of justice for the present and for posterity. While many applaud the "miracle" of the South African transition to democracy, the reality is that there was pain behind every story of hope and redemption. It has been nine years since the submission of the TRCG's report, and many Grenadians have never heard of its work or the report. While its genesis is commendable, the reality is that Grenada requires more than symbols to honestly deal with its political past. Even in the wake of the TRCG, Grenada as a society continues to struggle with properly locating the revolutionary period 1979–83 in its historical memory. The Keith Mitchell–led New National Party returned to power in February

2013, and it is worth looking to see whether that unfinished programme of national reconciliation will re-emerge from his government, since they were the ones who created the TRCG in 1999 when they found themselves in the position of winning all the contested seats in the general elections (as they have done again). It cannot be that the prospects for reconciliation and justice in Grenada ended in 2006 with the submission of the TRCG's report. The TRCG had the potential to really engage Grenadians, but, given its premature birth, its poor diet and poor eyesight, it ended up cataloguing the pain of the past without providing a basis on which Grenada could move forward. In the end, the report has helped to write the past into amnesia, and Grenadians and others involved are still "keeping silence", almost as a solemn vow.

Acknowledgements

The author wishes to thank the Office of Planning and Institutional Research and the Principal's Office at the University of the West Indies, Mona, for the Mona Research Fellowship which provided funding. The Faculty of Social Sciences at the University of the West Indies, Mona, initially supported the research.

NOTES

1.   Rwandan official quoted in Priscilla Hayner, *Unspeakable Truths: Transitional Justice and the Challenge of Truth Commissions* (New York: Routledge, 2010), 1. Hayner is the leading authority on truth commissions.

2.   The TRC was established based on the Promotion of National Unity and Reconciliation Act, No. 34, 1995.

3.   Jermaine McCalpin, "Prospects for a Truth Commission", *Sunday Gleaner*, 20 July 2008.

4.   Priscilla Hayner, *Unspeakable Truths: Confronting State Terror and Atrocity* (New York: Routledge, 2001), 2.

5.   Neil Kritz's groundbreaking 1995 edition is one of the first works on the field of transitional justice. See *Transitional Justice: How Emerging Democracies Reckon with Former Regimes* (Washington, DC: USIP Press, 1995).

6.   Hayner, *Unspeakable Truths*, 2.

7.   Bernard Coard, interview by Raoul Pantin, *Sunday Express* (Trinidad), reprinted in the *Jamaica Gleaner*, 20 September 2008.

8.   Derrick James (former Grenadian consul general), interview by the author, Manhattan, New York, 5 October 2012.

9.   It is interesting to note that Coard and the other fourteen political prisoners tied to the October 1983 episode were released under the minister responsible for the advisory committee on the Prerogative of Mercy, which was signed into law by Prime Minister Tillman Thomas, who was once a political prisoner of the People's Revolutionary Government under Bishop and Coard.

10. Truth Commission 2001, Chapter 58, Commission of Inquiry Act, Laws of the Government of Grenada.

11. Terms of Reference, in *Truth and Reconciliation Commission Grenada: Report on Certain Political Events which Occurred in Grenada, 1976–1991* (St George's: TRCG, 2006), 1:2.6. Hereafter referred to as *TRCG Report*. Volume 1 available online at http://www.thegrenadarevolutiononline.com/trccontents.html.

12. Ibid.

13. Introduction to *TRCG Report*, 1:12.

14. Ibid., 1:13–15.

15. Ibid.

16. Ibid.

17. Jermaine McCalpin, "For the Sake of Justice: Restorative Justice, Forgiveness and Reconciliation in Deeply Divided Societies", *Proteus: A Journal of Ideas* 24, no. 2 (2007): 35–42; Jermaine McCalpin, *No Truth, No Trust: Democracy, Governance and the Prospects for Truth-Telling Mechanisms in Jamaica* (Kingston: United Nations Development Program and the Jamaica Council of Churches, 2011), 10–75. http://www.jm.undp.org/content/dam/jamaica/docs/researchpublications/governance/TruthTellingMechanismsInJamaica.pdf.

18. McCalpin, "Prospects".

19. The multiple letters and documents sent to the TRCG by the Grenada 17 at various times challenged the legality or necessity of the truth commission. They claimed that it was established to "stall on the issue of allowing our case to go before the Privy Council". See a document authored by them entitled "The Grenada 17 and the TRC: Yet Another 'Broken Promise' in the Making", appendix 10 of *TRCG Report*, 2:2.

20. Field Officers' Report, appendix O of *TRCG Report*, 2:2.

21. Ibid.

22. Ibid.

23. Ibid.; emphasis in the original report.

24. Father Mark Haynes, interview by the author, Grand Anse, Grenada, 5 June 2013.

25. Field Officers' Report, 2:2.

26. Ibid.

27. Ibid., 1:20.

28. Out of the eight documents that represent the Grenada 17's position on many issues, two are explicit in taking some kind of responsibility for the tragedy – "Reflections and Apologies to All Detainees of the PRG from Some Former Leaders of the NJM" and "Apology to the Families of the Victims of the October 1983 Crisis, and to the Grenadian People by Bernard Coard", appendix 2 of *TRCG Report*, 2:1–5.

29. *TRCG Report*, 1:39.

30. Amnesty International, October 2003, https://www.amnesty.org/en/documents/amr32/001/2003/en/ (accessed 12 May 2015).

31. A specially created forum, with selected guests, organized by the Caribbean Studies Association was held on 5 June 2013. Six members of the Grenada 17 attended, spoke and responded to questions. They included: Chalky Ventour, Liam James, Christopher Stroude, Kamau McBarnette, Selwyn Strachan and Ewart Layne. Another member arrived later but offered no public comments.

32. Raoul Pantin, "Elated Coard Speaks on Freedom", *Sunday Express* (Trinidad), reprinted in *Jamaica Gleaner*, 20 September 2009.

33. Roy L. Brooks, *When Sorry Isn't Enough: The Controversy Over Apologies and Reparations for Human Injustice* (New York: New York University Press, 1999), 2–6.

34. Jon Elster, *Closing the Books: Transitional Justice in Comparative Perspective* (New York: Cambridge University Press, 2004), 22–24.

35. This list is further developed in *TRCG Report*, 1:41–55.

36. Ibid., 1:44–45.

37. Rajeev Bhargava, "The Moral Justification of Truth Commissions", in *Looking Back, Reaching Forward: Reflections on the Truth and Reconciliation Commission of South Africa*, ed. Charles Villa-Vicencio and Wilhelm Verwoerd (Cape Town: University of Cape Town Press, 2000), 65–67.

38. *TRCG Report*, 1:43.

39. Ibid., 1:44–45.

40. Ibid.

41. Ugur Ungor, "Organizing Oblivion in the Aftermath of Mass Violence", *Armenian Weekly*, 26 April 2008.

42. *TRCG Report*, 1:46–51.

43. Ibid.

44. "Nadia Bishop Speaks on Forgiveness and Reconciliation", *Grenada Today*, Internet edition, 12 January 2008, http://www.belgrafix.com/gtoday/2008news/Jan /Jan12/Nadia-Bishop-speaks-of-forgiveness-and-reconciliation.htm (accessed 12 May 2015).

45. *TRCG Report*, 1:94.

46. Wendy Grenade, interview by the author via teleconference, 25 October 2012.

47. Freeman attempts to distinguish commissions of inquiry from truth commissions but argues that they share certain key features: typically vested with subpoena powers, powers to conduct public and in-camera hearings and discretion to determine responsibility and make recommendations in a report. However, it appears that the key determination is the legislation that establishes either body. He argues that, in the cases of South Africa and Sierra Leone, their truth commissions emerged out of new legislation rather than existing commission of inquiry acts. Mark Freeman, *Truth Commissions and Procedural Fairness* (New York: Cambridge University Press, 2006), 22–24.

48. "Nothing Really Startling", editorial, *Grenada Today*, 8 July 2006, http://www .belgrafix.com/gtoday/2006news/Jul/Jul08/Nothing-really-startling.htm (accessed 12 May 2015).

49. David Scott, "Preface: The Silence People Keeping", *Small Axe: A Journal of Criticism* 11, no. 22, special issue on Grenada (2007): v–ix.

50. Scott, "Preface", vi.

51. *TRCG Report*, 2:1, appendix 1.

52. Bhargava, "Moral Justification", 65–67.

53. The South African TRC Report addresses four types of truth: factual and forensic truth, personal and narrative truth, social truth, and healing and restorative truth.

54. *TRCG Report*, 1:97.

11.

Party Politics and Governance in Grenada

An Analysis of the New National Party (1984–2012)

WENDY C. GRENADE

ABSTRACT

This chapter examines party politics and governance in post-revolutionary Grenada, using the case of the New National Party. The central question is: what does the evolution of the New National Party suggests about governance and democracy in post-invasion Grenada? The chapter traces four phases of the New National Party since its formation in 1984 – (1) externally imposed marriage of convenience; (2) intra-party conflict and splintering; (3) rebranding, consolidation and dominance; and (4) short-lived electoral defeat – and contends that Grenada has transitioned to formal democracy and the New National Party is a significant actor. Yet, despite this transition, Grenada has not become the showcase for democracy that the United States said it would, in 1984.

Introduction

This chapter analyses politics in post-revolutionary Grenada, tracing the New National Party (NNP) from its formation in 1984 to the present. A comprehensive analysis of the NNP requires an understanding of Grenada's modern political history that weaves together three interrelated periods: decolonization and early independence, the 1979–83 revolution and the post-revolutionary era. Each period cannot be analysed in isolation from the others.

First, decolonization involved, inter alia: the rise of trade unions and protest movements, which later became mass-based political parties; the emergence of new indigenous leadership; and the rise of nationalism. In the 1950s, Eric Gairy emerged as a charismatic leader who challenged the colonial establishment and fought for justice and social benefits for the majority black working class. While Gairy initially championed the plight of the poor and led Grenada to independence, he failed to transform the postcolonial state. Instead, a new authoritarian state emerged. Gairy's excesses were then challenged by the radical New JEWEL Movement (NJM), and a clash of forces led to the 1979 revolution.

In the second period, the Grenada Revolution was beset by the interplay of external and internal forces. Revolutionaries had to simultaneously defend the revolution in the context of the Cold War and Grenada's close proximity to the United States, forge a non-capitalist path to development and transform the postcolonial authoritarian state they overthrew. While the revolutionaries built on the social gains Gairy initiated in the 1950s and successfully managed the Grenadian economy, they strengthened the authoritarian state they inherited, through arbitrary detentions and militarization. The internal contradictions of the revolution, combined with pressure from the United States, led to its implosion in 1983. Subsequently, the United States invaded Grenada with the intention of turning that country into a showcase for democracy and free-market enterprise.

Within this broad context, this chapter concentrates on the third period. In 1984, there was an urgency to construct a new political and economic order in Grenada. The US and Caribbean governments that participated in the invasion successfully pursued an amalgamation of the centrist parties to form the NNP, "whose leaders on their own efforts had been unable to coalesce".[1] The objective of this chapter is to explore the twists and turns of the NNP from 1984 to 2013, given its electoral dominance and impact on Grenada's post-invasion political landscape.

Data for this study came from three sources: direct and participant observations, elite interviews and document analysis. The sample of elites is quite purposive, chosen to reflect a balance between ideological, political and sociocultural perspectives. Some interviewees consented to have their identity revealed; others requested anonymity. The study also examines a wide range of archival sources that include official documents from the Government of Grenada, reports from international organizations, political party manifestos, press releases and newspaper articles.

The remainder of the chapter is arranged as follows. The next two sections examine two distinct periods of the NNP: Blaize-led NNP (1984–89) and Mitchell-led NNP (1995–2013). These periods are further categorized into four phases: (1) externally imposed marriage of convenience; (2) intra-party conflict and splintering; (3) rebranding, consolidation and dominance; and (4) short-lived electoral defeat. The subsequent section discusses the implications for governance and democracy in Grenada. The final section presents conclusions and lessons.

Blaize-Led New National Party (1984–1989)

Externally Imposed Marriage of Convenience (1984)

In 1984, the re-establishment of the multi-party system ushered in the rebirth of traditional political parties, the formation of new ones and political mobilization. The Grenada United Labour Party (GULP) and the Grenada National Party (GNP) were resuscitated under the leadership of pre-revolutionary political opponents: Eric Gairy and Herbert Blaize. Four new parties were also formed under the leadership of new political figures. It was felt that Gairy's GULP was far from moribund and that, if the centrist parties did not get together, Gairy would win a number of seats and even hold the balance of power if the results of the election were inconclusive.[2]

Therefore, in 1984, the United States and three Caribbean prime ministers (James Mitchell of St Vincent and the Grenadines, John Compton of St Lucia and Tom Adams of Barbados) orchestrated the Union Island Accord, which created the NNP – a merger of the GNP led by Blaize, the National Democratic Party led by George Brizan, and the Grenada Democratic Movement led by Francis Alexis. In his autobiography, James Mitchell recounted that they had to resolve three issues: creating an anti-Gairy alliance, deciding its leadership and giving a name to the party. He reported that Blaize's former experience as a chief minister and his age, inter alia, allowed the younger men to concede him the leadership. Importantly, Blaize's emergence as leader was sanctioned by the United States. According to Mitchell, the creation of a single party proved more bothersome, and they settled for NNP and agreed on the metaphoric symbol of a "house" as a hopeful image for Grenada's reconstruction.[3] Blaize's emergence as political leader was supported by 61.9 per cent of respondents, while Brizan and Alexis received 35 and 0.6 per cent support, respectively.[4]

In Grenada, alliance formation is not new. As political leader of the conservative GNP, Blaize had entered into an anti-Gairy alliance with the NJM to contest the 1976 general election, but, as one interviewee reported, "there was deep mistrust among Blaize's conservative faction and the radical NJM comrades".[5] In 1984, the NNP represented an anti-Gairy alliance of strange bedfellows, who held opposing world views. Whereas Blaize was an ultra-right conservative, Brizan and Alexis were left of centre.

The NNP won the 1984 general election. Given the distortions of the first-past-the-post electoral system, it amassed 58.4 per cent of the popular vote but gained fourteen of the fifteen parliamentary seats. Gairy's GULP won 36.1 per cent and one seat. Voter turnout was relatively high, at over 85 per cent, which can be explained by the fact that this was the first election since 1976 and, as one interviewee pointed out, "many Grenadians believed that the NNP would be a political party to lead the political transformation, which was necessary for the country at that time".[6] Another interviewee supported that view and saw the NNP "as a worthwhile attempt at unity at a time when Grenada needed healing and reconciliation".[7] Other interviewees held varying views. One interviewee was ambivalent about the NNP and saw it "as a reincarnation of the GNP and worried that its interest would be to solidify the power of the merchant and propertied classes".[8] For another, "it was created by the Americans and was not representative of the people".[9] It was also viewed as "a shot gun marriage arranged by the invading and occupying powers".[10]

The NNP's ability to function as a cohesive team was threatened from the start. In his autobiography, Mitchell reported on a conversation he had with Blaize in the immediate aftermath of the 1984 general election. Mitchell recounted his dismay that Blaize had kept key portfolios such as finance, foreign affairs, security, trade and leadership of the parliament. Mitchell recalled advising Blaize that he was chairman of a hurried coalition, he was old and he had to give the young people elected around him some work to do or there would be trouble. Mitchell indicated that Blaize refused to change. "Right away . . . I knew his Government would fall apart. In despair I called John Compton . . . 'All is lost,' I told him. He called Grenada, to no avail. We went to the opening of their parliament for a few hours. I could not face with any ease the honourable men whom I had persuaded to join this unworkable Alliance."[11]

Intra-Party Conflict and Splintering (1987 and 1989)

The NNP fractured within the first three years, as a result of several factors. First, the Cold War was ending, and Grenada was no longer of strategic interest to the United States. Second, there were ideological differences and distrust within the NNP. Brizan confirmed that "Prime Minister Blaize favoured the GNP faction of the NNP and this was a major source of contention in the party".[12]

Another source of conflict was the neo-liberal economic policies that were pursued by Blaize. In 1986, the government implemented a fiscal reform programme to boost private sector growth.[13] By 1987, the Government of Grenada had embarked on a public sector reform programme designed to reduce the public service by 25 per cent or by 1,800 positions. The programme was subsequently suspended by the government, and only 450 to 500 positions were eliminated. According to the World Bank,[14] the programme was counterproductive because qualified and highly mobile civil servants left the service on account of the low salaries paid. Brizan[15] recalled that he and Alexis strongly disagreed with the government's decision to sack workers. He recounted that, as an economist, he advised Blaize that retrenchment was wrong and suggested a different approach. Brizan explained that Blaize did not listen and went ahead with the retrenchment programme. It was at this point that Brizan, Alexis and Tillman Thomas left the NNP and formed the National Democratic Congress.

In 1989, the NNP splintered further when Keith Mitchell defeated Blaize at the NNP's annual convention and became the party's political leader, while Blaize remained as prime minister.[16] Mitchell regularly criticized Blaize for making major decisions without consulting his cabinet.[17] Blaize's final year was marked by the threat of a no-confidence motion and defections from his government, which reduced the number of NNP members of parliament to nine against an opposition of six. With growing friction within the party, Blaize prorogued the parliament, withdrew from the NNP and, with a group of members loyal to him, launched the National Party. At the National Party's first convention on 17 December 1989, Blaize was officially elected as the party's political leader, but he died two days later, and his long-standing deputy, Ben Jones, was appointed political leader of the party and prime minister.

Therefore, the NNP, in its original formation, disintegrated within its first term. This marriage of convenience was short-lived. For James Mitchell, "All the hand-wringing around the world about the American invasion of Grenada was over. Blaize's government had crumbled cookie fashion. His country had collected no crumbs from America's victory. . . . Grenada was falling unceremoniously off the strategic map. Invaded and then ignored. President Reagan got his second term."[18]

The splintering of the NNP in 1987 and 1989 led to the creation of two new parties – the National Democratic Congress (NDC) and the National Party – and a reconfigured NNP, under the leadership of Keith Mitchell. Within this multi-party context, none of the parties won a clear majority in the 1990 general election. The NDC received 34.6 per cent of the popular vote and seven seats. It formed the government with support from GULP members of parliament. The Mitchell-led NNP had not yet mobilized a mass base and received 17.5 per cent of the vote and two seats. Voter turnout stood at 68.4 per cent. The decline in voter turnout can surely be attributed to voter disillusionment with politics at that time.

Keith Mitchell–Led NNP (1995–2012)

Rebranding, Party Consolidation and Dominance (1995–2008)

After 1990, Keith Mitchell resuscitated the NNP, and the party then significantly shaped politics in post-invasion Grenada. Five parties contested the 1995 general election. Voter turnout stood at 61.3 per cent, slightly lower than in 1990. Again, given the distortions of the first-past-the-post electoral system, the NNP gained 32.37 per cent of the popular vote but eight seats in the fifteen-seat parliament. The results of the 1995 general election may have symbolized defeat for the ruling NDC rather than victory for the NNP. The NDC was only able to gain one term in office, given a combination of factors: intra-party conflict; sound economic policies that were poorly communicated and, as such, were perceived as austerity measures; and a growing detachment between the government and the Grenadian people. Thus, the NNP gained electoral advantage.

The NNP formed the government and entered into a strategic partnership with Gairy's GULP. Tangible evidence of this was the appointment of Gairy's daughter as high commissioner to Britain. A product of the working class, "Mitchell maintained solid links with the black working class, and as a result, frequently received praise from Gairy who referred to him publicly as 'my son'."[19] Gairy's death in 1997 marked the end of the GULP in its traditional formation, but the NNP was able to win over many of GULP's supporters.

Mitchell astutely balanced neo-liberal principles, technocratic leadership and populism to consolidate a solid mass-based party. One of the high points for the NNP was its unprecedented election victory in January 1999, when it won all fifteen parliamentary seats. Mitchell had been forced to call elections eighteen months early when his party saw its then nine-to-six majority reversed to an eight-to-seven split in favour of the opposition after two of his ministers defected to the opposition over corruption allegations. Foreign minister Fletcher alleged that the prime minister was "corrupt, dictatorial and an egomaniac".[20] However, the opposition parties were ill-prepared for the snap election. It is significant to note that the rate of voter turnout was 56.47 per cent, the lowest in Grenada's post-independence history.

When asked how he was able to govern in a parliamentary democracy, which assumes a parliamentary opposition, Mitchell indicated that his government believed that the most important opposition was really the opposition coming from the people. He pointed out, "We've seen a deepening of the democratic process in the country."[21] Mitchell referred to the social partnership, where the business community, the trade union movement and non-governmental organizations met with government on a regular basis to consult on issues of national concern. He also referred to the weekly face-to-face programmes that encouraged participatory democracy. However, when asked to describe the relationship between the NNP government and civil society, a non-governmental organization representative lamented that the relationship between government and civil society was "lukewarm and grow-ing cold".[22] Ferguson observed that international institutions had tied donor support to good governance and inclusiveness and governments were being forced to create greater space for civil society. She argued that in many cases this was "tokenism".[23]

The 2003 general election was held against a number of visible achieve-ments by the NNP administration. In its seven-and-a-half years in office, the NNP government undertook a number of development projects: a stadium, a new hospital, a ministerial complex, an education complex, a number of new and refurbished schools, an improved road network, enhanced telecommu-nications and a modernized fisheries complex, among other achievements. Yet, the NNP was almost defeated in 2003. It amassed 46.8 per cent of the popular vote and won eight of the fifteen parliamentary seats. The opposition NDC was able to secure 44.1 per cent of the vote and seven parliamentary seats. There was a difference of six votes between them in the decisive Car-riacou constituency.

A major reason for the close contest was the fact that the opposition NDC had regrouped. Key members of the NDC leadership were former members of the disbanded revolution, who were alleged to be sympathizers of the Grenada 17.[24] The new-look NDC leadership represented an alliance of sorts between the members of the erstwhile GNP, remnants of the NJM and other forces. While the 1976 alliance was forged to combat Gairy's excesses, the motivation in 2003 was to remove Keith Mitchell's NNP from power. The NDC's 2003 manifesto focused on "softer issues" such as good governance, transparency, inclusion, accountability, national unity, integrity in public life and insti-tutional development.[25] However, the incumbent NNP leadership was very critical of the former members of the People's Revolutionary Government who had assumed leading and visible roles in the NDC. The 2003 campaign was dubbed "the politics of hatred" by a leading non-governmental organiza-tion representative.[26] The "ghost of the revolution" was said to be haunting Grenadian politics.[27]

The 2003 campaign was also marked by confrontations between the gov-ernment and influential sectors such as the medical and legal professions, as well as some labour unions. A *Caribupdate* article observed that, in the past four years (1999–2003), the NNP had found ways to appear to be at war with significant sections of society. The article noted that this was the result of an arrogance that had grown out of the NNP's amazing 1999 victory. According to *Caribupdate*, "many outsiders who have not followed Grenadian politics closely cannot understand how a government that has done so much and only four and a half years ago won all the seats in a general election, can be fighting for its survival. An administration that had instituted face-to-face, made for television community meetings, missed the point that the best public relations is human relations."[28] Allegations of corruption were also central to the campaign. Perhaps more than any other prime minister in Grenada's recent history, Mitchell was accused of several corruption allegations. However, a commission of inquiry reported subsequently that the allegations could not be substantiated.

In September 2004, Grenada was devastated by Hurricane Ivan.[29] The opposition NDC proposed a government of national unity, but the Mitchell government rejected the proposal, indicating that the cabinet is a special element of the government that must comprise "like-minded" people.[30] The NNP, with assistance from international and regional donors and partners, successfully spearheaded the post-hurricane recovery.[31]

Despite the ravages of Hurricane Ivan and, later, Hurricane Emily (July 2005), there was tangible evidence of "progress" under the NNP government. The International Monetary Fund reported that the Grenadian authorities had made significant progress on fiscal measures, but warned that the budgetary situation remained challenging, as Grenada's public debt level remained high.[32] Based on 2011 country data from the Caribbean Development Bank, Grenada's debt-to-GDP ratio increased from 44.7 to 83.5 per cent for the period 2001–8.

Short-Lived Electoral Defeat (2008–2013)

After thirteen years of electoral dominance, the NNP was defeated on 8 July 2008. The opposition NDC mounted a successful campaign against the NNP on allegations of corruption, authoritarianism and economic mismanagement. Again, based on distortions of the first-past-the-post electoral system, the NNP amassed 47.68 per cent of the popular vote but gained only four of the fifteen parliamentary seats. The NDC secured eleven seats with 50.85

per cent of the popular vote. Voter turnout stood at a relatively high 80.3 per cent. Therefore, despite visible signs of infrastructural development and some minor democratic reforms, Grenadians did not return Mitchell's NNP to power in 2008. The 2008 general election centred around a referendum on Mitchell's high-handedness. As Hinds argues, "[t]he incumbent lost not so much because the NDC presented a better alternative but the better half of the electorate turned on a government that had gotten out of control".[33] Although the NNP was defeated electorally, there was still widespread support for the party and its leader. The electorate was divided almost equally between the NNP and the NDC, with a clear return to the two-party system that was present prior to the 1979 revolution. By 2008, small parties had been virtually eliminated from electoral politics.

However, the NDC's victory was short-lived. On 19 February 2013 the NNP again overwhelmingly won all fifteen parliamentary seats in the general election. As was the case during 1990–95, the NDC was plagued with internal wrangling and splintered into two factions. The source of the contention surrounded divergent world views within the cabinet and the prime minister's inability to manage dissent and build consensus. The prime minister survived a no-confidence motion that was tabled by the opposition NNP in May 2012. However, in September 2012, parliament was prorogued to avert a second no-confidence motion against the prime minister, which was to be tabled by his former foreign affairs minister, who resigned from the cabinet along with three other members. At the party convention in September 2012, the Tillman Thomas faction of the NDC expelled ten senior members from the party (five of whom were members of parliament). Unmanaged intra-party conflict combined with the impact of a chronic global economic recession led to the electoral defeat of the NDC and the return to electoral dominance by the NNP.

Finally, political competition in post-revolutionary Grenada has been dominated by the NNP and NDC. However, neither party has translated formal democracy into a deeper, substantive democracy.

Implications for Governance and Democracy

The case of the NNP has implications for governance and democracy in Grenada, in particular, and the Caribbean, in general. First, political life in post-revolutionary Grenada is consistent with the argument that, since independence, Commonwealth Caribbean states (except Guyana, 1968–92, and Grenada, 1979–83) have sustained a tradition of liberal democracy and have creatively adapted the Westminster system.[34] Grenada has transitioned to formal democracy, and the NNP has played a critical role in the transition. Seven elections were held in Grenada during the period 1984–2013; the military was disbanded; and constitutional rights and civil liberties were restored.

Second, one of the major contradictions of the Caribbean is its ability to sustain formal democracy within a political culture that lacks a genuine democratic ethos. Politics in post-revolutionary Grenada has been "chaotic, confusion-making, very sectarian and very tribal".[35] Several scholars have critiqued the quality of democracy in the Caribbean and have questioned the Westminster model as it has evolved in the region.[36] Benign authoritarianism is a constant feature of Caribbean politics. In countries that had experienced long periods of colonialism, with the attendant institutions of the plantation and slavery, it is difficult to overcome deeply ingrained authoritarian legacies in order to promote and consolidate democracy.[37] This is exacerbated by the first-past-the-post, winner-take-all electoral system.[38] Electoral outcomes in Grenada in 1984, 1999, 2008 and 2013 attest to the distortions of the first-past-the-post electoral system. There is need for electoral reform as part of a larger process of democratic renewal.

Conclusion

In the aftermath of the implosion of the Grenada Revolution and the US invasion, the formation of the NNP was intended to break with the past. The majority of Grenadians and many Caribbean people hoped for a new dawn in Grenada. The United States intended to turn Grenada into a showcase for democracy and free enterprise. Initially, the NNP managed the transition to electoral democracy and disbanded the military, with US support. However, by 1989, given geopolitical realities, Grenada was no longer of strategic interest to the United States, and US financial assistance declined. Additionally, internal wrangling resulted in the collapse of the original NNP, and a multi-party system emerged in Grenada from the late 1980s into the mid-1990s.

Within this context, Keith Mitchell resuscitated a new NNP, which dominated electoral politics in Grenada from 1995 to 2008 and 2013 to the present.

The NNP's evolution brought to the fore some of the challenges that confront small states in the twenty-first century: vulnerability to natural disasters; the tension between sovereignty, policy autonomy and dependency; high public debt; and threats to governance, such as corruption. What has emerged in the last thirty years is a new neo-liberal state. The NNP continued the tradition whereby each permutation of the Grenadian state threw up possibilities and contradictions.

Several lessons emerge from the NNP's case. First, political party formation must be organic, as externally imposed arrangements are not easily sustained. Second, political coalitions among disparate forces are complex, and their sustainability requires political astuteness, common values and trust. Importantly, electoral competition is a basic ingredient for democracy. Yet, it is insufficient, because it cannot guarantee true freedom and societal wellbeing. Finally, the United States was unable to turn Grenada into a showcase for democracy, as it is a challenge for small, postcolonial developing states to simultaneously consolidate democracy and balance economic, social and human development in the context of neo-liberalism.

NOTES

1. P.A.M. Emmanuel, F. Brathwaite and E. Barriteau, *Political Change and Public Opinion in Grenada 1979–1984* (Cave Hill, Barbados: University of the West Indies, 1986), 83–84.

2. S. Ryan, *Winner Takes All: The Westminster Experience in the Caribbean* (St Augustine, Trinidad and Tobago: Institute of Social and Economic Research, 1999), 85.

3. J. Mitchell, *Beyond the Islands: James Mitchell; An Autobiography* (Oxford: Macmillan Education, 2006), 202.

4. Emmanuel, Brathwaite and Barriteau, *Political Change*, 88.

5. Bernard Coard, interview by the author, 10 June 2012.

6. M. Creft, interview by the author, 6 June 2012.

7. J. Purcell, interview by the author, 10 June 2012.

8. I. Baptiste, interview by the author, 8 June 2012.

9. C. Charles, interview by the author, 8 June 2012.

10. Coard, interview.

11. Mitchell, *Beyond the Islands*, 203.

12. G. Brizan, interview by the author, 6 February 2010.

13. M. Williams, "Economic History of Grenada 1960–1990" (paper, Eastern Caribbean Central Bank, Basseterre, August 2003).

14. World Bank Grenada: Updating Economic Note, Report No. 8270-GRD 1990, World Bank, Washington, DC).

15. Brizan, interview.

16. L. Mackoon, "Political Turmoil Shaking Grenada", South–North News Service, *Sun-Sentinel.com*, 19 February 1989, http://articles.sun-sentinel.com/1989-02-19/news/8901100039_1_gairy-grenada-grenadians (accessed 23 June 2012).

17. "The World: Party Oust Grenada Chief", *Los Angeles Times*, 22 January 1989, http://articles.latimes.com/1989-01-22/news/mn-1357_1_centrist-party (accessed 23 June 2012).

18. Mitchell, *Beyond the Islands*, 264.

19. W.M. Will, "From Authoritarianism to Political Democracy in Grenada: Questions for US Policy", *Studies in Comparative International Development* 26, no. 3 (1991): 44.

20. Ryan, *Winner Takes All*, 97.

21. K. Mitchell, interview by David Hinds, Caribnation Television, St George's, Grenada, November 2000.

22. S. Ferguson (executive director of Agency for Rural Development, Grenada), interview by the author, 14 August 2003.

23. Ibid.

24. The "Grenada 17" refers to the seventeen military, political and civilian personnel who were convicted for the murder of Maurice Bishop, some members of his cabinet and others on 19 October 1983. They were all released by September 2009.

25. See Manifesto, National Democratic Congress, St George's, Grenada, 2003 (brochure).

26. S. Ferguson, "The Politics of Hatred", *Grenada Today*, 10 October 2003.

27. A. Johnson, "The Ghost of Maurice Bishop: Grenadian Leader Haunts Election Process 20 Years after His Murder", *Trinidad Express*, posted on GuyanaCaribbeanPolitics.com, October 2003, http://www.guyanacaribbean politics.com/grenada/grenada_elections.html (accessed November 2003).

28. Article posted on Caribupdate.com, 9 November 2003, http://www.caribupdate .com (accessed 15 November 2003).

29. See Organization of Eastern Caribbean States, *Grenada: Macro-Socio-Economic Assessment of the Damages Caused by Hurricane Ivan, 7 September 2004* (St Lucia: OECS, 2004), 1–28.

30. "Opposition Wants Cabinet Roles", BBCCaribbean.com, last updated 24 September 2004, http://www.bbc.co.uk/caribbean/news/story/2004/09/040924_grenada -opposition.shtml (accessed 15 May 2008).

31. See International Monetary Fund (IMF), "Statement by IMF Staff at the Conclusion of the 2007 Article IV Consultation Discussions with Grenada", Press Release No. 07/162, 16 July 2007, http://www.imf.org/external/np/sec/pr/2007/pr07162 .htm (accessed 10 May 2008).

32. Ibid.

33. D. Hinds, "A Referendum on Highhanded [*sic*] Rule: The 2008 Grenadian Election in Perspective", GuyanaCaribbeanPolitics.com, 11 September 2008, http://www.guyanacaribbeanpolitics.com/commentary/hinds_091108.html, 1 (accessed 10 November 2012).

34. J. Domínguez, R. Pastor and D. Worrell, eds., *Democracy in the Caribbean* (Baltimore: Johns Hopkins Press, 1993); E. Huber, "The Future of Democracy in the Caribbean", in Domínguez, Pastor and Worrell, *Democracy in the Caribbean*, 74–95; and A. Payne, "Westminster Adapted: The Political Order of the Commonwealth Caribbean", in Domínguez, Pastor and Worrell, *Democracy in the Caribbean*, 57–73.

35. G. Brizan, interview by the author, 24 July 2004.

36. D.C. Peters, *The Democratic System in the Eastern Caribbean* (New York: Greenwood, 1992); J. Haynes, *Democracy and Civil Society in the Third World* (Cambridge: Polity Press, 1997); T. Munroe, *Renewing Democracy into the Millennium* (Kingston: University of the West Indies Press, 1999); Ryan, *Winner Takes All*; S. Ryan, "Reforming Caribbean Democracy in the Era of Globalization", in *Caribbean Survival and the Global Challenge*, ed. R. Ramsaran (Boulder: Lynne Rienner), 237–63; D. Hinds, "Beyond Formal Democracy: The Discourse on Democracy and Governance in the Anglophone Caribbean", *Commonwealth and Comparative Politics* 46, no. 3 (2008): 388–406.

37. T.J. D'Agostino, "Caribbean Politics", in *Understanding the Contemporary Caribbean*, ed. R. Hillman and T.J. D'Agostino (Kingston: Ian Randle, 2003), 85–127.

38. See C. Barrow-Giles and T. Joseph, *General Elections and Voting in the English-Speaking Caribbean 1992–2005* (Kingston: Ian Randle, 2006).

12.

Coming in from the Cold
Grenada and Cuba since 1983

JOHN WALTON COTMAN

ABSTRACT

The Grenada Revolution's radical course was stamped by the bold turn to Cuba in April 1979. Cuban commitment to Maurice Bishop's regime was crucial to its consolidation. In 1983, counter-revolution and invasion ruptured Grenada-Cuba ties and damaged Havana's relations with CARICOM states. Since the demise of the Cold War, Havana's survival strategy has prioritized regional integration and cooperation in the Americas. In the anglophone Caribbean, Grenada has been at the centre of this rapprochement since 1993. Despite Washington's disapproval, Grenada champions expanded ties with socialist Cuba. The rekindled alliance brings tangible mutual benefits and validates the strategy of South-South cooperation advocated by Maurice Bishop's People's Revolutionary Government and the New Jewel Movement.

Introduction: Grenada Charts a New Course: 1979–1983

The Grenada Revolution established the second workers' and farmers' government[1] in the Americas – twenty years after the first, led by Fidel Castro, and four months before the third, created by Nicaragua's Sandinista National Liberation Front. For Havana, "Nicaragua and Grenada, with their victorious revolutions, have reaffirmed the validity of the road to power opened by

Cuba".[2] This assessment placed consolidation of the Grenadian prime minister Maurice Bishop's fledgling regime atop Cuba's foreign-policy agenda.

The New Jewel Movement (NJM)–led People's Revolutionary Government (PRG) advocated a "basic needs" strategy, seeking to enhance well-being and human capabilities as foundations for socially equitable economic growth. The PRG prioritized literacy, technical/scientific education, health and living conditions and sought a long-term transition to socialism. Public policy emphasized: (1) rural reforms to aid small farmers, increasing food self-sufficiency and raising agricultural productivity; (2) industrialization via agro-industry; (3) a state-of-the-art airport to jump-start tourism; (4) state-led full employment with a broad social safety net; (5) broadening and deepening international alliances in the Caribbean, Global South, Europe and Soviet bloc, especially with Cuba; (6) participatory politics based on elected local assemblies and voluntary grass-roots institutions of workers, farmers, women and youth; (7) a political alliance led by workers and peasants and aligned with Grenada's small capitalist class; and (8) professionalizing and enlarging the military, while creating a citizens' militia.[3]

South-South cooperation[4] highlighted Cuba's commitment and capacity to provide multifaceted aid programmes. For example, from 1979 to 1983, Cuban civilian aid totalled US$45.6 million, US$30.3 million of which went to the Point Salines International Airport Project, equating to 42 per cent of its cost. Havana's aid amounted to 64 per cent of civilian grants, 20 per cent of military grants and 36 per cent of foreign aid, in total, that the PRG received. Havana's aid was not free. Grenada had financial obligations. The PRG spent over US$17 million to support Cuba's 636-person airport construction team in Grenada. The net value of Cuban aid was US$31.56 million or US$354 per capita.[5]

Havana's swift provision of civilian aid, diplomatic support and military assistance were crucial to the revolution's consolidation. The scope of human development projects was inconceivable without Castro's commitment. Grenada was the showcase for Cuban internationalism in the Caribbean.

Agonies of Autumn 1983

The NJM's inability to institutionalize direct and representative democracy made it impossible for Bishop and his allies to reverse the consolidation of authoritarian politics within the NJM and PRG. This set the stage for bloody counter-revolution, days of terror and US-led invasion. On 13 October 1983, the Grenada Revolution was overthrown by the deputy prime minister Bernard Coard's coup d'état. Bishop was imprisoned. Supporters mobilized outraged citizens to release him. The second Grenada Revolution of 19 October was short-lived. Around fifteen thousand people defied the putschists and army; several hundred then freed Bishop and occupied St George's fort. When the army tried to retake the fort, NJM founder Vincent Noel was killed in the initial skirmish. PRG ministers Maurice Bishop, Unison Whiteman, Jacqueline Creft, Norris Bain and Fitzroy Bain were then executed by firing squad. Caught by surprise, Havana ordered its 762 civilian and 22 military-aid personnel to its compound at Point Salines, attempted to mobilize world opinion against the coming invasion and showed its open contempt for the coup leaders by refusing to coordinate defences as US forces approached.[6]

Recriminations and Distancing: 1983–1992

American troops invaded on 25 October 1983. Cuban personnel were attacked by surprise, resisting for twenty-seven hours before surrendering. Havana ignored Governor General Paul Scoon's initial order to remove its personnel by 2 November, but, by 9 November, all except one diplomat had been flown home. Castro denounced the invasion as "unjustified, treacherous and criminal".[7]

Cuba's Caribbean ties, already deteriorating, by 1980, with the Bahamas, Barbados and Jamaica, frayed further after the invasion. Belize, Guyana, the Bahamas, and Trinidad and Tobago opposed the invasion, but a combined four-hundred-member military/police force from Jamaica, Barbados, Antigua and Barbuda, Dominica, St Kitts and Nevis, St Lucia, and St Vincent and the Grenadines supported US troops. The rise and fall of the PRG damaged the rapprochement between Havana and CARICOM begun by Jamaica, Trinidad and Tobago, Guyana, and Barbados in 1972.[8]

Grenadian Nicholas Brathwaite took power as Chair of the Interim Advisory Council on 5 December 1983. US combat forces left ten days later. Brathwaite backed expelling all Cubans and ending aid programmes. He closed Grenada's embassy in Havana and suspended – but did not sever – diplomatic

ties. Castro, meanwhile, refused to recognize Grenada's interim regime, arguing it was imposed by Washington. Worldwide, Cuba sought to stymie diplomatic accreditation of the Interim Advisory Council.[9] Postal and telecommunications links continued for two hundred Grenadian youth studying in
Cuba, but, after graduation, they were banned from "sensitive" positions. The
two governments were also at loggerheads over a damaged Cubana aircraft
and Cuban construction equipment. In Grenada, on 20 August 1984, Cuba
filed a suit for detention of property, seeking US$5.2 million for construction
equipment and nearly US$2 million for the plane. Grenada's High Court of
Justice ruled that Cuba must pay a security fee for lawsuit costs.[10]

When elections were held in Grenada in November 1984, Herbert Blaize
of the New National Party was chosen as prime minister. From the outset,
his view of Cuba was extremely negative. For example, he viewed Cuba as a
national security threat, blocked Havana's application to the Caribbean Tourism Organization, denied medical licences to ten Cuban-trained doctors and
blacklisted writings of Castro and "Che" Guevara. However, not all links were
severed. During the Blaize era, Cuba embraced the Maurice Bishop Patriotic Movement. Reaffirming its commitment to Grenada, Havana continued
civilian aid, albeit on a much smaller scale, via the Maurice Bishop Patriotic
Movement. It received up to five scholarships annually to Cuba, free medical
care in Cuba for those who could not be treated locally, and US$11,000 worth
of dental equipment for a medical clinic.[11]

In March 1990, new elections were held and Nicholas Brathwaite of the
centre-left National Democratic Congress (NDC) became prime minister,
and it was in Cuba's interest to recognize the new government. Unless it
did, membership in the Caribbean Tourism Organization and improved
CARICOM relations were impossible. In late 1991, Havana dropped its legal
suit, signalling a willingness to normalize ties. By May 1992, Grenada had
resumed diplomatic ties and ceased opposing Havana's application to the
Caribbean Tourism Organization. Cuba joined the organization that June.
Brathwaite's commitment to Caribbean cooperation in the context of globalization that threatened Grenada, the Soviet Union's collapse, and Cuba's
decision to save socialism via South-South regionalism and tourism led to
warmer relations.[12]

Coming in from the Cold: 1992–1995

With growing marginalization from the European Union, US-Canada-Mexico and Japan-Pacific trade blocs, CARICOM pushed regional solidarity, sending a delegation to Cuba in March 1992. With its traditional alliances in tatters, Havana had, by 1991, reaffirmed the importance of regional integration.[13] As CARICOM opted for constructive engagement, Washington tightened its embargo with the Cuba Democracy Act in October 1992.[14] Cuba's attempts to woo Caribbean policymakers made progress,[15] as evident in voting records of CARICOM states on UN General Assembly resolutions against the embargo. In 1992, only Barbados and Jamaica voted against the embargo. Seven CARICOM nations abstained. Grenada, Dominica, and St Kitts and Nevis did not vote. One year later, CARICOM votes were ten against the embargo with one abstention (Antigua). Grenada did not vote.[16]

In July 1993, Prime Minister Brathwaite criticized Washington's pressure to halt the pending CARICOM-Cuba Joint Commission.[17] The commission was launched in December 1993 and established "a permanent and formal frame-work for the advancement of cooperation" between Cuba and the English-speaking Caribbean.[18] Joint commissions became the principal institution for bilateral cooperation between Cuba and its Caribbean neighbours.[19]

Grenada's minister of tourism at the time was Tillman Thomas. In 1978, he and Maurice Bishop had led the Human Rights and Legal Aid Programme, which provided legal support to people in need. Thomas was jailed (11 July 1981) by Bishop's regime for supporting the *Grenadian Voice* newspaper, which openly criticized the PRG.[20] In March 1995, he reflected: "Cuba contributed substantially to our development, in particular in its contribution to the development of our international airport, which is vital for the country's thriving tourist industry."[21] Thomas reaffirmed the NDC government's constructive engagement policy and supported Cuba's CARICOM membership if it "can meet all the criteria that CARICOM sets down". He added, "We could benefit from the technology of Cuba and Cuba could benefit from our experience in tourism."[22] Havana's diplomatic recognition of Grenada allowed CARICOM to fully embrace constructive engagement via the CARICOM–Cuba Joint Commission.[23] Havana's route to regional integration had to pass through St George's.

Cold Warrior Mitchell Consolidates Cooperation: 1995–1998

The NDC was defeated in 1995 by the conservative New National Party under the leadership of Keith Mitchell. He continued the rapprochement: "With the new world order every country needs to start optimizing its potential and relations with other countries so that they will be able to take maximum advantage of the opportunities internationally."[24] In November 1996, Grenada re-established full diplomatic ties with Havana, despite the tightening United States embargo. St George's then sought support for several human development projects, such as a much-needed hospital, and for scholarships.[25]

In Havana, in April 1997, Mitchell and Fidel Castro signed the Basic Agreement on Economic and Technical Cooperation, with an initial emphasis on health care and sports. Castro agreed to provide more than 150 scholarships over eight years.[26] Mitchell was the first Grenadian prime minister to visit Cuba since Maurice Bishop. Mitchell noted:

> Our traditional friends have indicated that the days of grants, aid and soft loans are gone. . . . We have to be able to strike strategic relationships with those who are willing to help us in charting a course of serious development. I believe in getting all the available help you can in the building of your country, so long as it is done on your terms and does not interfere with your independence and sovereignty. . . . When we look back at the relationship with Cuba, I think most Grenadians of all ages and groups will agree that overall, the role and presence they played in Grenada was positive.[27]

By May 1997, two Cuban medical specialists had arrived in Grenada, and sixty Cuban scholarships had been announced. The local press reported broad approval of constructive engagement. Mitchell was confident the Havana partnership would not damage US–Grenada relations; Grenada's policy reflected a regional consensus.[28] In Mitchell's opinion, the most important gain for Havana was political solidarity at a time of increased US hostility.[29] An indication of this came in October 1997, when Grenada backed a UN resolution against Washington's embargo.[30]

Impacts of the post–Cold War global order were apparent: once an avowed enemy of Cuba and the PRG, Mitchell led the ratcheting up of South-South cooperation. This cooperation attained levels not observed since the PRG years. Fidel Castro, determined to reintegrate Cuba into the Americas, reaffirmed commitments made to his esteemed former ally Maurice Bishop and to the Grenadian people as Grenada again became a showcase for Cuban internationalism – an example of what normalized relations with Havana could bring.[31]

Castro's First Visit to the Spice Isle

In April 1998, the Cuba-Grenada Joint Commission met for the first time to carry out the terms of the Basic Agreement on Economic and Technical Cooperation. In July, former PRG opponents denounced the Cuban president's forthcoming visit. Leader of the opposition Democratic Labour Party, Francis Alexis, argued that Castro was not welcome until Havana's human rights situation improved. Herbert Preudhomme of the Grenada United Labour Party – whose founder, Eric Gairy, was deposed by the revolution – and former PRG political prisoners also protested.[32] Notwithstanding, Mitchell, speaking in July 1998, asked Grenadians to welcome Castro "regardless of [their] political views", adding that he understood and empathized with "those Grenadians who suffered during the People's Revolutionary Government regime. But President Castro or any other foreign leader cannot be held responsible for the negative aspects of the PRG's leadership. It must be understood that Grenadians led and executed the revolution."[33]

Nearly fifteen years after the US invasion – Cuba's greatest foreign-policy defeat in the Caribbean – Fidel Castro landed at Point Salines International Airport in August 1998. Welcomed by the prime minister and hundreds of cheering Grenadians, he received a twenty-one-gun salute. Reflecting on acrimonious relations after the invasion, Cuba's president said, "It is a source of special satisfaction for the Cubans to observe the Grenadian people's willingness to leave behind that chapter of their history and to look with their eyes to the future. We are, and will forever, be brothers."[34]

Castro's visit was historic. It signified that Grenadian and CARICOM support of constructive engagement was unshakeable, despite heightened opposition from Washington. Havana could point to Grenada, for those at home who – under pressures of economic hardship – questioned the wisdom of expending scarce resources on internationalism. Grenada showed that foreign aid opened and cemented new political alliances, built up regional goodwill and laid the basis for mutually beneficial economic and diplomatic ties essential for Cuba's survival. The visit reaffirmed the strategy of basic-needs development and South-South cooperation championed by Maurice Bishop as a viable alternative to neo-liberal orthodoxy.

Mitchell Reaps the Fruits of Rapprochement: 1999–2008

Mitchell was re-elected in January 1999 and led a delegation to Cuba two months later. Castro bestowed the José Martí Order upon the prime minister in recognition of his efforts in promoting constructive engagement.[35] By year's end, embassies were reopened in both capitals for the first time since 1983. The Cuba-Grenada Joint Commission continued to meet annually. Indeed, from 1999 until 2008, Mitchell's turn towards Cuba brought substantial benefits in health, education, disaster relief, agriculture and diplomacy. In 2003, the forty-nine Cuban internationalist volunteers on Grenada included sixteen health specialists and twenty educators.[36] The highlights of the health collaboration were the St George's General Hospital Project and Operation Miracle. In March 1999, Grenada received plans from Cuban engineers to build a US$20 million hospital; Havana would provide consultants and physicians during its first three years of operation.[37] In January 2003, the rehabilitated and enlarged St George's General Hospital opened. The 270-bed facility provides complicated surgical procedures, including open-heart surgery, previously unavailable on the island.[38] Phase II of Grenada's New Hospital Project was announced in 2007. This joint venture between Grenada and Venezuela relied on engineering consultants from Cuba and the Pan American Health Organization.[39]

Operation Miracle, meanwhile, began in 2004 as a bilateral Cuba-Venezuela programme to restore vision free of charge for those who could not take advantage of literacy campaigns due to reversible conditions leading to blindness or visual impairment. Operation Miracle aims to reverse blindness and vision loss for six million people in Latin America and the Caribbean by 2016.[40] The programme came to Grenada in October 2007. One thousand people participated, with all procedures performed in Grenada. Previously, Grenadians travelled to Cuba for eye care. Owing to its popularity, Operation Miracle returned to Grenada in 2008.

Further, educational aid programmes took place on both islands. In 2002, sixteen Cuban teachers arrived to train students in carpentry, horticulture, plumbing and automotive mechanics. Three secondary schools hosted Cuban Spanish teachers.[41] Post-secondary education opportunities for Grenadians in Cuba have been extensive. By 2001, over one hundred and fifty Grenadians were earning professional credentials there, including twenty-seven medical students; one hundred had already completed their studies.[42] Between 1998 and 2008, over three hundred Grenadians had been trained in Cuba, most at university level.[43]

The "Yes I Can" Adult Literacy Programme commenced in Grenada in November 2006. Free to youth and adults, this was the first use of Cuban literacy pedagogy in the English-speaking Caribbean.[44] In 2008, the first 112 graduates received diplomas, and phase two was launched.[45] However, Cuban education aid has not yet reached the levels of 1979–83.

After Hurricane Michelle struck Cuba in November 2001, Grenada donated US$60,000 for medical supplies. In September 2004, Hurricane Ivan devastated Grenada; thirty-nine people were killed, sixty thousand affected, and damage reached US$889 million.[46] Cuba sent electricians to rebuild the electrical grid, while Cuban technicians aided forest biodiversity and conservation, and agriculture irrigation management.[47] The goodwill and political capital engendered by Cuban foreign aid were invaluable for policymakers in both countries. In 2004, Grenadian foreign affairs minister Elvin Nimrod stated:

> Our health sector, our education system, our infrastructuwre and our human resource stock have all been positively affected by Cuban involvement and intervention. . . . The Government of Grenada is most definitely prepared to cooperate and collaborate with the Government of Cuba. . . . Indeed, the success or failure of our countries in our effort to confront the current challenges posed by globalization, will depend to a large extent on the kind of alliances we establish.[48]

Grenada Changes Leadership, Reaffirms Cuba Alliance

The NDC leader Tillman Thomas led his party to victory in the July 2008 elections, and he maintained the close ties with Cuba.[49] In May 2009, Thomas greeted Cuban vice president Esteban Lazo Hernández at Point

Salines International Airport. Lazo brought messages from President Raúl Castro and Fidel Castro commemorating the renaming of Grenada's key tourism facility as the Maurice Bishop International Airport.[50] Thomas – jailed for two years without trial under the PRG – fulfilled the commitment made by the NDC in 2003 to name the airport after the fallen leader.[51] In November 2009, now leader of the opposition, Mitchell reiterated his support for constructive engagement, adding: "What is significant about the contributions made to Grenada by Cuba is that there were never any strings attached."[52] An example of the continuity in the relationship was seen in the Grenada-Cuba Joint Commission, which met in 2010 and 2011.[53]

In relation to diplomacy, table 12.1 illustrates the increasing similarity of foreign-policy preferences in St George's and Havana, as measured by UN General Assembly resolution votes. The US Department of State

Table 12.1. UN General Assembly Voting Coincidence with United States: 2000, 2006–2008 (in percentages)

	Cuba		Grenada		All UN	
Year	Overall	Important	Overall	Important	Overall	Important
2000	21.2	22.2	39.3	50	43	47.9
	(83.6)		(85.7)		(87.6)	
2006	13.3	0	14.6	0	23.6	27.2
	(69.7)		(70.6)		(75.4)	
2007	2.6	0	15.1	66.7	18.3	36
	(66.7)		(71.4)		(73.5)	
2008	12.2	0	17.3	12.5	25.6	27.6
	(73.3)		(76.3)		(78.6)	
2006–2008 average	9.4	0	15.7	26.4	22.5	30.3
	(69.9)		(72.8)		(75.8)	
Net change 2000–2008	−9	−22.2	−22	−37.5	−17.4	−20.3
	(−10.3)		(−9.4)		(−9)	

Note: "Overall" means non-consensus issues, that is, those on which a vote was taken. Figures in parentheses include consensus resolutions. "Important" refers to votes considered important to US policymakers.

Source: J.W. Cotman, "The Havana Consensus: Cuba's Ties with Five CARICOM States", in CARICOM: Policy Options for International Engagement, ed. K. Hall and M. Chuck-A-Sang (Kingston: Ian Randle, 2010), 200–217.

monitors resolutions deemed "important". Between 2006 and 2008, Havana and Washington had polar opposite positions. The coincidence in votes fell from 22 per cent in 2000 to 0 per cent in 2008. For 2006–8, Grenada voted with the US on "important" resolutions 26.4 per cent of the time on average, down significantly from 50 per cent in 2000 and below the average voting coincidence of all UN countries. Although there is no evidence of Grenada and Cuba coordinating votes, the convergence of UN voting patterns is indicative of growing estrangement from Washington's primary foreign-policy goals. A similar trend is also evident for the CARICOM 'Big Four': Jamaica, Trinidad and Tobago, Guyana and Barbados.[54]

Visions of the global good society, as held in both St George's and Havana, still display striking similarities, as measured by UN votes. In 2010, on average, UN members voted with Washington on "important" resolutions 51.1 per cent of the time. For Grenada and Cuba, it was 37.5 and 10 per cent, respectively. The figures for 2011 were 52.9 per cent (all UN members), 33.3 per cent (Grenada) and 0 per cent (Cuba).[55]

Conclusion

Mutually beneficial South-South cooperation between Grenada and Cuba – institutionalized via the joint commission – is a lasting and positive legacy of the Grenada Revolution. In Grenada, the commission was established in July 1979, disbanded in October 1983 and reintroduced in April 1998. Grenada followed the lead of Barbados and Jamaica in re-establishing South-South cooperation with Cuba after the US invasion and the end of the Cold War.

The evolution of Cuban ties to Grenada since 1979 is based on three tenets of Havana's foreign relations: (1) alliance with states based on socialist property relations that respect Cuban sovereignty; (2) alliance with states and movements with an anti-capitalist, pro-socialist trajectory; and (3) promotion of normal diplomatic ties and favourable economic relations with capitalist countries that respect Cuban sovereignty.[56] During the Cold War, tenets (1) and (2) received the highest priority, resulting in Cuba's close alliance with the PRG. With the demise of the PRG, the consequent collapse of the anglophone Caribbean revolutionary Left and the Soviet Union's disintegration, Cuba prioritized tenet (3).

For Grenada, close ties with Cuba provide: (1) a proven ally in regional integration, collective bargaining and South-South cooperation; (2) an essential partner in sustainable human development that provides generous aid programmes and assistance in health, education, natural-disaster preparedness and relief, agriculture and food self-sufficiency, energy conservation, and science and technology; (3) a regional power that respects the sovereignty and importance of microstates; (4) an ally in tourism that supports a sustainable, equitable vacation industry; and (5) an irreplaceable friend committed to the production, promotion and preservation of Caribbean arts and culture. For Cuba, the alliance brings: (1) a proven ally in regional integration, collective bargaining and South-South cooperation; (2) an outspoken advocate of Cuba's full inclusion in hemispheric and international affairs; and (3) a neighbour that respects Cuba's right to pursue socialist development.

Despite disapproval from policymakers in Washington who sought to isolate Havana, Grenada's constructive engagement policy embraces close ties with socialist Cuba. The twenty-first-century alliance between St George's and Havana validates the strategy of South-South cooperation advocated by Maurice Bishop's PRG and NJM over thirty years ago.

NOTES

1. M. Waters, "The Workers' and Farmers' Government: A Popular Revolutionary Dictatorship", *New International* 1, no. 3 (1984): 15–100.
2. M. Piñeiro, "Imperialism and Revolution in Latin America and the Caribbean", *New International* 1, no. 3 (1984): 112.
3. J.W. Cotman, "Grenada 'New Jewel' Revolution (1979–1983)", in *The Encyclopaedia of Political Revolutions*, ed. J. Goldstone (Washington, DC: Congressional Quarterly, 1998), 205–7.
4. H.M. Erisman, *Pursuing Postdependency Politics: South-South Relations in the Caribbean* (Boulder: Lynne Rienner, 1992), 105–31.
5. J.W. Cotman, *The Gorrión Tree: Cuba and the Grenada Revolution* (New York: Peter Lang, 1993), 132–34.
6. Cotman, *Gorrión Tree*, 207–22; Cotman, "Grenada 'New Jewel' Revolution", 205–7; and G. Williams, *US–Grenada Relations: Revolution and Intervention in the Backyard* (New York: Palgrave Macmillan, 2007), 77–99.

7.   Cotman, *Gorrión Tree*, 221.

8.   J.W. Cotman, "Cuba and the CARICOM States: The Last Decade", in *Cuba's Ties to a Changing World*, ed. D.R. Kaplowitz (Boulder: Lynne Rienner, 1993), 145–64; J.W. Cotman, "Caribbean Convergence: Cuba and CARICOM Relations through 1995", *Global Development Studies* 1, no. 3 (1999): 197–222; Williams, *US–Grenada Relations*, 69 and 140–42.

9.   Cotman, "Cuba and the CARICOM States",153.

10.   Ibid., 154.

11.   Ibid., 154–55.

12.   Ibid., 155; and J.W. Cotman, "Caribbean Convergence: Cuba and CARICOM Relations", *Granma International*, 12 October 1994, 15.

13.   Cotman, "Cuba and the CARICOM States", 147.

14.   Cotman, "Caribbean Convergence: Cuba and CARICOM Relations", 197–98.

15.   J.W. Cotman, "Caribbean Convergence: Contemporary Cuba–CARICOM Relations", in *Redefining Cuban Foreign Policy: The Impact of the "Special Period"*, ed. H.M. Erisman and J. Kirk (Gainesville: University Press of Florida, 2006), 121–49.

16.   "UN Passes Cuban Resolution against U.S. Embargo", *Cubainfo*, 4 December 1992, 1–3; "UN Votes to End U.S. Embargo", *Cubainfo*, 5 November 1993, 1; "This Is How the Vote Went", *Granma International*, 6 December 1992, 5; "This Is How the Vote Went", *Granma International*, 6 December 1993, 7; "Stop Press: The World Condemns the Blockade", *Granma International*, 10 November 1993, 1.

17.   *Caribbean Update*, September 1993, 2.

18.   Byron Blake, assistant secretary general, Regional Trade and Economic Integration, CARICOM Secretariat (address delivered at the Sixth Meeting of the CARICOM-Cuba Joint Commission, Santiago de Cuba, 28 February 2000).

19.   J.W. Cotman, "The Havana Consensus: Cuba's Ties with Five CARICOM States", in *CARICOM: Policy Options for International Engagement*, ed. K. Hall and M. Chuck-A-Sang (Kingston: Ian Randle, 2010), 200–217.

20.   Government of Grenada, "Biography: Tillman Joseph Thomas", http://www.gov.gd/biographies/tillman_thomas_bio.html (accessed 28 May 2012).

21.   "Sister Nations of Sun, Sea and Land", *Granma International*, 1 March 1995, 14.

22.   Ibid.

23.   Cotman, "Caribbean Convergence: Contemporary Cuba–CARICOM Relations", 127–28.

24.   M. Bascombe, "Trade, Social Needs Pave Over Cold War Fields as Cuba, Grenada Mend Fences", Agence France-Presse, 5 November 1996; and "Grenada-Politics: Government Embraces Cuba . . . Again", Inter Press Service, 15 October 1996.

25. Bascombe, "Trade, Social Needs"; *Caribbean Update*, February 1997, 13.

26. "Leaders of Cuba, Grenada Come in from the Cold War", Agence France-Presse, 19 April 1997; *Caribbean Update*, June 1997, 7; L. Noel, "Minister Heads Delegation to Cuba", *Caribbean News*, 14 April 2004, 1.

27. L. Rohter, "U.S. Calm over Cuba-Grenada Ties", *New York Times*, 11 May 1997, 6; L. Rohter, "Cool to U.S., Caribbean Hails Castro All the More Warmly", *New York Times*, 2 August 1998, 3.

28. P. Smikle, "Caribbean Politics: Regional Leaders Move Closer to Cuba", Inter Press Service, 30 May 1997; L. Rohter, "Guns Bellow Again on Grenada, Giving Warm Welcome to Castro", *New York Times*, 3 August 1998, 1.

29. Ibid.

30. W. Gibbings, "Caribbean Politics: Closing Ranks with Cuba", Inter Press Service, 17 October 1997.

31. Cotman, "Havana Consensus", 204–10.

32. "Grenada: Opposition Expressed to Planned Visit by Cuba's Castro", Caribbean News Agency, 17 July 1998; R. Simon, "Castro Returns to Scene of Fighting between U.S., Cuban Forces", Associated Press, 24 July 1998.

33. Rohter, "Guns Bellow Again", 1.

34. L. Faul, "Castro Arrives in Grenada amid Cheers", Associated Press, 2 August 1998.

35. "Cuban President Fidel Castro Awards Visiting Grenadian Prime Minister Keith Mitchell with José Martí Order", Radio Havana Cuba, 10 March 1999; "Prime Minister of Grenada Arrives in Cuba", Radio Havana Cuba, 8 March 1999; Inter-Parliamentary Union, "Grenada, Elections Held in 1999", http://www.ipu.org/parline-e/reports/arc/2127_99.htm (accessed 28 May 2012).

36. "Cuba/Grenada: 6th Cuba-Grenada Intergovernmental Joint Commission Concludes", Prensa Latina, 14 May 2003; "Grenadian Foreign Affairs Minister Begins Visit to Cuba", Prensa Latina, 12 May 2003.

37. *Caribbean Update*, April 1999, 11.

38. *Cuba Source/Chronicle on Cuba*, 30 January 2003, 17.

39. K. Mitchell, "Addressing Sustainable Growth, Human Resource Development and Alleviating the High Cost of Living" (Budget Speech 2008, 30 November 2007).

40. C. Gorry, "Sight for Sore Eyes: Cuba's Vision Restoration Program", *MEDICC Review* 10, no. 2 (2008): 49–51.

41. "Brigada de maestros Cubanos colabora con educación en Granada", *Trabajadores*, 3 September 2002.

42. "Cuban Foreign Minister Signs Agreements during Visit to Grenada", Prensa Latina, 18 February 2000; "News Update: Cuba and Grenada Sign Bilateral

Agreements", Radio Havana Cuba, 12 April 2001; "Grenada's Prime Minister Mitchell to Visit Cuba", EFE [Spain], 16 April 2002.

43. "Closing Statement by PM Thomas at XI Session of the Grenada-Cuba Joint Commission", *Spiceislander*, 25 November 2008.

44. Budget speech 2007, Government of Grenada, 15–16.

45. "Cuban Teaching Method Bears Fruit in Grenada", *Caribbean Net News*, 9 April 2008, http://www.islandjournal.net/reportc.htm?section=caribbean-newsnow&story=Cuban-teaching-method-bears-fruit-in-Grenada&id=7080&-catid=32 (accessed 28 May 2012); "Closing Statement", *Spiceislander*.

46. Emergency Events Database, *Country Profile for Natural Disasters: Grenada* (Brussels: Centre for Research on the Epidemiology of Disasters, 2007).

47. "Cubans Help Restore Grenada's Electric System", Agencia de Información Nacional, 21 October 2004; C. Jaquith, "Cuban Volunteers Help Grenada Repair Storm-Damaged Electric Grid", *The Militant*, 30 November 2004; "Cuba Sends a Helping Hand to Power-Deprived Grenada", Prensa Latina, 27 September 2004.

48. Elvin Nimrod, Minister of Foreign Affairs and International Trade, New National Party (statement at opening ceremony of the Seventh Meeting of the Cuba-Grenada Joint Commission, St George's, 13 April 2004), New National Party News.

49. Inter-Parliamentary Union, "Grenada House of Representatives, Last Elections, 2008", http://www.ipu.org/parline-e/reports/2127_A.htm (accessed 10 July 2010).

50. R. Titus, "Grenada Hails Gateway to the Future as It Pays Tribute to the Past", CSMEnetwork.com, 7 June 2009, http://office.spoonlabs.com/dev/jasmina/test/premium-news/news-features/38549-cmcfeature-grenada-politics-country-hails-gateway-to-the-future-as-it-pays-tribute-to-the-past.html (accessed 28 May 2012).

51. Prime Minister, address on the occasion of the renaming of the Point Salines International Airport, 30 May 2009, Government of Grenada/Office of the Prime Minister.

52. "Opposition Leader Dr. the Hon. Keith Mitchell Has Again Expressed His Gratitude to the Government and People of Cuba", New National Party News, 11 September 2009; "Designado embajador en Granada", *Granma*, 8 October 2009; "Dr. Mitchell Meets New Cuban Ambassador", *Spiceislander*, 11 November 2009.

53. "Grenada's Parliament President Meets with Cuba's Ambassador to His Country", Agencia de Informacion Nacional (Havana), 19 February 2011.

54. Cotman, "Havana Consensus", 202.

55. United States Department of State, *Voting Practices in the United Nations, 2010*,

Washington, DC, 31 March 2011; *Voting Practices in the United Nations, 2011,* Washington, DC, 14 May 2012 http://www.state.gov/p/io/rls/rpt/c44269.htm (accessed 29 May 2012); http://www.state.gov/p/io/rls/rpt/2011/practices/index .htm (accessed 29 May 2012).

56.   Cotman, *Gorrión Tree,* 245.

Selected Bibliography

Aberdeen, Michael. *Grenada under the PRG*. Port of Spain: People's Popular Movement, 1983.

Andersen, R. *A Century of Media, A Century of War*. New York: Peter Lang, 2007.

Antrobus, Peggy. "Caribbean Women: Zoning in on Peace". CARICOM Perspective 22 (November–December 1983): 10–11.

Arend, A.C., and R. Beck. *International Law and the Use of Force: Beyond the UN Charter Paradigm*. London: Routledge, 1993.

Barrow-Giles, C., and T. Joseph. *General Elections and Voting in the English-Speaking Caribbean 1992–2005*. Kingston: Ian Randle, 2006.

Bartow, J.R. *Subject to Change: The Lessons of Latin American Women's Testimonio for Truth, Fiction, and Theory*. Chapel Hill: University of North Carolina Press, 2005.

Beck, R. *The Grenada Invasion: Politics, Law and Foreign Policy Decision-Making*. Boulder: Westview, 1993.

———. "Grenada's Echoes in Iraq: International Security and International Law". *The Long Term View* 6 (2004): 73–87.

———. "The 'McNeil Mission' and the Decision to Invade Grenada". *Naval War College Review* 44 (1991): 93–112.

Bennett, Ralph K. "Grenada: Anatomy of a 'GO' Decision". *Reader's Digest*. February 1984.

Bhargava, Rajeev. "The Moral Justification of Truth Commissions". In *Looking Back, Reaching Forward: Reflections on the Truth and Reconciliation Commission of South Africa*, edited by Charles Villa-Vicencio and Wilhelm Verwoerd, 60–67. Cape Town: University of Cape Town Press, 2000.

Bishop, Maurice. "Imperialism Is the Real Problem". In *Selected Speeches, 1979–1981*, edited by Maurice Bishop, 189–200. Havana: Casa de las Americas, 1982.

———. "Maurice Bishop Speaks to U.S. Working People". In *Maurice Bishop Speaks: The Grenada Revolution 1979–83*, edited by Bruce Marcus and Michael Taber, 287–312. New York: Pathfinder, 1983.

————. "Women Step Forward". In *Maurice Bishop Speaks: The Grenada Revolution 1979–1983*, edited by Bruce Marcus and Michael Taber, 32–41. New York: Pathfinder, 1983.

Brooks, Roy L. *When Sorry Isn't Enough: The Controversy Over Apologies and Reparations for Human Injustice*. New York: NYU Press, 1999.

Campbell, Horace. "The Grenadian Revolution and the Challenges for Revolutionary Change in the Caribbean". *Journal of Eastern Caribbean Studies* 35, nos. 3–4 (2010): 32–74.

Campbell, M. "Media Access to United States Military Operations: Grenada and Beyond". Thesis submitted to Kansas State University, School of Journalism and Mass Communications, 1989.

Caribbean Development Bank. Country Reports. Wildey, St. Michael, Barbados. CDB 2011.

Caruth, Cathy. *Unclaimed Experience: Trauma, Narrative and History*. Baltimore: Johns Hopkins University Press, 1996.

Cassell, P.G. "Restrictions on Press Coverage of Military Operations: The Right of Access, Grenada, and 'Off-the-Record' Wars". *Georgetown Law Journal* 73 (1985): 931–73.

CCBH. "Britain and the Grenada Crisis, 1983: Cold War in the Caribbean". Centre for Contemporary British History/LSE IDEAS Witness Seminar. 29 May 2009.

Chesterman, S. *Just War or Just Peace? Humanitarian Intervention and International Law*. Oxford: Oxford University Press, 2001.

Clarridge, D. *A Spy for All Seasons: My Life in the CIA*. With Digby Diehl. New York: Scribner, 1997.

Coard, Phyllis. Memo to NJM Board. 1979. Public Library, St George's, Grenada.

Collins, Merle. *The Governor's Story: The Authorized Biography of Dame Hilda Bynoe*. London: Peepal Tree, 2013.

————. "Grenada: A Political History, 1950–1979". PhD thesis, London School of Economics and Political Science, 1990.

Cooper, S.D. "Press Controls in Wartime: The Legal, Historical, and Institutional Context". *American Communication Journal* 6, no. 4 (2003). http://129.11.76.45/papers/pmt/exhibits/958/cooper.pdf. Accessed 18 November 2012.

Cotman, J.W. "Caribbean Convergence: Contemporary Cuba–CARICOM Relations". In *Redefining Cuban Foreign Policy: The Impact of the "Special Period"*, edited by H.M. Erisman and J. Kirk, 121–49. Gainesville: University Press of Florida, 2006.

————. "Caribbean Convergence: Cuba and CARICOM Relations through 1995". *Global Development Studies* 1, nos. 3–4 (Winter 1998–Spring 1999): 197–222.

————. "Cuba and the CARICOM States: The Last Decade". In *Cuba's Ties to a Changing World*, edited by D.R. Kaplowitz, 145–64. Boulder: Lynne Rienner, 1993.

———. *The Gorrión Tree: Cuba and the Grenada Revolution*. New York: Peter Lang, 1993.

———. "Grenada 'New Jewel' Revolution (1979–1983)". In *The Encyclopaedia of Political Revolutions*, edited by J. Goldstone, 205–7. Washington, DC: Congressional Quarterly, 1998.

———. "The Havana Consensus: Cuba's Ties with Five CARICOM States". In *CARICOM: Policy Options for International Engagement*, edited by K. Hall and M. Chuck-A-Sang, 200–217. Kingston: Ian Randle, 2010.

Creft, Jacqueline. "The Building of Mass Education in Free Grenada". In *Grenada Is Not Alone: Speeches by the PRG at the First International Conference in Solidarity with Grenada*, 49–60. St George's: Fedon, 1982.

D'Agostino, T.J. "Caribbean Politics". In *Understanding the Contemporary Caribbean*, edited by R. Hillman and T.J. D'Agostino, 85–128. Kingston: Ian Randle, 2003.

Danticat, Edwidge. *The Farming of Bones*. New York: Soho Press, 1988.

Davis, Miranda. *Third World Second Sex: Women's Struggles and National Liberation*. London: Zed Books, 1983.

Domínguez, J., R. Pastor, and D. Worrell, eds. *Democracy in the Caribbean*. Baltimore: Johns Hopkins University Press, 1993.

Ecumenical Program for Interamerican Communication and Action (EPICA) Task Force. *Grenada: The Peaceful Revolution*. Washington, DC: EPICA, 1982.

Elster, Jon. *Closing the Books: Transitional Justice in Comparative Perspective*. New York: Cambridge University Press, 2004.

Emergency Events Database. *Country Profile for Natural Disasters: Grenada*. Brussels: Centre for Research on the Epidemiology of Disasters, 2007.

Emmanuel, P.A.M., F. Brathwaite, and E. Barriteau. *Political Change and Public Opinion in Grenada 1979–1984*. Institute of Social and Economic Research (Eastern Caribbean). Cave Hill, Barbados: University of the West Indies, 1996.

Erisman, H.M. *Pursuing Postdependency Politics: South-South Relations in the Caribbean*. Boulder: Lynne Rienner, 1992.

Farber, S. *Cuba since the Revolution of 1959: A Critical Assessment*. Chicago: Haymarket Books, 2011.

Ferguson, J. *Grenada Revolution in Reverse*. London: Latin American Bureau, 1990.

Freedom House. "Grenada Overview". In *Freedom in the World*. Washington, DC: Freedom House, 2012. https://freedomhouse.org/report/freedom-world/2012/grenada#.VVRuav7bLcs. Accessed 13 May 2015.

Gilmore, W. *The Grenada Intervention: Analysis and Documentation*. London: Mansell, 1984.

Gordon, K. *Getting It Write: Winning Caribbean Press Freedom*. Kingston: Ian Randle, 1999.

Gorry, C. "Sight for Sore Eyes: Cuba's Vision Restoration Program". *MEDICC Review* 10, no. 2 (2008): 49–51.

Grenade, W. "Reflections on Politics in Post Revolutionary Grenada (1984–2008)". *Journal of Eastern Caribbean Studies* 35, nos. 3–4 (2010a): 109–40.

———. "Retrospect: A View from Richmond Hill Prison: An Interview with Bernard Coard". *Journal of Eastern Caribbean Studies* 35, no. 3/4 (2010b): 146–82.

Hall, S., C. Critcher, T. Jefferson, J. Clarke, and B. Roberts. *Policing the Crisis*. London: Macmillan, 1978.

Hayner, Priscilla. *Unspeakable Truths: Confronting State Terror and Atrocity*. New York: Routledge, 2001.

———. *Unspeakable Truths: Transitional Justice and the Challenge of Truth Commissions*. New York: Routledge, 2010.

Haynes, J. *Democracy and Civil Society in the Third World*. Cambridge: Polity, 1997.

Hickey, N. "Access Denied". *Columbia Journalism Review* 1, no. 27 (2002). http://cjrarchives.org/issues/2002/1/afghan-hickey.asp.

Hinds, D. "Beyond Formal Democracy: The Discourse on Democracy and Governance in the Anglophone Caribbean". *Commonwealth and Comparative Politics* 46, no. 3 (2008): 388–406.

———. "The Grenada Revolution and the Caribbean Left: The Case of Guyana's Working People's Alliance (WPA)". *Journal of Eastern Caribbean Studies* 35, nos. 3–4 (2010): 75–108.

Huber, E. "The Future of Democracy in the Caribbean". In Domínguez, Pastor, and Worrell, *Democracy in the Caribbean*, 74–95.

Hunt, Nigel. *Memory, War and Trauma*. Cambridge: Cambridge University Press, 2010.

Joseph, Rita. "The Significance of the Grenada Revolution to Women in Grenada". *Bulletin of Eastern Caribbean Affairs* 7, no. 1 (1981): 17.

Joseph, Tennyson. "C.L.R. James' Theoretical Concerns and the Grenada Revolution: Lessons for the Future". *Journal of Eastern Caribbean Studies* 35, no. 3/4 (2010): 4–32.

Joyner, C. "Reflections on the Lawfulness of Invasion". *American Journal of International Law* 78 (1984): 131–44.

Kritz, Neil. *Transitional Justice: How Emerging Democracies Reckon with Former Regimes*. Washington, DC: USIP Press, 1995.

Kurlansky, Mark. *1968: The Year that Rocked the World*. New York: Ballantine Books, 2004.

Le Mon, C. "Unilateral Intervention by Invitation in Civil Wars: The Effective Control Test Tested". *New York University Journal of International Law and Politics* 35 (2003): 741–93.

Lewis, Patsy. "Remembering October 19: Reconstructing a Conversation with a Young Female NJM Candidate Member about Her Recollections of October 19, 1983". *Journal of Eastern Caribbean Studies* 35, no. 3/4 (2010): 141–45.

———. "Revisiting the Grenada Invasion: The OECS' Role, and Its Impact on Regional and International Politics". *Social and Economic Studies* 48, no. 30 (1999): 85–120.

Lewis, Rupert. *Walter Rodney's Intellectual and Political Thought*. Kingston: University of the West Indies Press, 1998.

Lewis, Sybil Farrell, and Dale T. Matthews, eds. "Documents on the Invasion of Grenada". *Caribbean Monthly Bulletin* 17, nos. 11–12, supp. 1 (November–December 1983): 1–84.

Lewis-Meeks, Patsy. "An Analysis of the Legal Justification for the United States' Invasion of Grenada on the Basis of the Invitation from the OECS". MPhil thesis, Cambridge University, 1988.

MacKinnon, Catherine A. "Feminism, Marxism, Method, and the State: An Agenda for Theory". *Signs* 7 (1982): 45–54.

McCalpin, Jermaine O. "For the Sake of Justice: Restorative Justice, Forgiveness and Reconciliation in Deeply Divided Societies". *Proteus: A Journal of Ideas* 24, no. 2 (2007): 35–42.

———. *No Truth, No Trust: Democracy, Governance and the Prospects for Truth-Telling Mechanisms in Jamaica*. Kingston: United Nations Development Program and the Jamaica Council of Churches, 2011.

McNeil, F. *War and Peace in Central America: Reality and Illusion*. New York: Charles Scribner's Sons, 1988.

Midgett, Douglas. *Eastern Caribbean Elections, 1950–1982: Antigua, Dominica, Grenada, St Kitts–Nevis, St Lucia, and St Vincent*. Development Series 13. Iowa City: Center for Development Studies (Institute of Urban and Regional Research, University of Iowa), 1983.

Mitchell, J. *Beyond the Islands: James Mitchell: An Autobiography*. Oxford: Macmillan Education, 2006.

Moore, J. "Grenada and the International Double Standard". *American Journal of International Law* 78 (1984): 145–68.

Munroe, T. *Renewing Democracy into the Millennium*. Kingston: University of the West Indies Press, 1999.

Naparstek, A. "Partners in Conflict: The Media and the Military in Grenada, Panama and the Persian Gulf Wars". BA thesis, Washington University, Saint Louis, Missouri, 15 May 1993. http://www.naparstek.com/thetortoise/thesis/chap2.htm. Accessed 18 November 2012.

National Security Council. "Response to Caribbean Governments' Request to Restore Democracy on Grenada". National Security Decision Directive 110A, 23 October

1983. Declassified 6 February 1996. http://www.fas.org/irp/offdocs/nsdd/nsdd-110a.htm. Accessed 27 August 2012.

National Women's Organization (NWO). Draft Resolution on the Work Programme of the National Women's Organization for 1981. Public Library, St George's, Grenada.

———. Pamphlet. November 1981. Public Library, St George's, Grenada.

———. "The Part the NWO Must Play in the Development of Women in Grenada from 1983 to 1989". 1983. Public Library, St George's, Grenada.

Nolte, G. "Intervention by Invitation". In *Max Planck Encyclopaedia of Public International Law*, 282–88. Heidelberg and Oxford: Max Planck Institute for Comparative Public Law and International Law and Oxford University Press, 2011.

Office of Assistant Secretary of Defense. News Release Reference Number 2030. Washington, DC. 1984.

Olson, K.T. "The Constitutionality of Department of Defense Press Restrictions on Wartime Correspondents Covering the Persian Gulf War". *Drake Law Review* 41 (1992): 511–35.

Payne, A. "Westminster Adapted: The Political Order of the Commonwealth Caribbean". In Domínguez, Pastor, and Worrell, *Democracy in the Caribbean*, 57–73.

Peters, D.C. *The Democratic System in the Eastern Caribbean*. New York: Greenwood, 1992.

Pincus, R.W. "Press Access to Military Operations: Grenada and the Need for a New Analytical Framework". *University of Pennsylvania Law Review* 135, no. 3 (1987): 813–50.

Piñeiro, M. "Imperialism and Revolution in Latin America and the Caribbean". *New International* 1, no. 3 (1984): 103–30.

Porter, Rosemary. "Women and the State: Women's Movements in Grenada and Their Role in the Grenada Revolution 1979–1983". PhD thesis, Temple University, 1986.

Rowbotham, Sheila. *Hidden from History: Rediscovering Women in History from the 17th Century to the Present*. New York: Vintage Books, 1974.

———. *Women in Movement: Feminism and Social Action*. London: Routledge, 1992.

Ryan, S. W "Reforming Caribbean Democracy in the Era of Globalization". In *Caribbean Survival and the Global Challenge*, edited by R. Ramsaran, 237–63. Boulder: Lynne Rienner, 2002.

———. *Winner Takes All: The Westminster Experience in the Caribbean*. St Augustine, Trinidad and Tobago: Institute of Social and Economic Research, 1999.

Schlesinger, P., and H. Tumber. *Reporting Crime: The Media Politics of Criminal Justice*. Oxford: Clarendon, 1994.

Schoenfeld, M. "Military and the Media: Resolving the Conflict". Operations Department report, Naval War College, Newport, 19 June 1992. http://www.dtic.mil/dtic/tr/fulltext/u2/a253110.pdf. Accessed 18 November 2012.

Scoon, Paul. *Survival for Service: My Experiences as Governor General of Grenada*. Oxford: Macmillan Caribbean, 2003.

Scott, David. "Preface: The Silence People Keeping". *Small Axe: A Journal of Criticism* 11, no. 22, special issue on Grenada (2007): v–ix.

Seaga, Edward Phillip George. *The Grenada Intervention: The Inside Story*. Kingston: n.p., 2009.

Searle, Chris. *Grenada: The Struggle against Destabilisation*. London: Writers and Readers Publishing Cooperative, 1983.

Seib, P. *Beyond the Front Lines: How the News Media Cover a World Shaped by War*. New York: Palgrave, 2004.

Sharkey, J. "Will Truth Again Be First Casualty?" Paper, Institute of Communications Studies, University of Leeds, 2001. http://media.leeds.ac.uk/papers/vp018b90 .html. Accessed 29 May 2015.

Shultz, G. *Turmoil and Triumph: My Years as Secretary of State*. New York: Charles Scribner's Sons, 1993.

Tesón, F. *Humanitarian Intervention: An Inquiry into Law and Morality*. Dobbs Ferry: Transnational, 1988.

Thatcher, M. *The Downing Street Years*. London: Harper Collins, 1995.

Truth and Reconciliation Commission of Grenada (TRCG). *Truth and Reconciliation Commission Grenada: Report on Certain Political Events which Occurred in Grenada, 1976–1991*. St George's: TRCG, 2006.

Tumber, H. "Covering War and Peace". In *Handbook of Journalism Studies*, edited by K. Wahl-Jorgensen and T. Hanitzsch, 386–97. Oxford: Routledge, 2009.

Tumber, H., and J. Palmer. *Media at War: The Iraq Crisis*. London: Sage, 2004.

UK Parliament, House of Commons. *Foreign Affairs Committee, Second Report, Grenada Session 1983–84*. London: HMSO, 1984.

Waters, M. "The Workers' and Farmers' Government: A Popular Revolutionary Dictatorship". *New International* 1, no. 3 (1984): 15–100.

Wilder, A. "Free Press and the Role of the Media (10–12 November 1979)". Bishop speech excerpt. *The Grenada Revolution*. http://www.thegrenadarevolutiononline .com/bishtorchlightretro.html. Accessed 31 October 2012.

Will, W.M. "From Authoritarianism to Political Democracy in Grenada: Questions for U.S. Policy". *Studies in Comparative International Development* 26, no. 3 (1991): 29–57.

Williams, Dessima. "Grenadian Women under the New Jewel Movement". *Trans Africa Forum* 4, no. 3 (1987): 55.

———, ed. "Women Must Define Their Priorities: Grenada 1979–1983". In *Women in the Rebel Tradition: The English-Speaking Caribbean*, 24. New York: Women's International Resource Exchange, 1987.

Williams, G. "A Matter of Regret: Britain, the 1983 Grenada Crisis, and the Special Relationship". *Twentieth Century British History* 12 (2001): 208–30.

———. "The Tail That Wagged the Dog: The Organisation of Eastern Caribbean States' Role in the 1983 Intervention in Grenada". *European Review of Latin American and Caribbean Studies* 61 (1996): 95–115.

———. *US–Grenada Relations: Revolution and Intervention in the Backyard.* New York: Palgrave Macmillan, 2007.

Williams, M. "Economic History of Grenada 1960–1990". Paper. Eastern Caribbean Central Bank, Basseterre, St Kitts, Nevis. August 2003.

Woodward, G.C. "The Rules of the Game: The Military and the Press in the Persian Gulf War". In *The Media and the Persian Gulf War*, edited by R.E. Denton Jr, 1–26. Westport, CT: Praeger, 1993.

Worrill, C. "African People Should Not Forget Grenada". *Final Call*. 2003. Accessed 18 November 2012.

Contributors

Patsy Lewis is Professor, Sir Arthur Lewis Institute of Social and Economic Studies, University of the West Indies, Mona, Jamaica. Her publications include *Surviving Small Size: Regional Integration in Caribbean Ministates* and *Social Policies in Grenada*.

Gary Williams is Research Development Manager, University of Essex, United Kingdom. His publications include *US–Grenada Relations: Revolution and Intervention in the Backyard*.

Peter Clegg is Senior Lecturer, Department of Politics and International Relations, University of the West of England, United Kingdom. His publications include *Governance in the Non-independent Caribbean: Challenges and Opportunities in the Twenty-First Century* (with E. Pantojas-Garcia).

Robert J. Beck is Associate Professor of Political Science, University of Wisconsin-Madison, United States. His most recent publication is *Law and Disciplinarity: Thinking beyond Borders*.

Merle Collins is Professor of English (Caribbean Literature), University of Maryland, United States. Her most recent non-fiction publication is *The Governor's Story: The Authorized Biography of Dame Hilda Bynoe*.

John Walton Cotman is Associate Professor, Department of Political Science, Howard University, United States. His publications include *Redefining Cuban Foreign Policy: The Impact of the "Special Period"*.

Wendy C. Grenade is Lecturer in Political Science, Department of Government, Sociology and Social Work, University of the West Indies, Cave Hill, Barbados. Her publications include *The Grenada Revolution: Reflections and Lessons*.

Richard Hart (1917–2013) was a Jamaican historian, solicitor and politician. He was Grenada's attorney general in 1983. His publications include *The Grenada Revolution: Setting the Record Straight* and *The End of Empire: Transition to Independence in Jamaica and Other Caribbean Region Colonies*.

Laurie R. Lambert is Assistant Professor of African and American Studies, University of California at Davis, United States.

Jermaine O. McCalpin is Lecturer in Transitional Justice, Department of Government, University of the West Indies, Mona, Jamaica.

Nicole Phillip-Dowe is Head, University of the West Indies Open Campus, Grenada. Her recent publications include *Women in Grenadian History 1783–1983*.

Sir Shridath "Sonny" Ramphal was Commonwealth Secretary General from 1975 to 1990. His recent publications include *Caribbean Challenges: Sir Shridath Ramphal's Collected Counsel* and *Glimpses of a Global Life*.

Howard Tumber is Professor of Journalism, City University London, United Kingdom. His recent publications include *Media, Power Professionals and Policies*.

CPSIA information can be obtained
at www.ICGtesting.com
Printed in the USA
LVHW090840100820
PP16123500001B/5